Gregory D. Clark

Leadership & Organizational Performance

Research-Based Practices that Turn Potential into Results

Second Edition

Pearson Learning Solutions, 501 Boylston Street, Suite 900,
Boston, MA 02116
A Pearson Education Company
www.pearsoned.com

Printed in the United States of America

1 2 3 4 5 6 7 8 9 10 VOCR 18 17 16 15 14 13

000200010271770047

EEB/SK

PEARSON

ISBN 10: 1-269-32038-6
ISBN 13: 978-1-269-32038-2

For Anthony and Nathan

Table of Contents

Preface

In 1914 Ernest Shackleton set out to lead the first expedition to cross the Antarctic continent. He placed the following advertisement in the newspaper:

MEN WANTED: FOR HAZARDOUS JOURNEY.
SMALL WAGES, BITTER COLD, LONG MONTHS OF
COMPLETE DARKNESS, CONSTANT DANGER, SAFE
RETURN DOUBTFUL. HONOUR AND RECOGNITION
IN CASE OF SUCCESS.

Hundreds applied. Shackleton selected twenty-eight. The voyage was deemed the Imperial Trans-Antarctic Expedition and in December 1914, Shackleton and crew left their last port of call, South Georgia Island off the southern tip of South America (the crew was twenty-seven at this point as one sailor only traveled as far as South Georgia). Then, on January 18, 1915, only one day sail from the continent, Shackleton's ship, the *Endurance* (named after his family motto, "Through endurance we conquer") was frozen in the solid ice pack of the Weddell Sea. They were trapped; Shackleton's dream was thwarted. Without radio contact or modern rescue devices such as snowmobiles or specialized aircraft, the men had only to rely on each other if they were to survive. As the sun disappeared from the horizon and winter left days black as night, Shackleton planned the next move as they waited. Finally, on November 21, 1915 pressure from the slow moving ice pack became too much for the ship to bear as the beams and wooden planks of the *Endurance* creaked and cracked, then exploded sinking the ship forever. Shackleton calmly and with quiet resolve concluded that since the goal of crossing the Antarctic had vanished, he would set another goal: to bring all of his men home alive.

Prior to the *Endurance* sinking, the men lashed supplies into three lifeboats and began laboriously pulling the heavy boats toward the open sea over large, uneven ice crevices. They settled at Patience Camp and waited from January 1 to April 9, 1916. They had to keep moving toward the open sea and hope of rescue, so Shackleton made the decision to sail for an isolated, small, rocky sliver of land known as Elephant Island. The party landed on the island in late April. They were on solid ground for the first time in more than nine months; however, Elephant Island was off all the sailing routes and hope of signaling a ship was out of the question. Because most of the crew was exhausted, unfit for sea travel, and some even suffered from dementia, Shackleton knew he had to divide the party for the first time and sail for rescue to South Georgia Island. Shackleton selected five men to make the trip with him and they settled into one of the little boats named the *James Caird*. A seemingly impossible task loomed. They took supplies for six weeks, set their sights on crossing 870 miles of the most treacherous ocean on the planet, and launched for South Georgia on April 24, 1916. The remaining men stayed on Elephant Island under the leadership of Frank Wild, Shackleton's right-hand-man. Miraculously, after 16 days weathering gale force storms on the open ocean, the tiny boat and crew arrived safely on the shore of South Georgia Island. This was the same island they had sailed from 522 days earlier. The only problem: they were on the wrong side of the island. The whaling station was on the northern coast and they landed on its southern side.

A sea voyage of more than 130 miles around the western tip of the island would bring them to the whaling station, but the *Caird* wasn't fit for another sea journey. Instead, Shackleton decided to hike 20 miles over the interior of the island to reach the station. No one had ever crossed over the mountain ranges of South Georgia Island. In fact, it was uncharted and considered impassable. But it had to be done if they were to save their companion's lives. Three of the men weren't fit for the journey, so waiting for the weather to clear, at 3:10 a.m. on May 19, Shackleton, Frank Worsley, and Tom Crean set out to cross the interior of an island bursting with icy peaks of almost 10,000 feet. At one point, they were on a ridge at about 4,500 feet as nightfall began to set in. Shackleton knew that at this elevation the temperature at night would easily drop below zero. They had no way to build a protective shelter and their clothes were too thin to provide adequate heat; they had to either get down the ridge quickly or freeze to death. Shackleton suggested they slide down the mountain. They untied the rope that held them together, coiled parts of it up beneath each of them, locked legs and arms around each other and pushed off. The three men shot down the mountain gaining speed faster and faster until they came to an abrupt halt in a snow bank. They laughed wildly, brushed themselves off, had a quick meal, and charged ahead in the blackness of night.

The men had been hiking more than 12 hours when early the next morning they heard the faint sound of a factory whistle and knew they were close to civilization. Approaching the whaling station, they found themselves at the top of a steep grade that took three hours of careful climbing to descend. Finally, they ascended the top of the final ridge and looked down upon the bay and Stromness Whaling Station. They could just make out the tiny figures of men moving around the docks and sheds. When Shackleton and his companions arrived at the factory manager's house, the manager—who saw Shackleton and his team off close to a year and a half earlier—opened the door and stood shocked as he silently gazed at the men standing before him. Shackleton, Crean, and Worsley were unrecognizable. Their clothes were torn and filthy and their hair was matted with salt and blubber oil and hung down almost to their shoulders.

"Who the hell are you?" the station manager said at last.

"My name is Shackleton," came the reply.

They were safe. But what of their companions? The next day, Frank Worlsey boarded a ship to the other side of South Georgia to rescue their three companions from the *Caird*. Then, less than 72 hours after arriving at the whaling station, Shackleton, Crean, and Worsley set out to rescue the twenty-one men still on Elephant Island. This commenced a number of rescue attempts, each ending in failure, lasting more than three months. Once again it was Shackleton's old enemy that stood in the way: the ice. Each time he would get close to Elephant Island, the ice packs forced his return. Shackleton became unusually agitated and anxious. He appealed to the government in England to send a proper ice vessel that could make it through the pack. When the English government responded that they were sending a ship but it would take several weeks for her arrival, Shackleton petitioned the Chilean government to use one of their old tugboats. The request was granted and Shackleton set sail for Elephant Island yet again. It was now over four months since the *Caird* had sailed for South Georgia Island. Frank Wild and the men believed Shackleton and the others to be dead. Then, at 12:45 p.m. on August 30, everyone was gathered in the communal hut for lunch except George Marston. Suddenly, Marston poked his head in and asked in a breathless tone, "Hadn't we better send up some smoke signals?" Knowing what this meant, the men tumbled over each other on their way to the shoreline and saw a ship on the horizon. As Shackleton drew closer to the island, he saw the men one-by-one assembling at the water's edge. Peering through binoculars, Shackleton accounted for each man. They were all there. Everyone was alive. Only then did Shackleton feel a deep sense of relief. The journey was finally over.

(Source: Alfred Lansing (1999). Endurance: Shackleton's Incredible Voyage. Tyndale House Publishers, Inc.)

WHY THE STORY OF SHACKLETON AND THE ENDURANCE?

This fascinating story illuminates a number of important leadership lessons that are explored more deeply in the following pages of this book. The welfare of the crew was ultimately realized in no small part due to Shackleton's leadership abilities. Like all great leaders, he was competent, adaptive, inspirational, and earned the trust and loyalty of his followers. Also, under the most challenging of circumstances, Shackleton dealt with conflict assertively and constructively. Most important, he put the well-being of his men above his own personal ambitions. Shackleton understood that all leadership is situational. When circumstances change leaders must adapt, set new goals, and clearly communicate decisions to the rest of the team. Leaders also learn from experience. This was Shackleton's third expedition to the Antarctic. In 1901, he was a member of the National Antarctic Expedition under Robert F. Scott as they drove 745 miles from the Pole—deeper than any other expedition at that time. In 1907, Shackleton set out with three companions with the goal of being the first to reach the South Pole, but had to turn back only 97 miles from the prize because of food shortages. Everything is life is cumulative. Leaders build upon past experiences—even failures—and reinvent themselves in service to deep-seated goals.

ORGANIZATION OF THIS BOOK

This book gleans the most respected perspectives and research from the leadership literature to help you turn personal and organizational potential into results. While a comprehensive review of every leadership perspective would fill volumes, this book discards ideas learners find irrelevant or overly cumbersome in favor of concise reflections that get to the heart of everyday personal and organizational leadership challenges. For over 15 years, I have taught undergraduate and graduate leadership courses. Working with managers and executive teams from Fortune 500 companies, schools, non-profits, military, community, and religious organizations, I've seen which ideas from the leadership and organizational behavior literature help individuals and teams get results. This book includes new approaches and timeless practices that have helped hundreds of students and working professionals get the best out of themselves and others. The book also includes assessments, activities, and specific suggestions to improve individual and team performance. As a busy manager, parent, student, coach, or community leader, your time is valuable. The most effective leadership training is straightforward, thought-provoking, research-based, and most important, applicable to the real-world. The academic world is one of reflection; the business world is one of action. Leaders combine *reflection* with *action*. Reflection without action is folly. Action without reflection is dangerous. With this in mind, I have organized the book into the following sections.

Introduction. The first section sets the stage with sections on focus, getting results, being smart and being wise, born v. made leadership skills, and management and leadership perspectives.

Personal Leadership. This section builds on the premise that you are only as good a leader as you are—or are becoming—a person. You can't separate who you are as a person from who you are as a leader. Thus, leadership development *is* personal development. This section focuses on general leadership theory, modern leadership perspectives (such as servant leadership, authenticity, followership, and bad leadership), ethics, values, honesty, integrity, trust, transparency, how to think like a leader, innovation and creativity, and coping with failure.

Leading Others. Leadership is a collaborative endeavor. It's been said that if you are leading and nobody is following, then you are just out for a walk. Specifically, this section focuses on politics, vision, power, coalition building, conflict, change, motivation, employee engagement, job satisfaction, and the effective use of teams.

Organizational Culture. Culture is the glue that binds together tribes, communities, civilizations, and organizations. Also, culture provides the signposts that impart meaning, significance and direction to leaders, organizational members, and external audiences. Organizational culture consists of symbols, values, rituals, ceremonies, storytelling, and humor. This section also explores how information is communicated within cultures, organizational culture profiles, the role of culture on performance, and strategies to shape and change cultures.

Four Required Virtues of Leaders. The book concludes with a discussion of the four cardinal virtues that great leaders must possess: prudence, justice, fortitude, and temperance. Many leaders have either stumbled—or permanently fallen—because of inattention to one or more of these virtues.

One never quite achieves the status of a "fully developed leader." Great leaders understand that there is always more to learn; there are always new insights, skills, and behaviors to cultivate. It's the journey that counts. In the

Declaration of Independence, Thomas Jefferson saw the *pursuit* of happiness as what really matters. I wish you the best in your leadership pursuits. Let me know how I can help. The journey isn't always easy, but as Sir Ernest Shackleton reminds us, "*Through endurance we conquer.*"

Gregory D. Clark

INTRODUCTION

The introductory section examines the following leadership topics: focus, getting results, being smart and being wise, born v. made leadership skills, and management and leadership perspectives.

CHAPTER 1:
Building a Leadership Foundation

LEARNING OBJECTIVES

After studying this chapter, you should be able to:

1. Discuss the role of focus and avoiding distractions on leadership effectiveness.
2. Discuss why leaders are judged on the ability to get results.
3. Differentiate between being smart and being wise.
4. Show why potential isn't enough when it comes to being a leader.
5. Discuss whether leaders are born or made.
6. Compare management and leadership perspectives.

FOCUS

In a classic study, Darley and Batson (1973) set out to investigate if a person would stop to help a stranger in distress. They enlisted seminary students from Princeton University and divided them into groups. One group was asked to develop a short lecture on the jobs that seminary students enjoyed. Another group was given the parable of the Good Samaritan (a story about providing assistance to strangers) and told to deliver a short talk on anything they would like in response to the passage. Now, here is where things get interesting; some of the participants in each group were told that they were very late and needed to get over to another building to deliver their talk in a hurry. A second group was told they had plenty of time; while the third group was given a moderate amount of time to prepare their talk. In the alleyway between the buildings was an actor—in obvious need of help—sitting slumped in a doorway, head down, eyes closed, not moving. As the seminary students walked by, this person coughed twice and groaned while keeping his head down.

So, what did the researchers discover? Which students were more likely to stop and help the stranger? Well, the students in the "high-hurry" category were far less likely to offer help than subjects not in a hurry. The fact that some of the students were reflecting on the parable of the Good Samaritan did not significantly affect their helping behavior; the primary cause was being in too big a *hurry*. While we would expect students preparing to enter a helping profession (especially those preparing to deliver a talk on the Good Samaritan!) to stop and help a person in distress, this study revealed that a majority of the students failed to offer assistance (i.e., "do the right thing") not because they were callous or unethical, but simply because they were in too big a hurry. The management implications are immense.

Leaders and managers are thrust into a hurried and hectic environment of deadlines, meetings, and deliverables. In a classic study, Mintzberg (1980) found that managers led a daily routine marked by brevity, chaos,

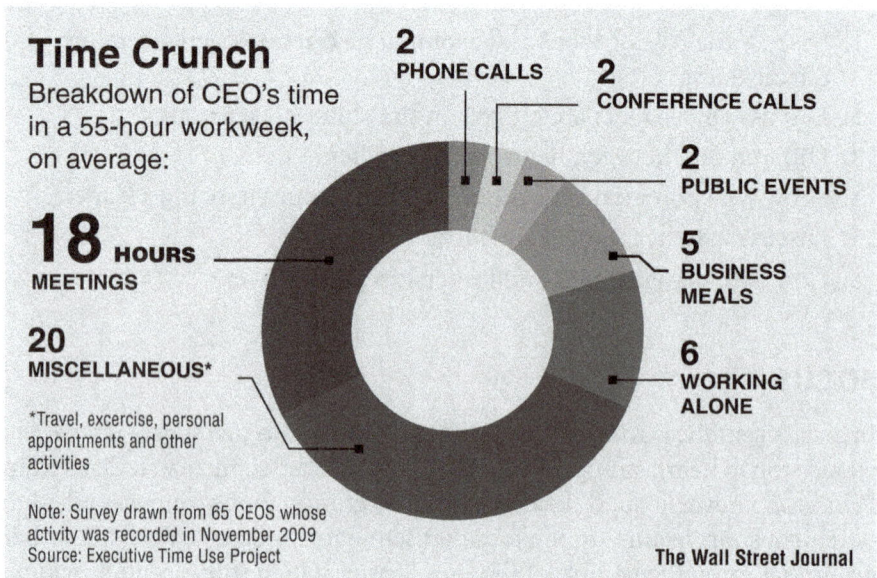

Time Crunch

Breakdown of CEO's time in a 55-hour workweek, on average:

2 PHONE CALLS

2 CONFERENCE CALLS

2 PUBLIC EVENTS

18 HOURS
MEETINGS

20
MISCELLANEOUS*

*Travel, excercise, personal appointments and other activities

5 BUSINESS MEALS

6 WORKING ALONE

Note: Survey drawn from 65 CEOS whose activity was recorded in November 2009
Source: Executive Time Use Project

The Wall Street Journal

Reprinted by permission of the *Wall Street Journal*, February 14, 2012.

interruptions, and fragmentation. In his observations of managers, half of the activities they engaged in (e.g., desk work, telephone calls, scheduled and unscheduled meetings) were completed in less than nine minutes and only one-tenth took more than an hour. "In effect, the managers were seldom able or willing to spend much time on any one issue in any one session" (Mintzberg, 1980, p. 33). A recent study found that CEOs spend most of their time in meetings or activities such as travel and personal appointments. CEOs spend an average of just six hours weekly working alone. These executives say they wish they had more time to sit back and think, strategize, or bounce ideas around "without a fixed meeting or fixed agenda" (Silverman, 2012). Distractions and a "high-hurry" pace can get in the way of doing the right thing; however, a more fundamental reason is our propensity as human beings to forget about the larger purpose behind our actions, lose focus, and behave in ways that complicate our effectiveness. Every day we must recommit ourselves to the important tasks that require our full attention. Every leader is operating under the same "high-hurry" stresses; the best leaders battle against this curse of forgetfulness through self-discipline and focus.

GETTING RESULTS

When you browse the management and leadership section of your local bookstore, you will find a cacophony of competing voices offering advice to current and aspiring leaders. There are titles related to leadership in business, the military, non-profits, schools, and politics as well as, numerous books outlining the qualities and practices of successful leaders. Amid the noise, one thing is clear: No matter what the setting, leaders are judged by their ability to deliver results. Sometimes the results are large-scale and have global implications such as George Mitchell's work to mediate a peace agreement in Northern Ireland between Protestants and Catholics. Other times, leaders focus on smaller issues closer to their own backyard. Take the case of Mayor Pro Tem Dick Daniels of Escondido, California who is intent on bringing an In-N-Out hamburger restaurant to his constituents. Commenting on the frustration of local community members (dating back to 1991), Daniels says if he can deliver an In-N-Out he "could be in office for life" (Perry, 2009, B3). Fair or unfair, at the end of the day, leaders are judged on results.

A leader's legacy is tied to delivering results; however, compensation structures often protect and even *reward* poor performance. It isn't uncommon to hear of a public official, teacher, or school administrator who failed to deliver results yet continued to draw a salary and stayed on the job for years. Even when public officials commit crimes, they can walk away with lucrative compensation packages still intact. Former Orange County,

California sheriff, Michael Corona, was found guilty of felony obstruction of justice and sentenced to 66 months in federal prison for witness tampering, yet he continues to receive taxpayer-assisted pension benefits. New York City schools were recently profiled for removing ineffective teachers from the classroom and placing them in district office "rubber rooms" where they report each day and continue to draw a full salary while replacement teachers are hired to take their place in the classroom. Many of these poor performing teachers have been reporting to these rooms for years while they wait out the dismissal process at a cost of hundreds of thousands of dollars to the school district.

The track record isn't any prettier in corporate America. Top executives that have resigned, or even been fired for poor performance, have walked away with multi-million dollar severance packages regardless of the health of the companies they left behind. For example, in 2009 Carol Bartz was hired as CEO at Yahoo to help turn around the company. She was given a sign-on package worth over $47.2 million in cash and stock and received a salary of $11.9 million in 2010. After three years on the job, Yahoo still struggled and she was fired by the board. Her exit package included large allotments of stock options and a cash severance worth $5.2 million. At Hewlett-Packard a revolving door of CEOs has led to tens of millions in severance payouts even as thousands of employees lost their jobs. In 2007, CEO Carly Fiorina left with more than $21 million in cash-stock severance after she struggled to achieve sustainable results during her tenure. Her successor, Mark V. Hurd, left with a severance of more than $12.2 million when he was forced to step down after accusations of an improper relationship. Then, Leo Apotheker, who struggled after just 11 months as CEO, was let go and given $13.2 million in cash and stock. After hiring Mr. Apotheker the company paid $2.9 million to relocate him to California; after letting him go, the company paid expenses to relocate him to Europe and cover loses on the sale of his house (Dash, 2011).

BEING SMART AND BEING WISE

It certainly takes a reasonable level of intelligence to be a successful leader. But great leadership is more than IQ. Daniel Golman, Codirector of the Consortium for Research on Emotional Intelligence in Organizations at Rutgers University, argues that *emotional intelligence* accounts for a greater percentage of success than traditional IQ measures (this idea is explored in the next chapter). Followers want a *wise* leader rather than a *smart* leader. But what does it mean to be wise? Socrates was deemed by the Oracle at Delphi to be the wisest person in ancient Greece. Socrates was puzzled by the Oracle's proclamation so he interviewed politicians, poets, and craftsmen trying to find someone wiser than himself. Ultimately, each interviewee failed the test of wisdom because they *thought* they knew things when in reality they lacked knowledge. Thus, Socrates declared himself wiser simply because he was conscious of his own ignorance. Plato, in his *Apology*, quotes Socrates as saying, "I am wiser than this human being. For probably neither of us knows anything noble and good, but he supposes he knows something when he does not know, while I, just as I do not know, do not even suppose that I do. I *am* likely to be a little bit wiser than he in this very thing: that whatever I do not know, I do not even suppose I know" (West & West, 1984, p. 70).

Socrates isn't bothered by the *lack* of knowledge in others; rather, it is the illusion that an individual *thinks* he knows something when in reality he doesn't that proves false wisdom. Socrates doesn't pretend. He doesn't put up a front. He is aware that there is always more to learn and the quest for knowledge is never ending. Great leaders follow Socrates' example. When leaders pretend to know something, they display more bluster than brains. Sometimes a simple, "I don't know but will find out" is the wisest response to a question. It's been said that with age comes wisdom; but sometimes age comes alone.

LEADERSHIP POTENTIAL

Everyone has leadership potential. Regardless of one's work history, current job title, or personality, we all have the ability to lead. However, whether or not one chooses to exercise that potential is another story. In fact, in athletics, potential is a dirty word. Coaches never want to hear that their team has *potential*. It makes them squirm. Why? Because it means that the team isn't *realizing* its potential and getting results. In fact, coaches have a saying: Potential gets you beat. The point is to turn potential into results. This idea is similar to the concept of potential energy in physics. Imagine a basketball sitting at rest at the top of a steep hill; even though the basketball is not moving, it has the potential to release energy and roll. However, it isn't until the ball is nudged or pushed that there is movement and the ball rolls down the hill. The same is true with our potential to become leaders. Often our talents and skills lie dormant until we are nudged or tapped on the shoulder and given the opportunity to strut our stuff.

There are good reasons why people sometimes wait in the background before exercising their leadership potential. Perhaps they want to gain more experience as a team member and learn by observing the successes and failures of others. Or they may want to focus on refining their own leadership skills by taking a class or participating in training workshops. Sometimes it is wise to pause before jumping into a formal leadership role;

it is a good idea to make sure you feel confident and prepared. Over the years much ink has been spilled trying to determine the best way to learn how to lead. In my opinion, the best way to learn how to lead is by *leading*. At some point all great leaders have emerged from the background and walked on stage. Yes, the beginning stages of exercising one's leadership potential can be risky and filled with mistakes and setbacks (we'll explore the role of failure on leaders in Chapter 6), but we don't know the depth of our strength and resilience unless we put ourselves in situations that draw out and reveal our true character and abilities. It is also worth pointing out: you have to *want* to be a leader. As simple as it sounds, you have to want it. No amount of encouragement from a teacher or mentor at work can kindle the leadership potential in you unless *you* decide to take initiative. As the Chinese proverb says, "A teacher opens the door, but you must walk through by yourself." These thoughts bring up the perennial question: Are some people born to lead?

ARE LEADERS BORN OR MADE?

What we are born with matters. We are all born with what Buckingham and Clifton (2001) call "unique and enduring talents" (p. 8). However, what we do with those talents and how we leverage them is up to us. Gandhi was born with a number of unique talents such as introspection, empathy, and resolve. While we remember the dramatic hunger strikes and rousing speeches during his leadership role in transforming India's independence from Great Britain, much earlier Gandhi struggled to find his voice and leadership message as a young lawyer in South Africa. It wasn't until he refined his innate talents and vision in India that he impacted history. Likewise, Abraham Lincoln possessed qualities such as foresight, resilience, and humility; however, historians note that he needed to learn how to draw strength from within to endure a life-long battle with depression, personal tragedies, and public defeat. Even Michael Jordan, one of the greatest professional basketball players of all time, had to work hard at developing his natural skills and talents after being cut as a sophomore from his high school varsity basketball team.

The common denominator with all of these leaders is that they made the choice to capitalize on their unique talents, conquer their insecurities, and find resolve and persistence in the midst of setbacks and failure. We can do the same. Great leaders, like great dancers, make their work look effortless and natural. This is because we only see the tip of the iceberg, the articulate and poetic speeches, the massive crowds of adoring followers, and the last-minute buzzer beating shots. What we don't see are the years of practice in isolation, the times of extreme self-doubt, and the many blunders and false starts that are the prerequisite to achieving levels of peak performance. What we are born with provides clues to our potential, but becoming a leader is more a mindset than a list of hardwired traits. Great leaders leverage their talents, focus on learning, and ultimately take responsibility for their actions and development. Describing the process of becoming a great teacher, Earl Pullias, education professor at the University of Southern California, says, "The central idea is that the teacher must be *growing toward* excellence in every phase of his life that relates to teaching" (p. 278). The same can be said of leaders; you are only as good a leader as you are—or are becoming—a person. In other words, you can't separate who you are as a person from who you are as a leader. Leadership development is personal development, a combination of study and practice. We learn to become a leader through feedback and reflection. We also learn by taking initiative and putting ourselves in situations that tap into and draw out our unique talents and skills. Today, leadership scholars and practitioners agree: leaders aren't born; they are made. Avolio (2005) cautions, "If you truly believe leaders are born to lead, you may avoid engaging in situations and experiences that trigger your full leadership potential. You may even engage in those situations and experiences, but fail to derive the deep meaning from those events that can enhance your leadership development. Your beliefs about leadership can become self-fulfilling and self-limiting" (pp. 2–3).

MANAGEMENT AND LEADERSHIP

Think about your manager at work. Do you consider this person to be a leader? Perhaps yes, perhaps no. How would others describe you? While it is certainly possible to posses both management and leadership qualities, distinct associations come to mind when you say each word. This is because there are clear differences between the functions and practices of managers and leaders; however, they are two sides of the same coin and both are necessary in a high-performing organization. I see it this way: management is a position and leadership is a mindset. While one can aspire to a management position, leadership is a process that can originate from anyone, at any level of an organization. Let's look more closely at the unique roles managers and leaders play in organizations.

Commenting on his landmark article *Managers and Leaders: Are they Different?*, Zaleznik (1992) says, "a crucial difference between managers and leaders lies in the conceptions they hold, deep in their psyches, of chaos and order. Leaders tolerate chaos and lack of structure and are thus prepared to keep answers in suspense, avoiding premature closure on important issues. Managers seek order and control and are almost compulsively addicted to disposing of problems even before they understand their potential significance" (p. 131). Kotter (1990) picks up on this distinction by saying, "management is about coping with complexity . . . leadership is about coping with change" (p. 104). Kotter defines management activities as: planning and budgeting, organizing and staffing, and controlling and problem solving. The equivalent leadership activities are: setting a direction, aligning people, and motivating and inspiring.

Bennis (2003) expands on the distinctions between managers and leaders:

- The manager administers; the leader innovates.
- The manager is a copy; the leader is an original.
- The manager maintains; the leader develops.
- The manager focuses on systems and structure; the leader focuses on people.
- The manager relies on control; the leader inspires trust.
- The manager has a short-range view; the leader has a long-range perspective.
- The manager asks how and when; the leader asks what and why.
- The manager has his or her eye always on the bottom line; the leader's eye is on the horizon.
- The manager imitates; the leader originates.
- The manager accepts the status quo; the leader challenges it.
- The manager is the classic good soldier; the leader is his or her own person.
- The manager does things right; the leader does the right thing.

(p. 39–40)

Bennis' dichotomy arguably paints managers in a negative light while showcasing the more desirable contributions of leaders. However, managers and leaders both play vital roles on the overall functioning of a high-performing organization.

Managers <u>and</u> Leaders Are Critical to Organizational Performance

Organizations need leaders to shake things up, make necessary changes, and motivate and inspire others around a shared vision. However, organizations also need managers to implement the change, design structures and systems that support the goals and mission of the organization, and measure progress in order to take corrective action where necessary. An imbalance of either function is unproductive. Gardner (1990) points out, "Many writers on leadership take considerable pains to distinguish between leaders and managers. In the process, leaders generally end up looking like a cross between Napoleon and the Pied Piper, and managers like unimaginative clods" (p. 3). Still, many employees are frustrated by managers that overplay the authority and control elements of the management paradigm at the expense of cultivating trust and respect. Some of us are naturally inclined toward management behaviors while others intuitively display leadership qualities. The skilled administrator realizes his or her shortcomings and develops a team with complementary leadership and management skills.

Ultimately, followers are looking for a supervisor that provides an uplifting vision for the future and develops constructive relationships with others (*leadership*) while holding everyone accountable to high standards of quality and performance (*management*).

Questions for Review

1. What role does focus and avoiding distractions play in effective leadership? How does this relate to your own leadership experiences?

2. Do you agree that leaders are ultimately judged on their ability to get results? Is judging a leader this way fair? Discuss.

3. What is the difference between being smart and being wise? How does this relate to leadership?

4. Why is potential not enough when it comes to individual or group performance?

5. Are leaders born or made? Discuss.

6. What behaviors and functions are associated with managers? What about leaders? What are the implications for high-performing organizations?

PERSONAL LEADERSHIP

Families, communities, organizations, and countries will always face difficult challenges. The measure of a leader is how he or she rises to meet these challenges. Furthermore, leadership is a dynamic relationship between the leader, followers, and the situation. In addition to a leader's personal accountability, he or she must articulate the collective responsibility and role others play in solving problems while constantly responding and reacting to ever-changing situational variables.

The following chapters explore: general leadership theory, modern leadership perspectives (such as servant leadership, authenticity, followership, and bad leadership), ethics, values, honesty, integrity, trust, transparency, how to think like a leader, innovation and creativity, and coping with failure.

CHAPTER 2:
General Leadership Theory

LEARNING OBJECTIVES

After studying this chapter, you should be able to:

1. Discuss early ideas about leaders and leadership.
2. Identify traits and qualities possessed by leaders.
3. Discuss the role of situation on leadership effectiveness.
4. Report attributes associated with Theory X and Theory Y.
5. Compare transformational and transactional leadership.

Let's begin with an activity. Take a moment to finish the sentence below. You can use words, phrases, complete sentences, or even draw a picture.

Great leaders . . .

_____

_____

_____

_____

_____

_____

_____

_____

_____

_____

How did you do? Was this activity harder than you thought? Take another look at your answer. Did you capture *everything* you believe about leadership? Chances are you didn't. (Perhaps I didn't give you enough space!) We'll revisit this activity at the end of this section, so let's move on for now.

One challenge in leadership research is the lack of a universally agreed upon definition of leadership. In fact, Rost (1991) found 221 definitions of leadership in his analysis of books, journals, and articles on leadership from 1900 through the 1980s. When it comes to defining leadership, there isn't one right answer. The study of leadership is—in essence—the study of human nature. People have the capacity to do great good and the capacity to do great harm. Leadership is a deeply human endeavor. Leaders can build up just as readily as they can tear down. Tyrants and villains have demonstrated the leadership qualities of communicating a vision and rallying massive amounts of people around shared beliefs; however, these leaders can hardly be called great. In this chapter, we will explore the progression of leadership thought from early perspectives to modern approaches.

EARLY IDEAS ABOUT LEADERS AND LEADERSHIP

Since people first roamed the planet, stories have been passed down to make sense of the human experience and the role of leaders. Joseph Campbell, in his book *The Hero with a Thousand Faces*, examined what he calls the "monomyth" or central framework that embodies the mythology of stories passed down from primitive civilizations to today. This monomyth is evident in stories from such wide-ranging sources as the Bible and Greek and Roman mythology, to modern interpretations in George Lucas' *Star Wars* episodes. In Campbell's analysis, the structure of all stories involves a hero (or leader) who possesses unique gifts. The hero may be revered by society, or he is frequently unrecognized or disdained. The hero then embarks on a journey where he must separate from familiar surroundings and depart into a world that is unfamiliar and strange. It is important to note that the hero has the choice of accepting the call to adventure or refusing the call, that is, the hero must take initiative and respond to the leadership quest. During this stage, usually some form of supernatural assistance is offered to the hero, many times in the form of an experienced mentor or teacher. The hero then progresses through a period of initiation marked by temptation, challenges, victories, and enlightenment. Finally, the hero returns and is reintegrated into society. Upon returning from the journey, the hero is transformed and as such, is equipped to transform the community. Campbell's "monomyth" provides clues to early interpretations of leadership and a leader's inner journey toward self-actualization and outward contributions to the larger community.

The Impact of "Great Men"

> "Because you are a nobleman you think you are a great man! What did you do to deserve it? You took the trouble to be born!" From Beaumarchais's *The Marriage of Figaro*

Based on observations in the animal kingdom, early notions of leadership can also be viewed from a dominance and deference perspective. Heifetz (1994, p. 53) reports five social functions provided by the dominant members of chimpanzee and gorilla societies: 1) choosing the direction of group movement, 2) protecting the group from predators, 3) orienting members to their status and place, 4) controlling conflict, and 5) maintaining norms, including norms of mating and resource allocation. In this context, some are destined to lead while others are destined to follow. In leadership studies, this idea is commonly referred to as the Great Man Theory. This theory claims that leaders (men in particular) have special gifts and even possess a divine right to command others. Thomas Carlyle, the 19th century Scottish essayist and social critic, wrote in *The Hero as King*:

> We come now to the last form of Heroism; that which we call Kingship. The Commander over Men; he to whose will our wills are to be subordinated, and loyally surrender themselves, and find their welfare in doing so, may be reckoned the most important of Great Men . . . he means

also the truest-hearted, justest, the Noblest Man: what he *tells us to do* must be precisely the wisest, fittest, that we could anywhere or anyhow learn;—the thing which it will in all ways behove us, with right loyal thankfulness, and nothing doubting, to do! (pp. 169–170)

Obviously, this perspective is outdated on a number of fronts. However, the Great Man belief continues to surface today in many Hollywood films. For example, in a number of action films, all is lost until the hero arrives on the scene to take control and save the day. This flawed perspective relegates leadership to only a select few, or even one person, while the rest of the community passively waits, is totally dependent on someone else, and gratefully relieved of any responsibility. This premise is most evident in the film *High Noon* when the cowardly townspeople shiver in their boots peering out of storefront and bedroom windows waiting for the town marshal, Gary Cooper, to save the day and catch the bad guys. The fact that *High Noon* is one of the most popular films requested by U.S. Presidents for screening in the White House is a telling comment about their leadership beliefs.

Trait and Personal Qualities

Identifying the trait and personal qualities of leaders is one of the oldest approaches in leadership research. The advantage of trait research is that it is an intuitive and easy to report method of understanding what makes leaders tick. After all, if one wants to become a leader, why not start by identifying the traits of people already in leadership roles? If it were only that simple! The major drawback to the trait approach is that a concise and consistently agreed upon list of traits doesn't exist. However, traits like honesty, integrity, and character are consistently represented in trait studies. With its significant drawbacks, the trait approach still provides a useful window on leadership. Let's look at a few of the most respected representations from the literature.

Kirkpatrick and Locke (1991) found six traits of effective leaders: drive (i.e., achievement, ambition, energy, tenacity, and initiative), leadership motivation (i.e., a desire to lead), honesty and integrity, self-confidence (including emotional stability), cognitive ability (i.e., intelligence but not necessarily brilliance), and knowledge of the business (i.e., technical competence). Regarding intelligence, new research has revealed that 24% of the changes in one's intelligence over a lifetime are linked to genes; the remaining fluctuations in intelligence between adolescence and old age are due to environmental factors (Naik, 2012, A3). Over multiple decades,

> **Drive:** achievement, ambition, energy, tenacity, initiative
> **Leadership Motivation** (personalized vs. socialized)
> **Honesty and Integrity**
> **Self-confidence** (including emotional stability)
> **Cognitive Ability**
> **Knowledge of the Business**
> **Other Traits** (weaker support): charisma, creativity/originality, flexibility
>
> Exihibit 1. Leadership Traits

Kouzes and Posner (2007) surveyed over 75 thousand people from six continents (Africa, North America, South America, Asia, Europe, and Australia) asking respondents to identify the characteristics they most admire in a leader. Their findings reveal the top four characteristics (in order) as: honesty, forward-looking, inspiring, and competent. Leaders that possess these four characteristics are seen as *credible* leaders. It is important to note that these same four characteristics have received the top four rankings in their research dating from 1987 to 2007.

In *Good to Great*, Jim Collins (2001) analyzed 1,435 *Fortune* 500 companies and found that only 11 companies achieved great results over an extended time period. Further analysis of the CEO's in each of these great companies revealed that they possessed a paradoxical blend of two qualities: extreme personal humility and intense professional will. Collins labels this "Level 5" leadership because it represents the highest level in a hierarchy of executive capabilities. For example, Level 5 leaders are modest and readily give credit to others (or luck) for the success of the organization and take the blame when things go poorly. They also act with a quiet resolve (rather than flagrant charisma) and accept nothing less than superb results associated with high standards. Finally, Level 5 leaders focus on the long-term success of the company and select highly capable successors when they retire or leave. In Japan, modesty is a virtue among political leaders. For example, Japanese Prime Minister, Yoshihiko Noda, known for his extreme humility, commented that his looks wouldn't win his party any votes but he promised to work hard anyway. In a display of humility and humor upon taking office, Noda compared himself to a loach, a less than attractive fish that scours the mud for food. He said, "Sweating ineptly, but with all my strength and all my heart, I will advance this country forward" (Fackler, 2011).

Goleman, Boyatzis and McKee (2002) argue that a leader's emotions are contagious and that the best leaders are "emotionally intelligent." In

LEVEL 5	LEVEL 5 EXECUTIVE Builds enduring greatness through a paradoxical blend of personal humility and professional will.
LEVEL 4	EFFECTIVE LEADER Catalyzes commitment to and vigorous pursuit of a clear and compelling vision, stimulating higher performance standards.
LEVEL 3	COMPETENT MANAGER Organizes people and resources toward the effective and efficient pursuit of pre-determined objectives.
LEVEL 2	CONTRIBUTING TEAM MEMBER Contributes individual capabilities to the achievement of group objectives and works effectively with others in a group setting.
LEVEL I	HIGHLY CAPABLE INDIVIDUAL Makes productive contributions through talent, knowledge, skills, and good work habits.

LEVEL 5 HIERARCHY

Reprinted from *Good to Great* (2001), by Jim Collins, by permission of the author.

other words, great leaders reveal and manage their emotions intelligently. There are two domains related to the personal competencies necessary for emotional intelligence: self-awareness and self-management. The self-awareness competencies include recognizing one's emotions and their effects, knowing one's strengths and limits, and a strong sense of one's worth and capabilities. Self-management consists of flexibility in dealing with changing situations, self-control, taking initiative, striving to do better, trustworthiness, and optimism. Unfortunately, it is commonplace to hear about a bright and talented leader that falls due to a lack of self-control and self-management. An old Cherokee story about a boy who was angry at a friend who had done him an injustice captures the essence of self-management:

> The grandfather sat him down and said, "I too, at times, have felt hatred toward those who have injured me, with no sorrow for what they did. But hate wears you down and does not hurt your enemy. It is like taking poison and wishing your enemy would die. I have struggled with these

CHARACTERISTICS OF ADMIRED LEADERS.

Characteristic	Percentage of Respondents Selecting Each Characteristic			
	2007 edition	2002 edition	1995 edition	1987 edition
HONEST	89	88	88	83
FORWARD-LOOKING	71	71	75	62
INSPIRING	69	65	68	58
COMPETENT	68	66	63	67
Intelligent	48	47	40	43
Fair-minded	39	42	49	40
Straightforward	36	34	33	34
Broad-minded	35	40	40	37
Supportive	35	35	41	32
Dependable	34	33	32	25
Cooperative	25	28	28	33
Courageous	25	20	29	27
Determined	25	24	17	17
Caring	22	20	23	26
Imaginative	17	23	28	34
Mature	15	17	13	23
Ambitious	16	21	13	21
Loyal	18	14	11	11
Self-Controlled	10	8	5	13
Independent	4	6	5	10

Note: These percentages represent respondents from six continents: Africa, North America, South America, Asia, Europe, and Australia. The majority of respondents are from the United States. Since we asked people to select seven characteristics, the total adds up to more than 100 percent.

Reprinted from *The Leadership Challenge*, by J. Kouzes and B. Posner (2007), by permission of John Wiley & Sons, Inc.

feelings many times." He continued, "It is as if there are two wolves inside of me. One is good and does no harm. He lives in harmony with all around him, and does not take offense when no offense was intended. He will only fight as the last resort, and in the right way. But the other wolf—ah, he is full of anger. The smallest thing will send him into a fit of temper. He fights everyone, all the time. He cannot think because his anger and hate are so great. It is helpless anger, for his anger will change nothing. Sometimes it is hard to live with these two wolves inside me, for both of them try to dominate my spirit." The boy then looked with great interest into his grandfather's eyes and asked, "Which one wins, grandfather?" The old man smiled and said, "The one I feed."

In addition to self-awareness and self-management, emotionally intelligent leaders exhibit social competence. The two domains of social competence are: social awareness and relationship management. The competencies related to social awareness are empathy, organizational awareness (including politics) and service to followers, clients, or customers. One way to demonstrate empathy in interpersonal communication is by capturing and reflecting back the emotional state of the person or people you are talking to. This goes beyond just indicating that you are hearing *what people say*; rather it is connecting with *what people are feeling*. For example, when a customer is upset and frustrated because the sole on a new pair of shoes split apart and they want a refund or exchange, it is wise for the salesperson to not only connect with the customer's request for a refund but also to say, "I can understand your frustration having just purchased these shoes and then having them fall apart. This is clearly a manufacturer defect and I would be happy to refund your money or exchange the shoes for another style." The second social competence, relationship management, involves inspiring others, persuasive influence, developing others, managing change and conflict, cultivating relationships, and team building. Each of these competencies is discussed more fully in the third section of this book.

Emotional Intelligence Domains and Associated Competencies

Personal Competence: These capabilities determine how we manage ourselves.

SELF-AWARENESS

- *Emotional self-awareness:* Reading one's own emotions and recognizing their impact; using "gut sense" to guide decisions
- *Accurate self-assessment:* Knowing one's strengths and limits
- *Self-confidence:* A sound sense of one's self-worth and capabilities

SELF-MANAGEMENT

- *Emotional self-control:* Keeping disruptive emotions and impulses under control
- *Transparency:* Displaying honesty and integrity; trustworthiness
- *Adaptability:* Flexibility in adapting to changing situations or overcoming obstacles
- *Achievement:* The drive to improve performance to meet inner standards of excellence
- *Initiative:* Readiness to act and seize opportunities
- *Optimism:* Seeing the upside in events

Social Competence: These capabilities determine how we manage relationships.

SOCIAL AWARENESS

- *Empathy:* Sensing others' emotions, understanding their perspective, and taking active interest in their concerns
- *Organizational awareness:* Reading the currents, decision networks, and politics at the organizational level
- *Service:* Recognizing and meeting follower, client, or customer needs

RELATIONSHIP MANAGEMENT

- *Inspirational leadership:* Guiding and motivating with a compelling vision
- *Influence:* Wielding a range of tactics for persuasion
- *Developing others:* Bolstering others' abilities through feedback and guidance

Reprinted from *Primal Leadership: Realizing the Power of Emotional Intelligence* (2002), by permission of Harvard Business School Publishing.

- *Change catalyst:* Initiating, managing, and leading in a new direction
- *Conflict management:* Resolving disagreements
- *Building bonds:* Cultivating and maintaining a web of relationships
- *Teamwork and collaboration:* Cooperation and team building

Building on Golman's (1995) research in emotional intelligence, Daniel Golman and Richard Boyatzis (2008) have turned their attention to the field of social neuroscience which studies what happens in the brain when people interact. While emotional intelligence focuses on theories of individual psychology, Golman and Boyatzis believe that effective leaders must also possess what they call *social intelligence.* They define social intelligence as a set of interpersonal competencies built on specific neural circuits that inspire others to be effective. The research in social neuroscience has identified "mirror neurons" in areas of the brain that act to mimic, or mirror, what another being does. Golman and Boyatzis say, "This previously unknown class of brain cells operates as neural Wi-Fi, allowing us to navigate our social world. When we consciously or unconsciously detect someone else's emotions through their actions, our mirror neurons reproduce those emotions. Collectively, these neurons create an instant sense of shared experience" (p. 76).

This is important for leaders because their actions and emotions are reflected in the behavior and feelings of others. Golman and Boyatzis cite Herb Kelleher, cofounder and former CEO of Southwest Airlines, as an example of social intelligence in action. Through video analysis of Kelleher strolling down the corridors of Love Field in Dallas, the airline's hub, Golman and Boyatzis observed how Kelleher's warm smile, handshakes with customers expressing his appreciation for their business, and hugs to staff members while thanking them for their work were greeted with reciprocal positive emotions. Golman and Boyatzis note that their research reveals large performance gaps between socially intelligent and socially unintelligent leaders. Can one learn to become more socially intelligent? Yes, but it is not easy and requires a willingness to change and deliberate actions. The best way to improve one's social intelligence is through 360-degree evaluation and coaching. Golman and Boyatzis provide examples of the unique path that each leader must take to identify their strengths and weaknesses, change behavior, and achieve better results.

Below are seven qualities of social intelligence followed by some of the questions the Hay Group uses to asses a leader's social intelligence.

Are You a Socially Intelligent Leader?

EMPATHY

- **Do you understand** what motivates other people, even those from different backgrounds?
- **Are you sensitive** to others' needs?

ATTUNEMENT

- **Do you listen attentively** and think about how others feel?
- **Are you attuned** to others' moods?

ORGANIZATIONAL AWARENESS

- **Do you appreciate** the culture and values of the group or organization?
- **Do you understand social networks** and know their unspoken norms?

INFLUENCE

- **Do you persuade others** by engaging them in discussion and appealing to their self-interests?
- **Do you get support** from key people?

DEVELOPING OTHERS

- **Do you coach** and mentor others with compassion and personally invest time and energy in mentoring?
- **Do you provide feedback** that people find helpful for their professional development?

INSPIRATION

- **Do you articulate a compelling vision,** build group pride, and foster a positive emotional tone?
- **Do you lead** by bringing out the best in people?

TEAMWORK

- **Do you solicit input** from everyone on the team?
- **Do you support** all team members and encourage cooperation?

Reprinted from *Social Intelligence and the Biology of Leadership* (2008), by permission of Harvard Business School Publishing.

TRAITS AREN'T ENOUGH: ALL LEADERSHIP IS SITUATIONAL

While personal traits and qualities are important, leadership success also involves interpersonal behaviors and actions in response to situational variables. Parents know that each of their children is unique and responds to different styles of parenting. One child may respond better to direct, less emotional forms of communication while another child needs a different approach. In athletics, coaches know that it takes a different motivational style to get the most out of his or her athletes. For example, one athlete wants to be left alone before a big game to reflect quietly on the task at hand; a lot of interference from the coach will undercut this athlete's performance. However, another athlete on the same team performs better with a more in-your-face approach from the coach with a lot of yelling, screaming, and aggressive confrontation challenging the athlete to show what they are made of in an effort to stoke peak levels of performance. Great managers also understand this fundamental point. Employees respond to different leadership styles and the best managers adapt and fine-tune their approach to the demands of a given situation. General George Patton's leadership style was perfect during wartime and ineffective during peacetime; he wasn't able to shift when the landscape around him had changed.

Sir Thomas More, famous for his refusal to recognize Henry VIII as head of the English Church, was described by his friend, the celebrated Dutch philosopher, Desiderius Erasmus as a "man for all hours." Erasmus meant that More was adaptable and able to get along with all kinds of people in any situation as circumstances change from hour to hour. Does this mean that a leader is like a chameleon and compromises his or her integrity? Of course not. Instead great leaders adapt their language, behavior, and approach in order to consider how best to relate to others. This requires leaders to eliminate ego and self-righteousness in relationships and reframe the way they interact with others. For example, if you are currently a manager, some of your employees probably like you to use blunt, straight talk when you are asking them to do something. Others respond best to a more delicate approach. Perhaps you stop by this employee's office and ask how their day is going or how they enjoyed their weekend before giving a directive. The point is that leaders need to get along with a variety of different people and your success as a leader is directly related to the performance of others.

One of the quickest ways to derail your management career is to rely on one style of leadership for every situation. For example, the manager who

	Very favorable			Intermediate in Favorableness			Unfavorable	
	I	2	3	4	5	6	7	8
Leader-member relations	Good	Good	Good	Good	Poor	Poor	Poor	Poor
Task structure	High	High	Low	Low	High	High	Low	Low
Position Power	Strong	Weak	Strong	Weak	Strong	Weak	Strong	Weak
Preferred Leadership Style	Task	Task	Task	Relation	Relation	Relation	Task	Task

FIGURE 2-1 Leader Situation Favorability and Preferred Leadership Style

Source: Adapted from F. E. Fiedler, *A Theory of Leadership Effectiveness*, 1967. New York: McGraw-Hill. [used by permission]

always competes without seeking ideas and suggestions from others will perform well in a crisis but stumble once the task turns to nurturing a shared vision for the future. This next section explores two of the most popular perspectives on leadership style. The first from Fred Fiedler argues that once a manager's style has been determined, he or she should be placed in environments that are a good match. The next approach from Paul Hersey and Ken Blanchard says that leaders must change their style depending on the environment and type of follower with whom the manager is working.

Fiedler's (1967) Contingency Model introduces the situational variables of leader-member relations, task structure, and position power as influences on leadership effectiveness. According to the model, these variables combine with the leader's tendency to be more task or relationship oriented and predict whether a situation is "favorable," "moderately favorable," or "unfavorable" according to the leader's individual style.

Fiedler's model measures preferred leadership style through a questionnaire entitled *Least Preferred Coworker (LPC) scale*. Respondents fill out the questionnaire with their least preferred coworker in mind. This person isn't a colleague that you don't like; rather, it is the person with whom you have had the most difficulty working. The model suggests that leaders with a higher LPC score are more relationship-oriented because, even under difficult conditions, the leader can see the person's strengths. Likewise, a low LPC score indicates a tendency to be more task-oriented in one's leadership behaviors because the leader focuses more on accomplishing the task than demonstrating empathy. Fiedler believes the goal in organizational settings is to match the person to the appropriate situation

Situational Leadership®
Influence Behaviors

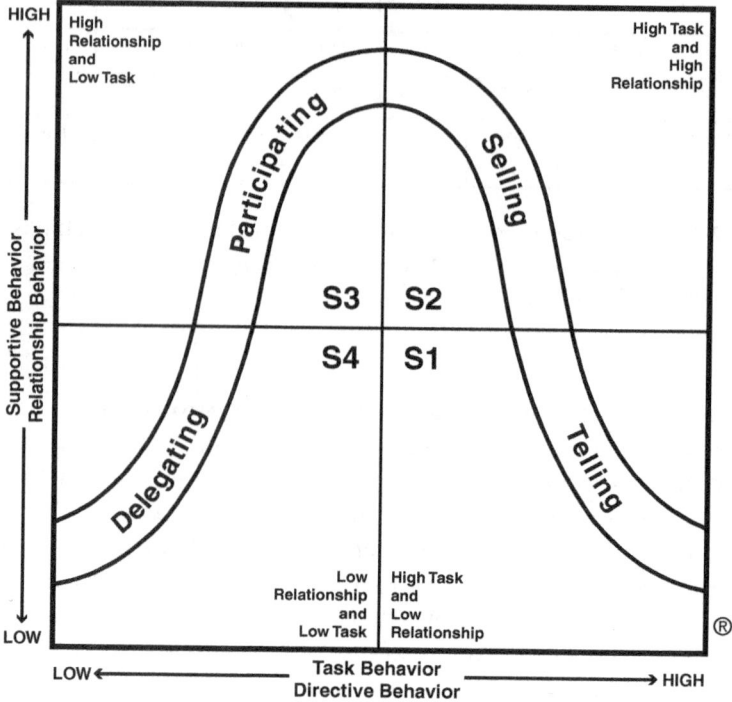

Performance Readiness®

HIGH	MODERATE		LOW
R4	**R3**	**R2**	**R1**
Able and Confident and Willing	Able but Insecure or Unwilling	Unable but Confident or Willing	Unable and Insecure or Unwilling

FIGURE 2-2   Expanded Situational Leadership Model

Source: Paul Hersey, *Situational Selling* (Escondido, Calif.: Center for Leadership Studies, 1985), p. 32.

Reprinted from *www.situational.com*, by Paul Hersey (2006), by permission of the Center for Leadership Studies.

rather than ask leaders to alter their own style to fit the situation. This means that an assessment of situational variables should be made and that leaders should be chosen deliberately when put in charge of projects so that their unique strengths are maximized while their weakness are minimized. This is a popular theory among researchers; however, it can be cumbersome to understand and difficult to implement because organizations usually can't reconfigure each job to match a leader's preferred style. However, the model is of value because it systematically accounts for situational variables that interact with a leader's style to influence outcomes of particular leadership endeavors.

Hersey and Blanchard (1993) created the Situational Leadership model as a practical tool for leaders to diagnose situational dilemmas and choose an effective course of action. They state, "according to Situational Leadership, there is no one best way to influence people. Which leadership style a person should use with individuals or groups depends on the readiness level of the people the leader is attempting to influence" (p. 185).

Identifying followers' "readiness level" is an important aspect to understanding effective leadership. Hersey and Blanchard define readiness as, "the extent to which a follower has the ability and willingness to accomplish a specific task" (p. 189). For example, if an employee is new to the organization, he or she may be at R1, unable and unwilling or insecure, on the continuum of follower readiness. This individual would best be served by engaging in S1 leadership behaviors with explicit directions and close guidance by the leader. However, if a follower has a readiness level at the R4 stage, he or she has the skills, abilities and confidence level to get the job done with little or no close supervision. In this case, the leader would engage in S4 behaviors by delegating responsibility for decisions and implementation. Criticism of this model emerges because it can be argued that engaging in high relationship behaviors (listening, facilitating, and supportive behaviors) are critical in all stages of follower readiness; however, the central idea of assessing a follower's readiness level and shifting one's leadership behavior depending on the situation is of paramount importance to leadership success.

HUMANISTIC PERSPECTIVES: THEORY X AND THEORY Y

Douglas McGregor's ideas ushered in the modern human relations approach to management and leadership. In his seminal work *The Human Side of Enterprise*, McGregor (1960) provides two dimensions to view leadership behaviors; he calls these perspectives Theory X and Theory Y. McGregor asserts that every management decision is a reaction to fundamental assumptions about human nature. Theory X assumptions include:

- The average human being has an inherent dislike of work and will avoid it if he can.

- Because of this human characteristic of dislike of work, most people must be coerced, controlled, directed, and threatened with punishment to get them to put forth adequate effort toward the achievement of organizational objectives.
- The average human being prefers to be directed, wishes to avoid responsibility, has relatively little ambition, and wants security above all.

McGregor links his Theory X and Theory Y to motivation. He equates Theory X with the "carrot and stick" process of motivation that works only on a very superficial level and then breaks down once higher order needs such as self-esteem and self-fulfillment are sought.

McGregor also describes Theory Y assumptions about human nature, which include:

- The expenditure of physical and mental effort in work is as natural as play or rest. The average human being does not inherently dislike work. Depending upon controllable conditions, work may be a source of satisfaction (and will be voluntarily performed) or a source of punishment (and will be avoided if possible).
- External control and the threat of punishment are not the only means for bringing about effort toward organizational objectives. People will exercise self-direction and self-control in the service of objectives to which they are committed.
- Commitment to objectives is a function of the rewards associated with achievement. The most significant of such rewards, e.g., the satisfaction of ego and self-actualization needs, can be direct products of effort directed toward organizational objectives.
- The average human being learns, under proper conditions, not only to accept but to seek responsibility. Avoidance of responsibility, lack of ambition, and emphasis on security are generally consequences of experience, not inherent human characteristics.
- The capacity to exercise a relatively high degree of imagination, ingenuity, and creativity in the solution of organizational problems is widely, not narrowly, distributed in the population.
- Under the conditions of modern industrial life, the intellectual potentialities of the average human being are only partially utilized.

The essence of Theory Y is that both the organization's and the individual's needs must be recognized and integrated. Theory X focuses on methods of control that emanate from one's positional authority, while Theory Y points to the possibility of lessening external control through a process of mutual commitment. In short, the assumptions managers and leaders make about people drive their behaviors which in turn create predictable and distinct work environments that affect organizational outcomes. For example, if a manager assumes that workers are lazy, he or she probably tends to micromanage using tight controls and threats. This will in turn create an oppressive and hostile work environment that decreases employee productivity (and, by the way, reinforces the manager's original assumption, "these people are lazy").

Theory Y assumptions about human nature will create different results. For example, if a leader believes that employees can be trusted to work hard, the manager will probably empower and coach team members. This in turn creates a dynamic, high-spirited environment where employees are productive and achieve results. Traditional critiques of managers usually focus on the manager's behavior and style; however, McGregor suggests that the critique needs to start one step earlier by considering one's fundamental assumptions about human nature. McGregor is careful to note that "the assumptions of Theory Y do not deny the appropriateness of authority, but they do deny that it is appropriate for all purposes and under all circumstances" (p. 56). In other words, Theory X isn't all bad and Theory Y all good. There is a time and place for both. Again, this is why the situation is of paramount importance.

Take the following self-assessment to measure your Theory X and Theory Y dimensions.

Assumptions About People

EXERCISE

The assumptions you make about people affect your leadership style. The purpose of this exercise is to help you better understand the assumptions you make about people and to recognize more fully your perceptions about human nature.

INSTRUCTIONS

- Assign a weight from 0 to 10 to EACH STATEMENT IN EACH PAIR to show the relative strength of your belief in the statement.
- The points assigned for each pair must total 10.
- Be as honest with yourself as you can and resist the natural tendency to respond as you would "like to think things are."

- This instrument is not a "test." There are no right or wrong answers. It is designed to be a stimulus for personal reflection and discussion.

1. _____   a. It's only human nature for people to do as little work as they can get away with.

_____   b. When people avoid work, it's usually because their work has been deprived of its meaning.

2. _____   c. If employees have access to any information they want, they tend to have better attitudes and behave more responsibly.

_____   d. If employees have access to more information than they need to do their immediate tasks, they will usually misuse it.

3. _____   e. One problem in asking for the ideas of employees is that their perspective is too limited for their suggestions to be of much practical value.

_____   f. Asking employees for their ideas broadens their perspective and results in the development of useful suggestions.

4. _____   g. If people don't use much imagination and ingenuity on the job, it's probably because relatively few people have much of either.

_____   h. Most people are imaginative and creative but may not show it because of limitations imposed by supervision and the job.

5. _____   i. People tend to raise their standards if they are accountable for their own behavior and for correcting their own mistakes.

_____   j. People tend to lower their standards if they are not punished for their misbehaviors and mistakes.

6. _____   k. It's better to give people both good and bad news because most employees want the whole story, no matter how painful.

_____   l. It's better to withhold unfavorable news about business because most employees really want to hear only the good news.

7. _____ m. Because a supervisor is entitled to more respect than those below him in the organization, it weakens his prestige to admit that a subordinate was right and he was wrong.

_____ n. Because people at all levels are entitled to equal respect, a supervisor's prestige is increased when he supports this principle by admitting a subordinate was right and he was wrong.

8. _____ o. If you give people enough money, they are less likely to be concerned with such intangibles as responsibility and recognition.

_____ p. If you give people interesting and challenging work, they are less likely to complain about such things as pay and supplemental benefits.

9. _____ q. If people are allowed to set their own goals and standards of performance, they tend to set them higher than the boss would.

_____ r. If people are allowed to set their own goals and standards of performance, they tend to set them lower than the boss would.

10. _____ s. The more knowledge and freedom a person has regarding his job, the more controls are needed to keep him in line.

_____ t. The more knowledge and freedom a person has regarding his job, the fewer controls are needed to insure satisfactory job performance.

Scoring
Add the points assigned to the following:
Theory X score = Sum of a, d, e, g, j, l, m, o, r, and s.
Theory Y score = Sum of b, c, f, h, i, k, n, p, q, and t.

Kolb, David A., Irwin M. Rubin, and James McIntyre. *Organizational Psychology: An Experimental Approach*, 2nd ed. Englewood Cliffs: Prentice-Hall, 1974. 241–242.
Used by permission of Prentice-Hall.

TRANSFORMATIONAL AND TRANSACTIONAL LEADERSHIP

Political scientist and respected leadership scholar, James MacGregor Burns defined two types of leadership: transactional and transforming. Both involve a relationship between leader and follower; however, each type of leadership is distinctly different. Transactional leadership "occurs when one person takes the initiative in making contact with others for the purpose of an exchange of valued things" (Burns, 1978, p. 19). Examples include, hard work in exchange for a salary bonus, a politician providing jobs in exchange for votes, or even hospitality in exchange for a listening ear. In these transactional leadership relationships, there is a connection between two people; however, the link is centered on the exchange rather than a deeper personal bond. As Burns puts it, "The bargainers have no enduring purpose that holds them together" (Burns, 1978, p. 20).

In contrast, transforming leadership "occurs when one or more persons engage with others in such a way that leaders and followers raise one another to higher levels of motivation and morality. Their purposes . . . become fused" (Burns, 1978, p. 20). Transforming leadership centers around a moral relationship where both leader and follower are challenged to raise one another's ethical aspirations. Burns cites Gandhi as a transforming leader who elevated the hopes of millions and whose life and personality were enhanced in the process.

Building on Burns' ideas, Bass (1985) introduced a model called transformational leadership. We'll spend the next few pages examining Bass's ideas because they are seen as some of the most credible perspectives in leadership studies. According to Bass, transformational leaders achieve superior results by employing one or more of the four core components of transformational leadership: idealized influence, inspirational motivation, intellectual stimulation, individualized consideration (Bass & Riggio, 2006).

Idealized Influence (II)

This leadership behavior focuses on leaders serving as role models for followers. Leaders with a great deal of idealized influence are admired, respected, and trusted. Idealized influence is determined by the leaders' behaviors and the qualities attributed to the leader by followers.

Inspirational Motivation (IM)

Transformational leaders inspire and motivate others by providing a clear vision, communicating expectations, and generating commitment to shared goals. Bass and Riggio (2006) note that idealized influence

TABLE 2-1   Descriptions of Participative Versus Directive Leadership and the Components of the Full Range of Leadership Model

	Participative	**Directive**
Laissez-faire	"Whatever you think is the correct choice is okay with me."	"If my followers need answers to questions, let them find the answers themselves."
Management-by-exception	"Let's develop the rules together that we will use to identify mistakes."	"These are the rules, and this is how you have violated them."
Contingent reward	"Let's agree on what has to be done and how you will be rewarded if you achieve the objectives."	"If you achieve the objectives I've set, I will recognize your accomplishment with the following reward . . ."
Individualized consideration	"What can we do as a group to give each other the necessary support to develop our capabilities?"	"I will provide the support you need in your efforts to develop yourself in the job."
Intellectual stimulation	"Can we try to look at our assumptions as a ground without being critical of each other's ideas until all assumptions have been listed?"	"You must reexamine the assumption that a cold fusion engine is a physical impossibility. Revisit this problem and question your assumption."
Inspirational motivation	"Let's work together to merge our aspirations and goals for the good of our group."	"You need to say to yourself that every day you are getting better. You must look at your progression and continue to build upon it over time."
Idealized influence	"We can be a winning team because of our faith in each other. I need your support to achieve our mission."	"*Alea icta ist* (i.e., "I've made the decision to cross the Rubicon, so there's no going back"). You must trust me and my direction to achieve what we have set out to do."

Note: From *The Full Range of Leadership Development: Basic and Advanced Manuals* (pp. 5.5–5.6), by B. J. Avolio and B. M. Bass, 1991, Binghamton, NY: Bass, Avolio, and Associates. Copyright 1991 by Bass, Avolio, and Associates. Reprinted with permission.

Reprinted from *The Full Range of Leadership Development: Basic and Advanced Manuals*, by Bruce J. Avolio and B. M. Bass (1991), by permission of Bruce J. Avolio.

leadership and inspirational motivation usually form a combined single factor of charismatic-inspirational leadership similar to the behaviors described in charismatic leadership theories.

Intellectual Stimulation (IS)

Transformational leaders challenge followers to think creatively, foster innovation, and reframe problems. Followers are encouraged to take risks and there is no public criticism when members make mistakes. Leaders that practice intellectual stimulation are not threatened when their own ideas are challenged by followers because the focus is on addressing problems and finding solutions.

Individualized Consideration (IC)

Leaders strong in individualized consideration pay special attention to the individual needs of each follower and develop constructive relationships with others. A specific focus is paid to developing followers' skills and effectiveness through coaching or mentoring. Leaders create a supportive climate that emphasizes followers' potential and unique differences. This leadership behavior stresses listening and two-way communication.

Bass's Full Range of Leadership model also includes several components of transactional leadership. Transactional leadership centers on rewarding and disciplining followers. These include two forms of contingent reinforcement, the positive form called contingent reward (CR) or the negative forms associated with management-by-exception (MBE-A or MBE-P). Rounding out the Full Range of Leadership model is laissez-faire leadership which constitutes the absence or avoidance of leadership all together.

Contingent Reward (CR)

Contingent reward leadership involves the leader designating a specific reward to motivate followers in accomplishing specific goals. This can include material rewards such as a bonus, paid time off, or tickets to a sporting event. Bass is careful to note that contingent reward leadership can be effective in motivating others, although not as much as any of the transformational leadership components.

Management-by-Exception (MBE)

When leaders take corrective action with employees, they are exercising management-by-exception. This transactional leadership behavior includes both active (MBE-A) and passive (MBE-P) forms. MBE-A behaviors are exhibited when leaders actively monitor an employee's behavior against the performance standards and then take corrective action when there are deviances, mistakes, or errors. MBE-A is active in that the leader's focus is on preventing deviations from the standards through direct observation of others' performance and then providing feedback to anticipate avoiding future errors. The passive form, MBE-P, occurs when leaders wait to take corrective action until after a mistake or error is made. Leaders may need to engage in both passive and active MBE depending on the situation. For example, if safety is of the utmost importance, then MBE-A should be practiced. Consequently, passive MBE may be required if large numbers of subordinates report to the leader.

Laissez-Faire Leadership (LF)

Laissez-faire leadership is the absence or avoidance of leadership. This style is very inactive and ineffective because the leader does not engage in situations where leadership is needed. As Bass and Riggio (2006) state, "Necessary decisions are not made. Actions are delayed. Responsibilities of leadership are ignored. Authority remains unused" (p. 9). In the Full Range of Leadership model, leaders engage in all of the behaviors at one time or another; however, the most effective leaders rely more frequently on the active leadership practices associated with the four core components of transformational leadership, followed by CR, MBE-A, MBE-P, and LF in successive order. Transformational leadership and the Full Range of Leadership are measured by the Multifactor Leadership Questionnaire (MLQ; Bass & Avolio, 2000).

Morality and Transformational Leadership

Over the years tension has surfaced over the question of morality and transformational leadership. In Burns' assessment, individuals can only be called transforming leaders if they act ethically and raise the moral conduct of others. Bass notes, that in his earlier writings, the dynamics of transformational leadership were expected to be the same, whether beneficial or harmful to followers. Since then, Bass has concluded that there are two types of transformational leaders: inauthentic and authentic. Inauthentic transformational leaders are also called pseudotransformational leaders. These types of leaders may exhibit many of the transformational qualities (e.g., motivating and inspiring others, cognitively challenging others, etc.); however, their aim is always self-serving, self-aggrandizing, exploitative, and power oriented. In contrast, the objectives of authentic transformational leaders are to benefit others. This may include the group or its individual members, their organization, or society in general. In turn, the authentic transformational leader also benefits him or herself and fulfills the challenges of the task or mission.

Beyond these practical concerns, authentic transformational leaders are also motivated by moral principles. Bass and Riggio (2006) state, "If a matter of moral principles, the objective is to do the right thing, to do what fits principles of morality, responsibility, sense of discipline, and respect for authority, customs, rules, and traditions of a society" (p. 14). They go on to declare that authentic leaders are best distinguished from inauthentic leaders in their use of individualized consideration—that is, the extent to which the leader is genuinely concerned with the welfare, needs, growth and development of followers.

See how you would answer the sample questions from the MLQ leadership instrument in Table 2-2.

TABLE 2-2 Sample Items From the MLQ (5X)

Factor	Sample Item
Idealized Influence (Attributed Charisma)	My leader instills pride in me for being associated with him or her.
Idealized Influence (Behaviors)	My leader specifies the importance of having a strong sense of purpose.
Inspirational Motivation	My leader articulates a compelling vision of the future.
Intellectual Stimulation	My leader seeks differing perspectives when solving problems.
Individualized Consideration	My leader spends time teaching and coaching
Contingent Reward	My leader makes clear what one can expect to receive when performance goals are achieved.
Management-by-Exception (Active)	My leader focuses attention on irregularities, mistakes, exceptions, and deviations from standards.
Management-by-Exception (Passive)	My leader shows that he or she is a firm believer in "If it ain't broke, don't fix it."
Laissez-Faire	My leader delays responding to urgent requests.

Reprinted from *Transformational Leadership* (2006), by permission of Taylor & Francis.

Questions for Review

1. What are some examples of early ideas about leaders and leadership?

2. According to research, what traits and qualities do leaders possess? What does it mean to be emotionally intelligent? How is this related to social intelligence?

3. How does situation affect leaders and leadership? What is meant by the "readiness level" of followers?

4. What assumptions about human nature do Theory X managers make? What about Theory Y managers? How does this theory influence leadership style and organizational performance?

5. What are the four core components of transformational leadership? How is this related to transactional leadership? What is the Full Range of Leadership model?

CHAPTER 3:
Modern Leadership Perspectives

LEARNING OBJECTIVES

After studying this chapter, you should be able to:

1. Define servant leadership and discuss the characteristics of servant leaders.
2. Define authenticity and discuss the qualities associated with authentic leaders.
3. Discuss the relationship between leaders and followers.
4. Describe seven types of bad leadership.

SERVANT LEADERSHIP

> "The first responsibility of a leader is to define reality. The last is to say thank you. In between the two, the leader must become a servant." Max DePree from *Leadership is an Art*

Servant leadership argues that the primary responsibility of leaders is helping others and contributing to the common good. Robert Greenleaf developed his theory of servant leadership as an executive at AT&T and subsequently lectured at MIT, Harvard Business School, Dartmouth College, and the University of Virginia. In 1977, Greenleaf published a short essay titled *The Servant as Leader*. This essay has since been reissued in numerous books and it has influenced many leadership scholars and managers over the decades. Greenleaf (1991) describes his philosophy of servant leadership as evolving from reading Herman Hesse's novel *Journey to the East*. Greenleaf summarizes:

> In this story we see a band of men on a mythical journey, probably also Hesse's own journey. The central figure of

the story is Leo who accompanies the party as the *servant* who does their menial chores, but who also sustains them with his spirit and his song. He is a person of extraordinary presence. All goes well until Leo disappears. Then the group falls into disarray and the journey is abandoned. They cannot make it without the servant Leo. The narrator, one of the party, after some years of wandering finds Leo and is taken into the Order that had sponsored the journey. There he discovers that Leo, whom he had known first as *servant*, was in fact the titular head of the Order, its guiding spirit, a great and noble *leader*. (p. 1)

Spears (1998) states, "Greenleaf concluded that the central meaning of this story is that great leaders must first serve others, and that this simple fact is central to his or her greatness. True leadership emerges from those whose primary motivation is a desire to help others" (p. 4). Greenleaf (1991) notes, "The servant-leader *is* servant first . . . It begins with the natural feeling that one wants to serve, to serve *first*. Then conscious choice brings one to aspire to lead. He is sharply different from the person who is leader first, perhaps because of the need to assuage an unusual power drive or to acquire material possessions" (p. 7). Greenleaf goes on to say, "The best test, and difficult to administer, is: do those served grow as persons; do they, *while being served*, become healthier, wiser, freer, more autonomous, more likely themselves to become servants? *And*, what is the effect on the least privileged in society; will he benefit, or, at least, will he not be further deprived?" (p. 7). Research reveals that authentic servant leaders are self aware, good listeners, practice empathy, heal rifts in relationships and one's own interior wounds, use persuasion rather than positional authority to accomplish goals, provide a vision for the future, act as stewards of the organization, cultivate personal and professional growth among those they lead, and build a sense of community (Spears, 1998).

Greenleaf's essay and contemplative master-work plumbs the depths of viewing leadership as an internal and external orientation toward service. This involves a symbiotic relationship between leaders and followers. In this context, followers act from a moral compulsion to follow leaders with a service focus and reject leaders and institutions lacking this focus. Greenleaf (2002) says, "Those who choose to follow this principle will not casually accept the authority of existing institutions. *Rather they will freely respond only to individuals who are chosen as leaders because they are proven and trusted servants*" (p. 24).

Greenleaf acknowledges that "the fusing of servant and leader" is a dangerous proposition. Many are tempted to see human institutions as corrupt and retreat away from involvement in the "system." Others take a more radical view and insist that institutions must be destroyed and replaced with perfect ones. The zeal for utopian perfection is unrealistic because the human condition involves both suffering and joy. (On this point it is important to note that the word "utopia" literally means "nowhere"; the word is an ironic impossibility.) Here Greenleaf turns for guidance to the French writer Albert Camus' last published lecture, *Create Dangerously*. Camus views the act of creating something new as a constant battle with little rest. The key is coming to terms with our own difficulties and struggles and pushing on like Sisyphus, the Greek mythological figure destined to move his rock up and down a hill for eternity. Camus closes his essay by saying:

> Great ideas, it has been said, come into the world as gently as doves. Perhaps, then, if we listen attentively, we shall hear, amid the uproar of empires and nations, a faint flutter of wings, the gentle stirring of life and hope. Some will say that this hope lies in a nation, others, in a man. I believe rather that it is awakened, revived, nourished, by millions of solitary individuals whose deeds and works every day negate frontiers and the crudest implications of history. As a result, there shines forth fleetingly the ever-threatened truth that each and every man, on the foundations of his own sufferings and joys, builds for them all.

Engaging in servant leadership behaviors is one way to gain the trust of followers. Sendjaya and Pekerti (2010) tested the hypothesis that a servant-focused, follower-centric, and moral-laden servant leadership approach would create stronger trust in followers toward their leaders. The authors defined six dimensions of servant leadership:

Voluntary subordination: lack of self-serving motives where the leader possesses a natural inclination to serve others;

Authentic self: leaders relate to others in a truthful, transparent manner by demonstrating humility and accountable behaviors;

Covenantal relationship: intensely personal bonds between people that foster genuine, profound, and lasting relationships;

Responsible morality: leader-follower relationships that appeal to higher ideals, moral values, and the betterment of oneself and others morally and ethically;

Transcendental spirituality: leadership behaviors which manifest an inner conviction that something or someone beyond self and the material world exist to make life complete and meaningful;

Transforming influence: followers are positively transformed in multiple dimensions, including emotionally, intellectually, socially, and spiritually.

Empirical tests in this study revealed that servant leadership is a significant predictor of trust. Three out of six dimensions of servant leadership (covenantal relationship, responsible morality and transforming influence) were found to correlate positively and significantly to trust with the strongest factor being transforming influence. Transforming behaviors include articulating a vision that followers can identify with, setting a personal example by modeling behaviors, appealing to shared values, showing concern and respect for followers, and perceptions of fairness in one's actions.

Servant leadership is not a theoretical model. Rather, it is a philosophy— a way of leading—that stems from a deep-seated belief in the value of serving others. According to Robert Greenleaf, all great leaders are *servants first* and *leaders second*. Kurt Takamine (2011) expands on this notion by referring to the idea of "Rushmorean Leadership" after the monument in South Dakota honoring presidents Abraham Lincoln, Thomas Jefferson, Teddy Roosevelt, and George Washington. Takamine says, "The Rushmoreans placed the highest concern on truly serving their constituency, and this required changing the mindset of followers. People will not willingly change their mind unless they feel that their leaders are persons of integrity, of respect, and values. This is one of the reasons that these four presidents are admired even in our modern society" (p. 85). Sometimes servant leaders transform the arc of history; however, more often, servant leadership is displayed by small acts of sacrifice, kindness, and generosity. In many ways, the small things *are* the big things: taking time out of your schedule to provide a listening ear, offering a genuine compliment, saying "thank you," holding the door open for others as they enter a building, or showing compassion to another person during a time of crisis. Each of these actions sends a powerful message and impacts others immeasurably. Paradoxically, when leaders give of themselves, they end up receiving much more in return. However, true servant leaders don't grandstand or seek personal glory through their actions.

QUALITIES AND CHARACTERISTICS OF THE SERVANT-LEADER

In his essay, *The Servant as Leader*, Robert Greenleaf outlines a number of qualities and characteristics of servant-leaders. The section below summarizes Greenleaf's examples of each characteristic. As you review each quality, use the scale to assess your strengths and opportunities for development.

Listening

Servant leaders engage in sustained and focused listening. Greenleaf (2002) says, "Only a true natural servant automatically responds to any problem by listening *first*. When one is a leader, this disposition causes one to be *seen* as servant first" (p. 31). Listening also requires leaders and followers to become comfortable with silence and adopt a relaxed approach to dialogue that includes periods of silence.

Mark on the scale below your listening skills.

```
5————————4————————3————————2————————1
Definite              Skilled              Significantly
Strength                                   Need to Improve
```

Withdrawal and Renewal

Whether you draw energy and inspiration from the pressures of holding a leadership role or if you don't naturally like pressure but want the opportunity to lead anyway, the practice of withdrawal is a valuable asset. Withdrawal provides a change of pace for those that move from one pressure-packed situation to another and is a necessary defense against exhaustion for those that do not naturally thrive under pressure. Withdrawal also provides opportunities for renewal and allows one to find the optimal balance of energy expenditure in order to avoid burnout. Greenleaf (2002) notes, "The servant-leader must constantly ask: How can I use myself to serve best?" (p. 33).

Mark on the scale below your ability to engage in withdrawal and renewing activities.

```
5————————4————————3————————2————————1
Definite              Skilled              Significantly
Strength                                   Need to Improve
```

Acceptance and Empathy

Greenleaf (2002) says, "The servant always accepts and empathizes, never rejects. The servant as leader always empathizes, always accepts the person but sometimes refuses to accept some of the person's effort or performance as good enough" (p. 34). This requires tolerating the imperfections of others since we are all imperfect and have to lead imperfect people. However, leaders must critically judge the performance of others in light of what they are capable of doing. This focus on acceptance and empathy (without reducing performance standards) is the basis of trust between leaders and followers.

Mark on the scale below your ability to practice acceptance and empathy.

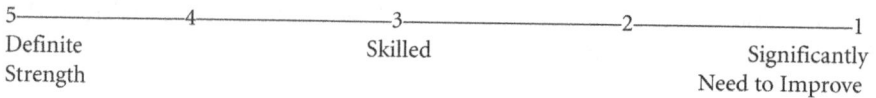

```
5———————————4———————————3———————————2———————————1
Definite                    Skilled                   Significantly
Strength                                              Need to Improve
```

Foresight

Foresight is "a better than average guess about *what* is going to happen *when* in the future" (Greenleaf, 2002, p. 38). This skill begins with a deep understanding of current events and trends and an intuition about what will happen in the future. Because every organization and industry is facing times of rapid and perpetual change, foresight is a critical leadership competency for organizational success now and into the future.

Mark on the scale below your ability to practice foresight.

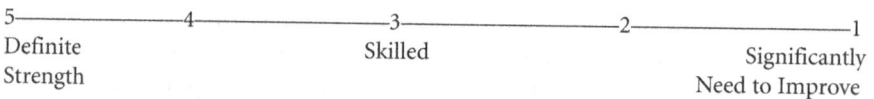

```
5———————————4———————————3———————————2———————————1
Definite                    Skilled                   Significantly
Strength                                              Need to Improve
```

Awareness

Awareness involves not only heightened consciousness of the environment, situations, and events around oneself, but also self-awareness. Greenleaf (2002) says, "Awareness is not a giver of solace—it is just the opposite. It is a disturber and an awakener. Able leaders are usually sharply awake and reasonably disturbed. They are not seekers after solace. They have their own inner serenity" (p. 41).

Mark on the scale below your ability to practice awareness.

5————————4————————3————————2————————1
Definite   Skilled   Significantly
Strength   Need to Improve

Persuasion

Servant-leaders demonstrate a persuasive communication style. They persuade in order to get people to go along with their vision; they pull rather than push. Greenleaf notes that this requires leaders to invest the time and effort to work with others one person at a time. Greenleaf uses the example of John Woolman, an American Quaker living in the middle of the eighteenth century, as a master in the art of persuasion. Woolman dedicated thirty of his adult years to ending the practice of slavery among Quakers by traveling the countryside, meeting with his Quaker neighbors and persuading them—person by person—to free their slaves. He practiced a gentle, yet clear and persistent, method of dialogue and interaction with others that achieved remarkable results. By 1770, nearly one hundred years before the Civil War, no Quakers held slaves.

Mark on the scale below your ability to practice persuasion in your communication style.

5————————4————————3————————2————————1
Definite   Skilled   Significantly
Strength   Need to Improve

Conceptualizing

This attribute involves having a visionary focus on the future; to be able to articulate and rally others around a compelling future-state for the organization is the practice of conceptualization. This characteristic compliments the earlier quality of foresight. While foresight focuses on using current trends and data to anticipate the future, conceptualization builds on this practice by articulating a vision of what the future *should* be and how to get there.

Mark on the scale below your ability to practice conceptualizing.

5————————4————————3————————2————————1
Definite   Skilled   Significantly
Strength   Need to Improve

Healing

Healing means "to make whole." When one practices healing, he or she is focused on building up and filling in deficiencies. These deficiencies could be in one's personal life, or healing can be used to repair and rebuild elements that are lacking in the leader's organizational life. Greenleaf notes that this is an interconnected process between the servant-leader and those being led. "There is something subtle communicated to one who is being served and led if, implicit in the compact between servant-leader and led, is the understanding that the search for wholeness is something they share" (Greenleaf, 2002, p. 50). Thus the servant-leader is continually engaged in a process of self-healing that emanates from within and serves to impact others.

Mark on the scale below your ability to practice healing.

5————————4————————3————————2————————1
Definite   Skilled   Significantly
Strength   Need to Improve

Community

Some people are better at tearing down rather than building up. Servant-leaders build up. They do this by creating a sense of community in the schools, neighborhoods, companies, and organizations they lead. In large, modern organizations it is common to experience a tension between feeling isolated and the need to connect within a supportive, integrated community. Greenleaf (2002) says, "All that is needed to rebuild community as a viable life form for large numbers of people is for enough servant-leaders to show the way, not by mass movements, but by each servant-leader demonstrating his or her own unlimited liability for a quite specific community-related group" (p. 53).

Mark on the scale below your ability to build a sense of community.

5————————4————————3————————2————————1
Definite   Skilled   Significantly
Strength   Need to Improve

Power

There are two ways of thinking about power: the ability to get people to do things through persuasion and example and the use of coercive force. Greenleaf (2002) says, "[persuasion] is used to create opportunity and alternatives so that individuals may choose and build autonomy" (p. 55).

In contrast, coercive force diminishes one's autonomy and strengthens resistance toward the leader and his or her objectives. Thus, servant-leaders use persuasion to build consensus, influence others, and achieve results.

Mark on the scale below your ability to use persuasion and example as a source of power rather than positional authority.

5————————4————————3————————2————————1
Definite   Skilled   Significantly
Strength   Need to Improve

AUTHENTICITY

Servant leaders act with authenticity; it is always about the cause rather than themselves. We have all been around a leader that—for whatever reason—we felt was not genuine. Just like in any relationship, before there is a lasting connection, one wants to know the true character and values of the other person. The same holds true in leadership. Followers want to know what their leader stands for; then they watch closely to see if there is alignment between words and action. Ronald Sugar, former CEO of Northrup Grumman Corporation says, "If people [are] going to follow you, they need to know more about you than the fact that you are their boss. They need to know your hopes, dreams, talents, and expectations . . . leadership is personal" (Pae, 2009). When leaders are hypocritical or keep their true feelings at arm's length, followers become confused, disengaged, or even cynical and angry. Choose any "super-leader" from history—Mohandas Gandhi, Martin Luther King Jr., Mother Teresa—and you find that they all possessed clear values, practiced what they preached, and in doing so, revealed their authentic selves and encouraged countless passionate and loyal followers. It may seem risky to reveal your true self to others, but authenticity is critical to forging deep, lasting relationships with followers.

AUTHENTIC LEADERSHIP

Great leaders have "it." They have that special something that makes them unique, special. But what is "it"? In *On the Road*, Jack Kerouac concluded that "it" was only expressed in the spontaneous music of jazz musicians. In 1964 the Supreme Court attempted to define what is "obscene" and the First Amendment implications under the law (what may be obscene to one person could be considered art to another). Struggling to define what is obscene or pornographic, Justice Potter Stewart famously declared "I shall not today attempt further to define the kinds of material I understand to be embraced . . . [b]ut I know it when I see it" (see JACOBELLIS v. OHIO).

The same holds true in leadership. We can get tongue tied trying to drill down on what exactly makes a leader, but like Justice Stewart, we know leadership when we see it. Most leadership writers have tried to definitively answer this question, so I'll give you my take. When we are around an admired leader and see and feel "it," what we are really experiencing is a person who truly knows himself. What we mistake for some magical and mysterious quality is actually the expression of a person that has figured out exactly what he was put on this earth to do; and he is doing it without pretense or self-consciousness. Thus, the essence of leadership is less about a definitive list of universal characteristics that all leaders must share and more about the authentic expression of one's true self. Few leaders do this, which is why it is so exhilarating when we come across someone who does. How authentic leaders express themselves—the enduring personal qualities they display and strategies they employ to build and exercise power—differ entirely from one leader to the next. At the center, when we feel "it," we feel authenticity.

Bill George, former CEO of Medtronic and business professor at Harvard University, offers five qualities that authentic leaders demonstrate: understanding their purpose, practicing solid values, leading with heart, establishing connected relationships, and demonstrating self-discipline. According to George, purpose stands in contrast to seeking leadership for the power and prestige it may offer. Instead, purpose stems from the leader's ability to serve others and values provide the solid bedrock from which action follows. George identifies integrity as the one value that is common among all authentic leaders. Leading with heart means that leaders are "open and willing to share themselves fully with us, and are genuinely interested in us" (George, 2003, p. 22). Authentic leaders also cultivate and sustain close relationships based on trust. George asserts that close relationships require an element of exposing one's weaknesses and vulnerabilities. Because leaders (especially men) fear having their weaknesses exposed, they "create distance from employees and a sense of aloofness" (George, 2003, p. 24). George calls this "creating a persona for themselves" rather than authentic leadership. Finally, authentic leaders practice self-discipline. Self-discipline is critical because it provides the ethos to translate values into consistent action. By practicing self-discipline, leaders also gain the respect of their followers.

1. Understand their purpose
   - Authentic leaders seek an environment that offers a fit between the organization's purpose and their own.
   - For example, David Packard led Hewlett Packard with openness, sincerity, and a commitment to make a difference through his work. He inspired employees to high levels of productivity

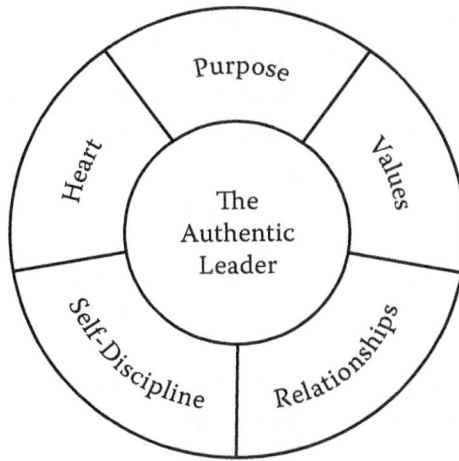

FIGURE 3-1 Dimensions of Authentic Leadership

Reprinted from *Authentic Leadership: Rediscovering the Secrets to Creating Lasting Value* (2003), by permission of John Wiley & Sons, Inc.

through the power of his purpose. At his death, Packard was one of the wealthiest people in the world yet one would never know this because most of his money went to fund philanthropic projects. His authentic purpose continues to inspire others today.

2. Practice solid values
   - Behaving with integrity is the one value that is required of all authentic leaders.
   - Integrity is the foundation of trust and it means communicating the "whole story" not just reporting positive information to others.
   - Leaders put themselves in situations (crucibles) where their values are challenged and then they have to make difficult decisions in the context of one's values.

3. Lead with heart
   - Leaders communicate their core beliefs and values with others and genuinely take an interest in followers (i.e., employees, constituents, etc.).
   - Respond to problems and negative feedback about the organization in a way that attends to the needs and concerns of others. This is done by behaving with compassion toward others.

4. Establish connected relationships

- Establish close and trusting relationships with colleagues. Many leaders shy away from this for fear of having their weaknesses and vulnerabilities exposed. Authentic leaders behave otherwise.

- This is done by leaders sharing their life story—their hopes, aspirations, personal and professional experiences, and even mistakes—in an open and honest environment. This behavior engenders trust and constructive relationships with others.

5. Demonstrate self-discipline

- Authentic leaders practice self-discipline with full knowledge that no one is perfect. When leaders fall short, they admit their mistakes.

- Leaders are highly competitive and driven to succeed in whatever they take on. This drive needs to be channeled through purpose and self-discipline.

- Authentic leaders don't let ego or emotions get in the way of appropriate action.

Gardner, Avolio, Luthans, May, and Walumbwa (2005) offer a framework for authentic leader and follower development. They claim that authenticity is achieved through self-awareness, self-acceptance, and authentic actions and relationships. This extends beyond the leader to include relations with followers and associates. These relationships with others are characterized by: a) transparency, openness, and trust; b) guidance toward worthy objectives; and, c) an emphasis on follower development. In this context, authentic leadership in organizations is defined as "a process that draws from both positive psychological capacities and a highly developed organizational context, which results in both greater self-awareness and self-regulated positive behaviors on the part of leaders and associates, fostering positive self-development" (p. 345). In other words, "by being true to one's core beliefs and values and exhibiting authentic behavior, the leader positively fosters the development of associates until they become leaders themselves" (p. 345). Authentic leaders demonstrate—and model for others—self-esteem, psychological well-being, confidence, optimism, hope, and resilience. The conceptual framework for authentic leader and follower development presented by the authors focuses on: communicating one's personal history, self-awareness, self-regulation, positive modeling, and an inclusive, ethical, caring and strengths-based organizational climate. Follower outcomes linked to authenticity are trust, engagement and workplace well-being.

Fields (2007) presents a model to determine the authenticity and integrity of leaders. According to the model, followers process both leader-specific and context specific variables when coming to consensus regarding the authenticity and integrity of the leaders they interact with. Six variables affect follower assessments of authenticity and integrity:

Number of follower observations of leader actions and interactions to gauge leader motives. Followers need frequent interactions with leaders in order to gain information about the leader and more importantly, to understand how the leader characterizes his/her motives underlying the actions. If followers have limited opportunities to directly observe or interact with the leader, the chances that followers will be able to reach consensus regarding the authenticity and integrity of the leader may be substantially reduced.

Multiple followers observe same actions of leader and gather similar information about motives. For followers to come to consensus regarding authenticity and integrity, leaders must not only provide opportunities for interaction with multiple follower groups, but they must demonstrate consistent behaviors during such interactions. If leader-follower interactions differ greatly, the likelihood for consensus will be reduced.

Stability of the leader's behavior and motives across instances. Consistency in the relationship between leader actions and motives across different situations will affect the judgments of followers. Followers may disagree about the actions a leader takes to address differing situations; however, if followers perceive a leader's motives to be consistent, the likelihood for consensus regarding authenticity and integrity will be increased.

Similarity in follower interpretations of leader actions and underlying motives. Differences among followers in interpretation of leader actions and motives and the consistency between actions and motives may in turn limit the extent of consensus about leader authenticity and integrity.

Extraneous information about leader available to the followers. Extraneous information obtained by followers, while unrelated directly to a specific leader, may limit consensus among followers. For example, poor organizational performance may be blamed by some followers on a leader's actions and/or motives, whether or not these results are causally related.

Communication among followers concerning the leader, the situation, and leader motives. The extent to which followers communicate with each other will influence the effects of information obtained from the leader. Because motives are not observable, communication among followers will influence any conclusions in this area. Followers may obtain information about leader motives directly from interaction with a leader or construct perceptions of motives from a number of indirect sources.

Bennis (2003) writes, "to be authentic is literally to be your own author (the words derive from the same Greek root), to discover your own native energies and desires, and then to find your own way of acting on them" (p. 45). Through experience and self-reflection, leaders discover their unique purpose and refine their talents and personal leadership message. Leaders can then be themselves and act with the confidence and freedom that authenticity provides. For example, in my leadership classes I have students participate in an activity called *Talented You*. The assignment requires students to identify a song, picture, story, poem, or any other symbol that reveals their authentic self and unique talents. Students then develop a short presentation where they stand in front of the class and share what they brought in and why. Sound pretty intimidating? When it comes time to present, it is amazing to watch what happens. People open up. Students share powerful stories about life experiences that range from overcoming adversity to experiencing times of pure bliss and joy. They share humorous stories about their personal lives, read poems they have written, play songs from a recording artist or bring their own instruments and play original compositions for the class. Some have even sung a-capella with beautiful voices and touching lyrics. The assignment challenges students to avoid, as Bill George says, "creating a persona for themselves" and get beneath the surface, revealing their authentic selves. It is worth the risk. Inevitably, from this class session forward students feel a deep connection with one another and a strong sense of community. Through their observation of others' presentations, students eliminate any prior misconceptions or false assumptions about their peers, develop a deep respect for one another, and understand the value of authenticity.

To be authentic, self-awareness is critical. The most popular major in colleges and universities is "undeclared" because students are figuring out who they are—and who they are becoming. The importance of self-awareness is not a new idea. In ancient Greece, one inscription above the Oracle at Delphi read: Know Thyself. Also, Chinese sage and founder of Taoism, Lao Tzu, is quoted as saying: One who knows others is wise; One who knows one's self is enlightened. Shakespeare adds the notion of *action* in alignment with *self-knowledge* in *Hamlet* when Polonius advises, "To thine own self be true/and it must follow as the night the day/though cannot then be false to any man." Ralph Waldo Emerson picks up on this idea in his 19th century essay *Self Reliance* exhorting, "Trust thyself, Every heart vibrates to that iron string." Authentic action aligned with self-awareness is a theme that resounds throughout the ages; it is up to us whether or not to listen.

FOLLOWERSHIP

Any parent understands the interplay between leadership and followership. When raising children, parents foster independence, critical thinking, and assertiveness in their children; but children also need to follow their parent's direction, listen, and suspend their own feelings of being all-knowing. It is a fine line. Parents don't want to squelch a child's independence, but at the same time, children must recognize the time and place to follow. Current leadership research has shifted the focus away from leader-centric approaches and toward the role and impact of followers. In fact, the threshold test of any leader is simple: Do you have followers? It's been said that if you are leading and no one is following, then you're just out for a walk. In Miguel Cervantes' masterpiece *Don Quixote,* even though Don Quixote embarked on a number of deranged and absurd journeys, he maintained a loyal and faithful follower in Sancho Panza. Bass (1990) asserts that a fundamental principle within military academies is that one must first learn how to follow before learning to lead. Bass believes that this idea can be traced back to philosopher G.W.F. Hegel's *Philosophy of Mind,* which, "argued that by first serving as a follower, a leader subsequently can best understand his followers" (p. 4). Kellerman (2008) argues that followers have not been given their due credit. She believes that we have been hardwired to accept that the real leadership force comes from holding a formal position of authority while being a "follower" is seen in a pejorative light. However, followers have the ability to affect change, influence others, and essentially, exercise leadership. Kellerman offers Sherron Watkins at Enron, Coleen Rowley at the FBI, and Cynthia Cooper at WorldCom as examples of followers that challenged their superiors and exposed unethical activities by senior leaders. These three women were not the formal leaders of their organizations; however, they have permanently become symbols of the power of followers since being recognized for their actions in 2002 by *Time* magazine as "Persons of the Year."

Followership can be described as the process and level of engagement between leaders and followers. Kelley (2008) shares two dimensions that define the way that people follow leaders:

1. Do they think for themselves? Are they independent critical thinkers? Or do they look to the leader to do the thinking for them?

2. Are they actively engaged in creating positive energy for the organization? Or is there negative energy or passive involvement?

Based on these dimensions, Kelley offers five basic styles of followership:

The sheep: passively look to the leader to do the thinking for them and to motivate them.

The yes people: these people are positive and always on the leader's side, but still look to the leader for what to think and do. Yes people will say, "I'm a doer; that's my job. The boss gets paid to think, and I'm the one who does the work." Kelley notes that there is more to being a good follower than simply doing.

The alienated: these followers think for themselves, but have a lot of negative energy. When leaders try to move the organization forward, these followers create roadblocks; they are skeptical and cynical about the current plan of action. The alienated see themselves as mavericks, the only people with the guts to stand up to the boss.

The pragmatists: pragmatists sit on the fence and see which way the wind blows. Once they see where things are headed, they'll get on board. They see themselves as preservers of the status quo. They do what they must to survive, but wait it out for the storms of change to blow over.

The star followers: star followers think for themselves, are very active, and have very positive energy. They do not accept the leader's decision without their own independent evaluation of its soundness. If they agree with the leader, they give full support. If they disagree, they challenge the leader, offering constructive alternatives that will help the leader and organization get where they want to go. Some people view these people as really "leaders in disguise," but this is basically because those people have a hard time accepting that followers can display such independence and positive behavior. Star followers are often referred to as "my right-hand person" or my "go-to person."

(pp. 7–8)

In consulting with executives, Kelley asks, "If you could have an ideal mix of the five follower styles in your organization, what percentage of each style would you prefer?" He says he is surprised at how many say they would like all yes-people. Other executives would prefer a mix. Kelley notes that these executives would, "start with a sprinkling of alienated because they keep the leader honest. Add a small group of star followers who would lead the charge, but avoid adding too many because they can get demanding, and they think for themselves too much. Then split the remaining majority among pragmatics who serve as an institutionalized, status quo base and yes-people who will get the job done" (p. 13). Kelley believes that organizations with large numbers of star followers perform better because they are intrinsically motivated.

BAD LEADERSHIP

Unfortunately, at work we have all been around someone we consider a bad leader. This brings up an interesting question: Can a person engage in destructive actions but still be called a leader? The leadership literature is full of debate about whether or not leadership is synonymous with doing good works. Kellerman (2004) believes that leadership is not inherently a moral concept and that bad leaders should still be referred to as "leaders." Kellerman has focused her research on understanding and categorizing types of bad leadership. She believes, "bad leadership falls into two categories: bad as ineffective and bad as unethical" (p. 32). Kellerman also acknowledges that sometimes leaders and followers are ineffective and unethical. She researched hundreds of cases involving bad leaders in the private, public, and nonprofit sectors and found that bad leadership falls into seven categories:

> **Incompetent:** the leader and at least some followers lack the will or skill (or both) to sustain effective action. With regard to at least one important leadership challenge, they do not create positive change.
>
> **Rigid:** the leader and at least some followers are stiff and unyielding. Although they may be competent, they are unable or unwilling to adapt to new ideas, new information, or changing times.
>
> **Intemperate:** the leader lacks self-control and is aided and abetted by followers who are unwilling or unable effectively to intervene.
>
> **Callous:** the leader and at least some followers are uncaring or unkind. Ignored or discounted are the needs, wants, and wishes of most members of the group or organization, especially subordinates.
>
> **Corrupt:** the leader and at least some followers lie, cheat, or steal. To a degree that exceeds the norm, they put self-interests ahead of the public interest.
>
> **Insular:** the leader and at least some followers minimize or disregard the health and welfare of "the other"—that is, those outside the group or organization for which they are directly responsible.

Evil: the leader and at least some followers commit atrocities. They use pain as an instrument of power. The harm done to men, women, and children is severe rather than slight. The harm can be physical, psychological, or both.

(pp. 40–46)

It is interesting to note that Kellerman's typology requires involvement by both leaders and followers. No leader can be bad without followers also going along. This point reinforces the fact that leadership—for good or ill—is dependent upon a relationship that requires collective action.

Questions for Review

1. What is servant leadership? What are the ten characteristics of a servant leader?
2. What is authenticity? What qualities and behaviors are associated with authentic leader?
3. What is the relationship between leaders and followers? What are the five basic styles of followership?
4. What are the seven types of bad leadership? How is bad leadership related to followership?

CHAPTER 4:
Ethics

LEARNING OBJECTIVES

After studying this chapter, you should be able to:

1. Differentiate between moral temptations and ethical dilemmas.
2. Compare and contrast the moral principles of care and justice.
3. Identify your top five core values.

ETHICAL BEHAVIOR IS A CHOICE

In Chapter 2 we learned about transforming and authentic transformational leadership. With regard to leadership theories, these are two of the most important ideas in the literature and the credibility of these two perspectives is axiomatic among researchers. Furthermore, a critical element of both transforming and authentic transformational leadership is ethics; more to the point, raising the ethical aspirations of both leaders and followers. Kidder (2009) has studied ways people resolve ethical issues. He offers a useful framework for understanding ethics. He believes that there are two domains: moral temptations (right vs. wrong) and ethical dilemmas (right vs. right). Usually one thinks of an ethical dilemma as fighting against doing the *wrong* thing. Kidder astutely reminds us that choosing not to engage in the wrong activity is merely refusing temptation. Think about it: if you are a cashier and do not take money from the till at the end of your shift, does that mean you acted ethically? No, it simply means that you avoided the temptation to do something wrong. Ethical dilemmas are more nuanced. They involve choosing between two "right" values. Kidder provides the following examples:

- It is right to provide our children with the finest public schools available—and right to prevent the constant upward ratcheting of state and local taxes.

- It is right to speak up in favor of a minority viewpoint in your club—and right to let the majority rule.
- It is right to "throw the book" at good employees who make dumb decisions that endanger the firm—and right to have enough compassion to mitigate the punishment and give them another chance.
- It is right to bench the star college quarterback caught drinking the night before the championship game—and right to field the best possible team for tomorrow's game.

(pp. 4–5)

Leaders must stand up and make a decision knowing that all parties are not going to be completely satisfied. Joseph Badaracco (1997) calls these right-versus-right leadership choices "defining moments." According to Badaracco, defining moments *reveal* a person's basic values and commitments, *test* those values, and *shape* one's character. "A right-versus-right decision can reveal a manager's basic values and, in some cases, those of an organization. At the same time, the decision tests the strength of the commitments that a person or an organization has made. Finally, the decision casts a shadow forward. It shapes the character of the person and, in some cases, the organization" (Badaracco, 1997, p. 7). The important thing to remember is that acting ethically (or succumbing to a moral temptation) is a choice and—as with any choice—leaders must be prepared to deal with the consequences.

Defining moments call forth doing the right thing, rather than what is easy or politically expedient. In an address at the state capitol of North Carolina, Harry S. Truman spoke about Andrew Jackson's courage in telling South Carolinians—people of his own blood and background—that their position on the Tariff of 1828 was wrong. Recalling this leadership moment, Truman said, "It takes courage to face a duelist with a pistol and it takes courage to face a British general with an army. But it takes still greater and far higher courage to face friends with a grievance. The bravest thing Andrew Jackson ever did was to stand up and tell his own people to their faces that they were wrong." Telling others what they *need* to hear instead of what they *want* to hear requires moral courage. Acting in alignment with these virtues can cause leaders to feel alone and isolated, but as the old joke goes: It's lonely at the top, but it's also lonely at the bottom and the top pays more. When leaders fail to take a stand on issues of consequence or change their positions to allay immediate criticism, they are labeled "flip-floppers." Former Democratic presidential nominee John Kerry was fatally labeled a "flip-flopper" when it came to making decisions. He didn't help his case when responding to a question about his vote against an $87 billion supplemental appropriation for military operations in Iraq and Afghanistan by implying that he was both for and against the bill. Astonishingly, Kerry declared, "I actually did vote for the $87 billion before I voted against it" (Roselli, 2004). Perhaps being remembered as a flip-flopper doesn't do justice to Kerry's full impact as a leader; however, followers would rather know where a leader stands on issues of consequence (even if they disagree with the leader) than experience uncertainty and ambiguity regarding a leader's beliefs.

Thirteenth century poet and writer Dante Alighieri addressed a number of ethical and leadership issues in his most famous work *The Divine Comedy*. In the first section of this work, *Inferno*, Dante the Pilgrim is escorted through Hell by the poet Virgil. When they enter the vestibule that leads to Hell itself, they encounter a group of souls that were rejected by God and not accepted by the powers of Hell. Hearing their screams of anguish, the Pilgrim asks Virgil: "Teacher, what are these sounds I hear? What souls are these so overwhelmed by grief?" Virgil responds, "This wretched state of being is the fate of those sad souls who lived a life but lived it with no blame and with no praise . . . undecided [they] stood but for themselves" (Musa, 1995; Canto III: 32–39). These are the only souls the Pilgrim and Virgil encounter who are "nowhere" because during their life—especially in times of moral crisis—they remained neutral and refused to make a choice.

Ethical Orientations: Care and Justice

White (2008) argues that resolutions to ethical issues are a function of our ethical orientation. Before we go further, circle your answers to the following questions:

1. Which is worse?
   a. Hurting someone's feelings by telling the truth
   b. Telling a lie and protecting their feelings

2. Which is the worse mistake?
   a. To make exceptions too freely
   b. To apply rules too rigidly

3. Which is it worse to be?
   a. Unmerciful
   b. Unfair

4. Which is worse?
   a. Stealing something valuable from someone for no good reason
   b. Breaking a promise to a friend for no good reason

5. Which is it better to be?
   a. Just and fair
   b. Sympathetic and caring

6. Which is worse?
   a. Not helping someone in trouble
   b. Being unfair to someone by playing favorites

7. In making decisions, you rely more on
   a. Hard facts
   b. Personal feelings and intuition

8. Your boss orders you to do something that will hurt someone. If you carry out the order, have you actually done anything wrong?
   a. Yes
   b. No

9. Which is more important in determining whether an action is right or wrong?
   a. Whether anyone actually gets hurt
   b. Whether a rule, law, commandment, or moral principle is broken

Use the chart below and score each of your answers as either C or J. For example, in question one, if your answer was a, circle the letter C; if it was b, circle the letter J. Do this for all nine of your answers and then count how many Cs and Js you have. You should have a total for your J score and C score at the end.

	a.	b.
1.	C	J
2.	J	C
3.	C	J
4.	J	C
5.	J	C
6.	C	J
7.	J	C
8.	C	J
9.	C	J

J score _____
C score _____

(Source: Thomas I. White (2008). *Discovering Philosophy* 2nd edition. pp. 389–390.)

According to Professor White, this self-inventory helps identify your ethical style. The J scores are based on the need for *justice*. This approach to understanding and acting upon ethical issues prizes reason, objectivity, and fairness. Similar to the statue of justice blindfolded, it doesn't matter what the circumstances are or who is involved, the same rules apply impartially across the board. The other style, C, combines reason with emotions. This is the moral principle of *care*. It takes into account circumstance and stresses responsibility to people in need. Those with a high C score are comfortable breaking away from black and white policies and establishing precedent. Some people are strongly oriented toward J or C and others have a more balanced score. Is one style better than the other? No. This self-assessment simply reveals heightened awareness of our own ethical orientation and the ethical orientations of others. Remember, true ethical dilemmas are right-versus-right choices. When we disagree with the ethical decisions of others, it is probably the result of different ethical orientations, rather than one person being wrong and the other right.

WHY PEOPLE CHEAT

Dan Ariely, a professor of Psychology and Behavior Economics at Duke University, has conducted a variety of experiments to study how dishonesty works. Ariely says, "Everybody has the capacity to be dishonest, and almost everybody cheats—just by a little. Except for a few outliers at the top and bottom, the behavior of almost everyone is driven by two opposing motivations. On the one hand, we want to benefit from cheating and get as much money and glory as possible; on the other hand, we want to view ourselves as honest, honorable people" (Ariely, 2012, C1). One of the experiments involves a "matrix test" where subjects are given sheets of paper containing boxes with different numbers to the hundredth decimal point. Subjects are told that each paper contains two numbers that add up to 10 and they have five minutes to solve as many of the matrices as possible. Most people can solve about four matrices in five minutes. However, when subjects are told to count their correct answers on their own and then put their work sheets through a paper shredder, something remarkable happens: people suddenly get a lot smarter! Participants in the "shredder condition" claim to solve an average of six matrices, two more than those in the control group. The increase in correct solutions isn't from a few people that cheat by a large margin; rather, the increase is the result of a lot of people that cheat by just a little.

So, what factors increase or decrease dishonesty? First, according to Ariely's research, the amount of money to be gained by cheating and the probability of being caught has no effect on dishonesty. When subjects took the matrix challenge and the reward for each solved matrix was increased from 50 cents to $10, the amount of cheating did not increase. In fact, when participants were promised the highest amount for each correct answer, incidents of cheating decreased slightly (Ariely notes that perhaps it was harder for participants to cheat and still see themselves as honest people). However, cheating increased when psychological distance was placed between the participant and the financial payoff. For example, when students received tokens—which could be redeemed for cash—subjects cheated twice as much as those lying directly for money. Furthermore, when participants were placed in an environment with a higher probability of being caught, again, there was no effect on cheating. Factors that increase dishonesty include: rationalization, previous immoral acts, others benefitting from our dishonesty (this is another form of rationalization, e.g., if cheating can help another person than that makes the cheater a virtuous person), being drained from the demands of a mentally difficult task, watching others directly behave dishonestly, and working in a culture where dishonesty is modeled.

One factor that significantly decreases dishonesty is being reminded of moral codes right at the point where people are making a decision. Ethics lectures and training appear to have very little effect on whether or not people cheat (after all, cheating exists every day in organizations that spend a lot of money putting managers through ethics training and have lofty sounding ethics and value statements framed on the walls of company buildings). A better approach is to infuse moral behavior into everyday activities—especially right before activities where people may be tempted to act dishonestly. Ariely and his colleagues tested this idea by administering their matrix task to two groups. One group was asked to recall the Ten Commandments and the other group to recall 10 books they had read in high school. There was the typical distribution of cheating among the group who recalled the 10 books, but no cheating whatsoever among those asked to recall the Ten Commandments. Other groups were reminded of their school honor codes instead of the Ten Commandments and even a group of self-declared atheists swore on a Bible that they would not cheat and under these conditions there was the same result: no cheating. Ariely's research also reveals that moving where people sign documents to the top of the form before they fill out information (rather than at the end of a form after people had already lied) reduced dishonesty.

VALUES

If you have chaperoned or attended a school dance lately, inevitably the issue of "freaking" has surfaced. If you are not familiar with this term, "freaking" occurs where dance partners press and gyrate their bodies against each other on the dance floor. A high school principal in Orange County, California took a strong stance in order to end this practice at school dances. At a back-to-school dance, where students were wearing sexually suggestive clothing and engaging in "freak" dancing, the principal became disgusted, ended the dance 30 minutes early, and sent an email to parents indicating that he was cancelling all dances until further notice. In the email, written just a couple of hours after the dance ended, he said, "I saw way too much of some of our young girls. Why do girls have to have themselves so exposed? Why are they wearing garters? Why do they have to have cleavage displayed so overtly and slits high up their thighs and then allow the boys (to) dance (and rub) up against them? This can happen no more . . . we need to slow this train down." The principal left open the possibility of bringing dances back only if parents and students implemented changes "that will clean up our dances" (Hernandez & Hardesty, 2006). Did this high school principal do the right thing in ending the dance early, immediately sending an email to parents expressing his concerns, and cancelling dances for the rest of the school year? One thing is clear: The principal stood up for what he believes in and acted in alignment with his values.

Where do our values come from? There are two major influences: inherited values and idealized values. Inherited values come from our parents, mentors, managers, and culture. Many times children will adopt (or rebel against!) the values of their parents. Either way, parental values have a strong influence on children. At work an employee may admire a supervisor or senior executive and pattern his or her value judgments after these people. Culture also influences values. For example, Europeans take many more vacation days than Americans and thus have different values regarding leisure and work-life balance. Inherited values are passed down through sayings. For example, a child may grow up in a household where a parent or grandparent asks, "What will you do for your country?" This child will probably grow up with values directed toward military service or patriotic expression. A master carpenter will tell an apprentice, "Learn the trade, not the tricks of the trade." In my own family I always tell my children, "Be nice, work hard, and no whining." Think about the sayings you've heard in your own family or workplace and I bet they have influenced your values. Idealized values are those that we aspire toward. We may lean on role models or heroes as examples of the values we try to integrate into our own life. Perhaps a religious or historical figure is a personal hero and we work hard to model his or her values in our thoughts, attitudes, and actions. We may not always successfully live up to our idealized values, but we use them as a guide to pull us back on track when we stumble or seek guidance and direction. In Ben Franklin's *Autobiography* he writes, "Imitate Jesus and Socrates." For Franklin these people were sources of idealized values.

Values are easy to deal with when interacting with others that share your same values. However, when an individual's personal values—or a group's values—conflict with others', problems arise. But does there always need to be strife and conflict when values collide? Consider the story of Charles and Emma Darwin. Charles was one of the most famous skeptics of religion and biblical teachings while his wife Emma fervently believed in God and living life in alignment with religious principles. They had a happy and fulfilling marriage that lasted 43 years. How was this possible? Deborah Heiligman (2009) studied the relationship between Charles and Emma Darwin and she believes they had a happy marriage because they communicated honestly, listened to each other, and—even though they disagreed on "the most important subject"—maintained a fundamental respect for one another. Heiligman says, "If it is the sign of intelligence to be able to hold two opposite thoughts or opinions in your head, then it is a mark of a successful marriage to be able to truly see the other person's point of view. This is also the mark of a successful society" (Heiligman, 2009, A19).

Honest communication, listening to others, and demonstrating respect are critical guideposts when value conflicts erupt. Leaders need to be more creative and work to find integrative solutions to seemingly intractable problems (we'll look at effective ways to deal with conflict in Chapter 8). Charles and Emma Darwin's relationship reminds us that value conflicts don't have to be destructive. As M. Scott Peck (1987) says, "A community is a group that can fight gracefully" (p. 71).

What Do You Think?

Step 1. Using the space below, brainstorm a list of 10 values that you passionately believe in. Examples might include: creativity, responsibility, playfulness, ethical behavior, recognizing others, diversity, teamwork, honesty, integrity, fairness, or any other values you think of on your own. When working with student leadership teams I always focus our first meeting on three values: be on time, be prepared, and be respectful. Focus on ten values that really resonate with you.

1.
2.
3.
4.
5.
6.
7.
8.
9.
10.

Step 2. Now comes the hard part! Remove five values from your list by drawing a line through them. I know these values are still important to you, but you are working to identify your top five core values.

List your top five core values.

1.
2.
3.
4.
5.

Step 3. Review your list of five core values. What did you learn from this activity? You can revisit this activity at a later date and make adjustments to your list. This list certainly isn't set in stone, the point is to get you started thinking about the core values that guide (or should guide) your behavior and set the tone for followers.

We've already seen how values impact transformational and authentic leaders. Additionally, followers want to know what leaders stand for. Values are a deeply personal expression of one's beliefs and principles. Clarifying one's core values is useful because values guide behavior and communicate expectations to others. For example, Bennis and Goldsmith (2003) offer five values that enable leaders to become more effective: clear communication, ethical practices, diversity in the workforce, ongoing recognition, and participatory empowerment. Complete the What Do You Think? activity to begin thinking about your top five core values.

Questions for Review

1. What is the difference between moral temptations and ethical dilemmas? What is a "defining moment" and how is this related to leadership?

2. What qualities and behaviors are associated with the moral principles of care and justice? How does your score on the ethical orientation assessment relate to experiences in your own leadership life?

3. What are your top five core values? How do your core values influence your decisions and behaviors? How should individuals and groups deal with value conflicts?

CHAPTER 5:
Honesty, Trust, and Integrity

LEARNING OBJECTIVES

After studying this chapter, you should be able to:

1. Summarize the relationship between honesty and leadership.
2. Discuss the risks and rewards when leaders are honest.
3. Summarize the relationship between trust and leadership.
4. Discuss the relationship between vulnerability and trust.
5. Identify how both trust and distrust influence relationships.
6. Identify trusting behaviors that reduce the risk of exploitation.
7. Define integrity and show how we can measure it.
8. Demonstrate how honesty, trust, and integrity are related to transparency.

HONESTY

Groucho Marx once quipped that the secret to life is honesty and fair dealing; if you can fake that, you've got it made. Let's revisit the Kouzes and Posner (2007) research study, discussed in Chapter 2, which identified *honesty, forward-looking, inspiring* and *competent* as the top four most admired leadership characteristics. How did they come to the conclusion that honesty was the most admired leadership quality? Well, in their surveys, Kouzes and Posner asked the following question, "What are the qualities of a leader that you most admire in someone you would willingly follow?" The word *willingly* is critical. The focus of their study is on the qualities we look for in people we choose to follow, those people that capture our heart, mind, and spirit. Findings were reported in 1987, 1995, 2002, and 2007, and the same characteristic always tops the list: *honesty*. This research is so important for leaders because honesty is the number one quality followers expect and demand in a leader (respondents also used trustworthy, character, and integrity as synonyms for honesty). These findings bring up an interesting dilemma: we say we want honesty in leaders but when leaders (and people in general) act candidly and honestly, they often get raked over the coals. Such was the case with the famous Dutch painter Rembrandt van Rijn.

In 1660, the town leaders of Amsterdam were commissioning artists to adorn the interior hallways and walls of the newly constructed Town Hall with paintings from Batavian antiquity. Rembrandt was no longer a favored son of the elite. At this point in his career, Simon Schama (1999) notes that Rembrandt was "treated rather like the eccentric uncle, soiled by disgrace, a little cracked, and with a poor sense of manners" (p. 628). Rembrandt lived sequestered in his apartment and needed money as he watched lesser contemporaries score jobs from wealthy patrons and town leaders. However, with the death of one of the Town Hall's commissioned painters, Govert Flinck, a slot opened up for someone to paint the oath-swearing scene of Claudius Civilis, and, against all odds, Rembrandt was selected. Civilis was a first century Batavian chieftain and Roman officer who rallied the ancestors of modern day Netherlands in a revolt against Roman rule in AD 69–70. Flinck left behind a pen drawing of his plans for the painting. The scene would be approached with regal daintiness. "Around a neatly dressed table, covered by white linen as though a lord were picnicking in the woods, the ritual handshake was being consummated. Civilis was seated at the end of the table, naked from the waist up, his face seen in profile, thus decently hiding his blind eye" (Schama, 1999, p. 629).

A gentlemanly and erudite scene if ever there was one. The only problem: this wasn't the way it happened. Tacitus, the Roman historian, recorded the "revelry that had fired their spirits" and noted that Civilis had assembled "the boldest of the common people." In reality, Civilis and his followers were earthy commoners forged together by the passion and spirit of liberation. When Rembrandt read Tacitus' reference to barbaric rites, "something other than this handshake came to mind: a clash of swords, a calyx slop-full of wine or blood or both" (Schama, 1999, p. 630). Rembrandt, "dreamt up a scene of barbarian uproar, hot with revelry, as Tacitus had said, drunk on freedom . . . gathering before some kind of screen, or within some sort of tent or tabernacle" (Schama, 1999, p. 631). With Rembrandt, Civilis's hollow eye isn't shielded from view; instead it confronts the viewer head-on while his good eye gazes fixed and resolutely outside the frame of the painting toward the future and us. This powerful, unvarnished honesty was too much for the local politicians. They wanted history communicated to the public and visiting dignitaries as they graced the Town Hall; it just wasn't this history.

So, they rolled up and returned the twenty-foot painting to Rembrandt. Simon Schama concludes the story this way:

> And yet he desperately needed to salvage something from the ruin. There was rent to pay, bread to be put on the table. Otherwise all his herculean labor would go for nothing; no fame and assuredly no fortune. His only hope was to try somehow to turn the white elephant into a salable commodity by cutting it down to a size that might be suitable for someone's house. Perhaps he could manage to find a buyer who could set it at the top of his own staircase, or over a grand mantel, if it were cut down. So there was nothing for it but to roll the twenty-foot masterpiece out on the floor (for Rembrandt could not have had any kind of table big enough to hold it) and have Titus [his assistant] secure one end while he knelt down with his knife and sliced through it, the tight weave fraying as he sheared, cut-away lengths falling on the floor like strips of shoddy in a tailor's shop. He must have crawled over it until the painting was pruned to the long, relatively narrow fragment that survives today in Stockholm (p. 633)

Imagine cutting up a Rembrandt original! Only time proved the virtue of Rembrandt's honesty as the remaining fragment of the once enormous original is considered one of Rembrandt's masterpieces.

Likewise, as pundit Michael Kinsley has observed, in politics, a gaff is when a politician tells the truth. For example, in 1976, Robert Scheer was conducting an interview with then presidential candidate Jimmy Carter. Scheer asked Carter to expand on the potential influence of his religious beliefs (Carter is Baptist) should he be elected president. Carter said, "Christ set some almost impossible standards for us. Christ said, 'I tell you that anyone who looks on a woman with lust has in his heart already committed adultery.' I've looked on a lot of women with lust. I've committed adultery in my heart many times." Carter was talking very openly and honestly about temptation, sin, and his own human frailty. Interestingly, the interview contained a number of comments about critical national and global issues, such as the war in Vietnam; however, the media focused exclusively on Carter's comments on lust. Here was a presidential candidate who in his honesty opened the door to attack from his political rivals. Although Carter eventually won the presidency, opponents used this revelation to attack Carter's morality and character. While honesty is a virtue, it often comes with significant political risk.

Leadership is all about relationships. As in any friendship or romantic relationship, there must be a strong foundation built on honesty, candor, and open communication. Honesty makes us vulnerable, but as we'll discover in the next section, vulnerability and trust go hand-in-hand.

TRUST

How long does it take for trust to develop in a relationship? Does it happen quickly or does it take a while? I think it takes a while. We need to spend time getting to know the other person—their authentic qualities—*and* observe how they act before there is a true connection. It takes time to cultivate trusting relationships, but trust can be fractured or lost in an instant—one misstep and trust quickly evaporates. Of course we can take steps to regain another's trust, but people have long memories and may forgive, but rarely forget. Solomon and Flores (2001) believe that trust, above all, is a conscious choice. It requires a willingness to make commitments and honor what you say. They offer that trusting relationships emerge by talking about trust and institutionalizing it in "the day-to-day rituals of a marriage or the well-organized routines of a global corporation" (p. 47). If trust is a "conscious choice," then it is the leader's responsibility to initiate conversations about trust and, more importantly, to act with integrity.

While there isn't a universal definition of trust in the scholarly literature, Rousseau, Sitkin, Burt, and Camerer (1998) suggest that a widely held definition of trust is, "a psychological state comprising the intention to accept vulnerability based upon positive expectations of the intentions or behavior of another" (p. 395). The emphasis on vulnerability is important because at the heart of any trusting action is the risk that one may be let down. Lewicki, McAllister, and Bies (1998) note that relationships are complex, multidimensional constructs where one can hold feelings of both trust and distrust simultaneously when interacting with others. Interactions with others operate within a given context, at a specific point in time, and around a given interdependency. This is because as specific facets in relationships change (through dialogue, interaction, joint decision making, common experience, and so on), these changes will have corresponding affects on the levels of trust and distrust in the relationship. In this model, trust and distrust exist as two separate dimensions. (see Table 5-1)

Low Trust/Low Distrust (Cell 1)

Under these conditions, one individual has neither reason to be confident nor reason to be wary and watchful of the other person. With increased interdependence, awareness of the other person will rise as will beliefs about

TABLE 5-1 Integrating Trust and Distrust: Alternative Social Realities

	High Trust/Low Distrust	High Trust/High Distrust

High Trust
 	
Characterized by
  Hope
  Faith
  Confidence
  Assurance
  Initiative
	High-value congruence
	
	Interdependence promoted
	
	Opportunities pursued
	
	New initiatives
		Trust but verify
		
		Relationships highly segmented and bounded
		
		Opportunities pursued and down-side risks/vulnerabilities continually monitored

	2 | **4** **1** | **3**	

Low Trust
 	
Characterized by
  No hope
  No faith
  No confidence
  Passivity
  Hesitance
	Low Trust/Low Distrust
	Casual acquaintances
	
	Limited interdependence
	
	Bounded, arms-length transactions
	
	Professional courtesy
		Low Trust/High Distrust
		Undesirable eventualities expected and feared
		
		Harmful motives assumed
		
		Interdependence managed
		
		Preemption; best offense is a good defense
		
		Paranoia

	Low Distrust
	Characterized by
	  No fear
	  Absence of skepticism
	  Absence of cynicism
	  Low monitoring
	  No vigilance
		High Distrust
		Characterized by
		  Fear
		  Skepticism
		  Cynicism
		  Wariness and watchfulness
		  Vigilance

Reprinted from "Trust and Distrust: New Relationships and Realities," *Academy of Management Review* 23, no. 3 (1998), by permission of the Academy of Management Review.

the other person's trustworthiness and untrustworthiness. Parties are not likely to engage in any relationship dynamics requiring complex interdependency. Conversation most likely is simple and casual, not violating the privacy of either party or suggesting the existence of any closeness or intimacy.

High Trust/Low Distrust (Cell 2)

One actor has reason to be confident in another and no reason to suspect the other. Relationships are characterized by high interdependence where parties are pursuing shared objectives. Parties are likely to continually develop and enrich the relationship and expand their interdependencies.

Conversations are complex and rich, reflecting shared values and verbalizations of support, appreciation, and encouragement.

Low Trust/High Distrust (Cell 3)

One actor has no reason for confidence in another and ample reason for wariness and watchfulness. It is extremely difficult (if not impossible) to maintain effective interdependent relationships under these conditions. This condition reflects a large number of negative experiences in which the aggregate experience has been distrust reinforcing. Significant time and resources are spent monitoring the other's behavior, preparing for the other's distrusting actions, and attending to potential vulnerabilities that might be exploited. Conversation is likely to be cautious, guarded, and often laced with sarcasm, cynicism, and sinister attributions of the other's intention and motives. High distrust relationships are most effectively managed by compartmentalizing relations and creating clearly specified parameters that constrain and guide each interaction. For example, if an employee feels high distrust toward another employee, the first party can approach the supervisor and request that the other party interact with him or her under specific conditions outlined by the employee. In this way, the relations are constrained to allow for trust relations to emerge and allow for functional interactions between the two individuals.

High Trust/High Distrust (Cell 4)

One party has reason to be highly confident in another in certain respects, but also has reason to be strongly wary and suspicious in other respects. In these relationships, partners are likely to have separate as well as shared objectives. The aggregate of experiences with the other party has proved both trust and distrust reinforcing. In order to sustain and benefit from this form of relationship, parties can take steps to limit interdependence to those areas where interdependence is critical and limit those interdependencies that may prove harmful. Lewicki, McAllister, and Bies (1998), note that when Boeing and the Japanese were engaged in a joint venture to build the Boeing 777, engineers shared large amounts of technical and proprietary information. However, Boeing protected itself by limiting the access of Japanese engineers to "secure" areas within Boeing buildings. This condition of high trust/high distrust is the most prevalent dynamic for working relationships within modern organizations.

Dirks and Ferrin (2002) report a number of positive associations related to trust in one's direct leader (e.g., supervisor, work group leader) and organizational leadership (e.g., executive leadership team, collective set of leaders). In their meta-analysis, Dirks and Ferrin found that trust in leadership is significantly related to attitudinal, behavioral, and performance outcomes. Trust demonstrated a substantial relationship with attitudinal variables such as job satisfaction, organizational commitment, and satisfaction with the leader. Trust also revealed a "bottom line" benefit indicating a significant relationship with employee performance.

Confidence and the Risk of Exploitation

Gaining the confidence of another person in order to cheat them is an age-old con. However, the term "Confidence Man" was first coined in 1849 to describe a real-life criminal named Thompson (The man later used other assumed names) who was arrested in New York City after Mr. Thomas McDonald complained that he had been tricked out of an expensive gold watch (see Bergmann, 1969). Thompson condensed all of the usual steps of the confidence game into a brief exchange. In his game, Thompson would gain the confidence of the other person by pretending to be an old acquaintance and gain the trust of the victim through his sheer confidence of expression (upon which the victim would feel embarrassed for having not remembered Thompson). Next Thompson would ask the victim to demonstrate his or her confidence by loaning him their watch which would be returned the next day. Of course the watch would not be returned and it was too late until the victim realized they had trusted too freely. From the "Original Confidence Man" to modern examples such as Bernard Madoff, who rather than gold watches swindled others out of millions of dollars from their life savings, the interplay between trust, confidence, and exploitation is worth exploring.

Kramer (2009) makes a compelling argument with fascinating examples as to why we are born social beings predisposed to trust others. He says:

> We enter the world "hardwired" to make social connections. The evidence is impressive: Within *one hour* of birth, a human infant will draw her head back to look into the eyes and face of the person gazing at her. Within a few more hours, the infant will orient her head in the direction of her mother's voice. And, unbelievable as it may seem, it's only a matter of hours before the infant can actually mimic a caretaker's expressions. A baby's mother, in turn, responds and mimics her child's expression and emotions within seconds. In short, we're social beings from the get-go: We're born to be engaged and to engage others, which is what trust is largely about. (p. 70)

So, what behaviors engender trust and why—at times—are we so bad at distinguishing con-artists from those who truly deserve our trust? Kramer claims that *biases, illusions,* and *simplistic (but powerful) trust cues* increase the propensity to make errors in our judgments about whom to trust.

Trust Biases

Biases surface in various forms. For example, if I am looking for a financial advisor and I have a trusted friend who recommends their financial advisor to me, I am more likely to trust the advisor based on my friend's recommendation. Kramer says, "We rely on trusted third parties to verify the character or reliability of other people" (p. 72). Bernard Madoff relied on trust biases to swindle smart, successful businesspeople. New York Mets professional baseball team owner Fred Wilpon dumped millions into Madoff's investment scheme and for years received steady returns of 10% to 12%. Wilpon suggested to Mets' general manager Steve Phillips that he should also join Madoff's fund once he had the $100,000 minimum investment. Reflecting on Wilpon's endorsement of Madoff, Phillips recounted, "I said to my wife, 'It sounds great.' I laugh about it now. But back then, here's Fred Wilpon, a tremendously wealthy and successful businessman. If he vetted it, I felt comfortable with it . . . " (Verducci, 2011).

Research also points to the fact that we are much more likely to trust others with similar physical characteristics (i.e., those that look like us) and members of our same social group. Kramer notes that "this in-group effect is so powerful that even random assignment into small groups is sufficient enough to create a sense of solidarity" (p. 70). Additionally, what psychologists call *confirmation bias,* or the inclination to see what we want to see, can skew our judgment. Kramer reports on a laboratory game he conducted where individuals who were primed to expect an abuse of trust looked more carefully for signs of untrustworthy behavior in others. Conversely, those who were primed to expect more positive and trusting interactions paid more attention to these aspects of their prospective partners. In short, the decisions about how much to trust (or not trust) the other person was largely determined by one's expectations.

Cognitive Illusions

In addition to biases that influence decisions on whom to trust, Kramer reports two cognitive illusions that increase our propensity to trust too readily, too much, and for too long. First is the *illusion of personal invulnerability.* Under this illusion we believe that bad things happen to other people but won't happen to us. For example, while we may read in the newspaper about the misfortunes of those that invested in Madoff's schemes, we tend to convince ourselves that we have taken the necessary precautions and steps to mitigate ever being victimized in such a way as those that suffered under Madoff, hence developing the illusion of personal invulnerability to ever being conned. A second illusion is *unrealistic optimism*. Kramer says, "Numerous studies have shown that people often overestimate the likelihood that good things will happen to them—that they will marry well, have a successful career, live a long life, and so on. Even when people are giving accurate information regarding the true odds of such outcomes, they still tend to think they will do better than average" (p. 73).

Trust Cues

The behaviors and cues used to engender trust can also be used—quite easily—to gain one's confidence for nefarious advantage. Kramer reports on his own lab experiments on deceptive behavior where he tells some participants to "fake" trustworthiness during a negotiation exercise. These "temporary con-men" tend to smile a lot; use direct eye contact; gently touch the other person's arm or hand; engage in cheery banter to relax the other person; and simulate openness during their actual negotiation by saying things like, "Let's agree to be honest and we can probably do better at this exercise" and "I always like to put all my cards on the table." Kramer reports that these efforts turn out to be pretty successful in getting the other person to believe that he is acting in an authentic and trustworthy manner. Kramer says:

> Additionally, even when students on the other side of the bargaining table were (secretly) forewarned that half the students they might encounter had been instructed to try to fool them and take advantage of them, their ability to detect fakers did not improve: They didn't identify fakers any more accurately than a coin flip would have. Perhaps most interesting, those who had been forewarned actually felt they'd done a better job of detecting fakery than did the other students. (p. 73)

So, with all of this evidence leading to the fact that we are probably worse at judging the trustworthiness of others than we think, how can we avoid being duped? Kramer says we need to practice "tempered trust." He provides seven rules to mitigate poor trust judgments by adjusting our mind-set and behavioral habits.

Rule One: Know Yourself

There are two general types of people with regard to trust: those who trust too readily and those who are too mistrustful of others. The first type may talk too freely and misread the trust cues of the other person assuming that person is a friend and consequently will reveal sensitive information or personal secrets too early in the relationship. The second type may assume too readily that other people cannot be trusted and avoid disclosing anything about themselves that might help create a social connection. We must decide which type we fall into and where we need to make adjustments so that we don't compromise ourselves or put up unnecessary barriers to forming trusting relationships.

Rule Two: Start Small

Measured trust begins with small acts that foster reciprocity. A good example of this dynamic was displayed by Hewlett-Packard in the early 1980s. Management allowed engineers to take equipment home whenever they needed to, without having to go through a lot of red tape. That sent a strong signal that the company trusted employees, yet it involved relatively little risk, because the policy was tied to employees' not abusing the trust.

Rule Three: Write an Escape Clause

With a clearly articulated plan for disengagement, people can trust more fully. In Hollywood, scriptwriters register their pitches with the Writers Guild—a simple act that hedges against the risk that others will claim a story as their own.

Rule Four: Send Strong Signals

Most of us mistakenly believe our trustworthiness is obvious. We actually need to signal it more clearly. By the same token, we have to retaliate strongly when our trust is abused. Sending weak signals about our willingness to engage in trust or punish abuse of it makes us more vulnerable to exploitation.

Rule Five: Recognize the Other Person's Dilemma

Because we worry so much about ourselves, we often forget that the people we are dealing with experience their own trust dilemmas and need reassurance about whether (or how much) they should trust. Good relationship builders are proactive about decreasing the anxiety and allaying the concerns of others.

Rule Six: Look at Roles as Well as People

A person's role or position can provide a guarantee of his expertise and motivation but be careful; people on Main Street USA trusted people on Wall Street for a long time because the financial systems seemed to be producing reliable results that were the envy of the world.

Rule 7: Remain Vigilant and Always Question

Many people whose trust is abused do conduct their due diligence initially. The trouble is they don't keep their due diligence up-to-date because they find that being vigilant and ambivalent about the people they trust is psychologically uncomfortable.

(Adapted from Kramer, R. (2009, June). Rethinking trust. *Harvard Business Review*, 69–77.)

INTEGRITY

Integrity means different things to different people. To some it means being moral or ethical, to others it means being trustworthy or a person of character. Still, to others it may imply authenticity or doing what you say you will do. Regardless of how one defines integrity, we know that integrity matters for leaders and organizations. Peterson (2004) found that the perceived integrity of leaders also impacts the ethical intentions of subordinates. This study investigated the degree to which a person believes in a universal set of moral rules (e.g., that not being truthful is always wrong regardless of the situation) or whether individuals believe ethics to be relative and assume that what constitutes ethical behavior depends on the situation or outcome of the behavior. Results of the study indicated that leader integrity and the ethical intentions of subordinates were only related for individuals who do not adhere to a belief in universal moral values. Individuals who believe in universal moral rules are expected to act in alignment with internalized principles rather than being influenced by the integrity of the leader. However, individuals who believe ethics are relative were found to be influenced by the perceived integrity of the leader. Thus, the integrity of leaders has a strong impact on the behaviors of employees under these circumstances.

Palanski and Yammarino (2007) note that integrity comes from the Latin term *integer*, which means wholeness or completeness. One example of integrity in this context is in relation to the hull of a ship having integrity—meaning that the hull is watertight. Palanski and Yammarino (2007) have identified four behavioral aspects in defining integrity: integrity as consistency of words and actions; integrity as consistency during times of adversity, temptation, or challenge; integrity as being true to oneself and acting in alignment with one's conscience and internalized values; and integrity as moral or ethical behavior (p. 175). Consistency between words and actions is one of the more common definitions of integrity. More to the point, integrity is consistency of an *acting entity's* words and actions and this *acting entity* can be an individual, a group, or an organization (Palansky & Yammarino, 2009, p. 408). Consistency between words and deeds has also been defined as *behavioral integrity* (BI). Simons (2002) contends that the perceived pattern of managers' word-deed alignment—or misalignment—is a critical organizational phenomenon because it serves as an antecedent to trust and credibility. Even small word-deed misalignments can have substantial consequences for the perceived integrity of leaders. Simmons also notes that the perception of BI is likely to be strongly influenced by hierarchical relationships because subordinates are far more likely to notice BI and its lack on the part of managers than the other way around. With the stakes so high regarding word-deed alignment, why might managers' espoused practices and values diverge from their actual actions? Simmons proposes three general observations:

1. *Diverse Demands*: Managers frequently are charged with satisfying multiple, often contradictory, constituencies both inside and outside the organization. Relaxed demands for consistency allow them to better accomplish this task.

2. *Wishful Thinking*: Language can help shape reality; therefore, managers might espouse their stretch goals and wishful thinking in an effort to elevate themselves and their organizations through processes similar to self-fulfilling prophecies and Pygmalion effects.

3. *Learning by Talking*: Managers often clarify their beliefs and values by reflecting on what they say and the demands placed upon them to act. For example, if a manager is being encouraged by a superior to support a change initiative he or she doesn't believe in, the manager may experience word-deed misalignment for a time while he or she reflects on this personal ambivalence, clarifies beliefs, and moves toward action.

In summary, consistency between what an individual, group, or organization says and does is a sign of integrity while inconsistencies signal an integrity gap.

MEASURING INTEGRITY

The following items concern your immediate supervisor. You should consider your immediate supervisor to be the person who you feel has the most control over your daily work activities. Circle responses to indicate how well each item describes your immediate supervisor.

Response Choices: 1 Not at all   2 Somewhat   3 Very much   4 Exactly

1. Would use my mistakes to attack me personally	1	2	3	4
2. Always gets even	1	2	3	4
3. Gives special favors to certain "pet" employees, but not to me	1	2	3	4
4. Would lie to me	1	2	3	4
5. Would risk me to protect himself/herself in work matters	1	2	3	4
6. Deliberately fuels conflict among employees	1	2	3	4
7. Is evil	1	2	3	4
8. Would use my performance appraisal to criticize me as a person	1	2	3	4
9. Has it in for me	1	2	3	4
10. Would allow me to be blamed for his/her mistakes	1	2	3	4
11. Would falsify records if it would help his/her work situation	1	2	3	4
12. Lacks high morals	1	2	3	4
13. Makes fun of my mistakes instead of coaching me as to how to do my job better	1	2	3	4
14. Would deliberately exaggerate my mistakes to make me look bad when describing my performance to his/her superiors	1	2	3	4
15. Is vindictive	1	2	3	4

	1	2	3	4
16. Would blame me for his/her own mistake	1	2	3	4
17. Avoids coaching me because (s)he wants me to fail	1	2	3	4
18. Would treat me better if I belonged to a different ethnic group	1	2	3	4
19 Would deliberately distort what I say	1	2	3	4
20. Deliberately makes employees angry at each other	1	2	3	4
21. Is a hypocrite	1	2	3	4
22. Would limit my training opportunities to prevent me from advancing	1	2	3	4
23. Would blackmail an employee if (s)he thought (s)he could get away with it	1	2	3	4
24. Enjoys turning down my requests	1	2	3	4
25. Would make trouble for me if I got on his/her bad side	1	2	3	4
26. Would take credit for my ideas	1	2	3	4
27. Would steal from the organization	1	2	3	4
28. Would risk me to get back at someone else	1	2	3	4
29. Would engage in sabotage against the organization	1	2	3	4
30. Would fire people just because (s)he doesn't like them if (s)he could get away with it	1	2	3	4
31. Would do things that violate organizational policy and then expect his/her subordinates to cover for him/her	1	2	3	4

Scoring Interpretation

The PLIS measures subordinates' perceptions of their leaders' integrity in organizational settings. Your responses on the PLIS indicate the degree to which you see your supervisor's behavior as ethical.

Score the questionnaire by doing the following. Sum the responses on all 31 items. A *low score* on the questionnaire indicates that you perceive your supervisor to be *highly ethical*. A *high score* indicates that you see your supervisor to be *very unethical*. The interpretation of what the score represents is given below.

Total score: _____

31-35	High ethical	If you scored in this range, it means that you see your supervisor as highly ethical. Your impression is that your supervisor is very trustworthy and highly principled.
36-66	Moderate	Scores in this range mean that you see your supervisor as moderately ethical. Your impression is that he or she sometimes engages in slightly unethical behaviors.
67-124	Low ethical	This range is descriptive of supervisors who are seen as very unethical. Your impression is that they do things which are dishonest, unfair, and unprincipled.

TRANSPARENCY: THE BEST WAY TO GAUGE HONESTY, TRUST, AND INTEGRITY IN ORGANIZATIONS

> Well you may throw your rock and hide your hand
> Workin' in the dark against your fellow man
> But as sure as God made black and white
> What's done in the dark will be brought to the light
>
> God's Gonna Cut You Down, Traditional Song

Transparency can mean different things to different people. Inevitably the term transparency brings to mind openness, candor, honesty, and integrity. Bennis, Goleman, and Biederman (2008) define transparency as "the free flow of information within an organization and between the organization and its many stakeholders, including the public" (p. 3). Transparency is inexorably linked with honesty, integrity and trust. Think about it this way:

if you are in an organization or work with leaders that are dishonest, lack integrity, or are untrustworthy, there will inevitably be a lack of openness, candor, and sharing of accurate information. Whether leaders want to create a culture of transparency or not, the rise of the Internet has forced the issue. We have entered a transparent world where anyone can post an online critique or review of organizations, businesses, or even other people. Web sites are dedicated to rating stores, restaurants, schools, doctors, teachers and college professors just to name a few. With the proliferation of blogs, information can be packaged and spread to millions of potential readers with lightening speed because anyone with a computer and Internet access can begin to generate thousands of followers. In fact, as of 2011 there are over 163 million blogs with thousands more being started each day (The Neilson Company, 2011).

Leaders and organizations are often criticized for not being "transparent" enough. Today's leaders are better off being proactive in creating systems and pathways for internal and external audiences to access information. Of course some information, such as employee personnel files, is confidential; however, claims against transparency usually revolve around how decisions are being made, and specifically, how money is being spent. Demonstrating transparency by posting copies of agendas and minutes online is a good start, but isn't enough. True transparency exists when leaders display a genuine commitment to honesty and openness and demand the same for all organizational members. Remember the old saying that you shouldn't do anything that you aren't comfortable seeing on the front page of the newspaper? Well, in today's world you shouldn't do anything that you aren't comfortable reading about on 163 million blogs!

As 2008 ushered in the largest recession since the Great Depression, aggressive calls for more transparency ensued in corporate and governmental organizations. For example, the nation's largest public pension fund— California Public Employees Retirement System (CalPERS)—CEO Anne Stausboll called for efforts within her organization to restore trust and transparency to markets both within the United States and globally. A centerpiece of the plan she is championing includes ensuring more transparency in often exotic and hard-to-comprehend investments and making sure that the private agencies that rate bonds and securities are not paid by the companies they are evaluating. Commenting on the leadership qualities necessary in a turbulent financial market, William D Crist, a long-time CalPERS board member says, "What's needed at the helm is common sense, intelligence, and pure stability. We don't need wizardry or magic bullets" (Lifsher, 2009, C1). This is good advice for any leader regardless of market conditions.

What Works for You?

Transparency is dependent on trust, honesty, candor, and openness with information. What changes can you and/or your organization implement to become more transparent?

_____

_____

_____

_____

_____

_____

_____

_____

_____

_____

Questions for Review

1. How is honesty related to leadership? What are the risks and rewards when a leader is honest?
2. What role does trust play in leadership relationships? How are trust and vulnerability related?
3. How do both trust and distrust influence relationships?
4. What behaviors contribute to building trust? What behaviors can reduce the risk of exploitation?
5. How is integrity defined? How can we measure integrity?
6. What is transparency? How is transparency related to honesty, trust, and integrity?

CHAPTER 6:
Think Like a Leader: Creativity, Innovation, and Reframing

LEARNING OBJECTIVES

After studying this chapter, you should be able to:

1. Compare L-Directed and R-Directed thinking.
2. Define janusian and paradoxical thinking.
3. Discuss the impact of technology on how people think.
4. Identify skills and practices that foster creativity and innovation.
5. Discuss the role of failure on leaders.
6. Discuss how reframing helps leaders manage paradox and ambiguity in modern organizations.
7. Apply the four-frame model to leadership and organizational performance.

THE MIND OF A LEADER

In which of the following subjects is the performance of American 12th graders the worst: a) science, b) economics, c) history, or d) math? According to the federal government's National Assessment of Educational Progress, the answer is history. Norm Augustine, a former undersecretary of the Army and retired chairman and CEO of Lockheed Martin, argues that this statistic should be a major wake-up call regarding how we are educating tomorrow's leaders. Schools, colleges, and universities have focused time and resources on bolstering the STEM subjects (science, technology, English and math); however, Augustine notes that as an executive leader, academic subjects like history train people in essential skills such as critical thinking, research, and the ability to communicate clearly and cogently. Also, acknowledging the impact of global-ization, Augustine says, "Having traveled in 109 countries in this global econ-omy, I have developed a considerable appreciation for the importance of knowing a country's history and politics" (Augustine, 2011, A. 17). This type of knowledge goes beyond reciting simple facts and dates in the timeline of a country or civilization. Rather it speaks to thinking critically: analyzing dis-parate, complex and, sometimes, conflicting perspectives, synthesizing numerous data points and ultimately communicating articulately and clearly. Augustine says, "In my position as CEO of a firm employing over 80,000 engineers, I can testify that most were excellent engineers—but the factor that most distinguished those who advanced in the organization was the ability to think broadly and read and write clearly" (Augustine, 2011, A17). We are living in a time of unprecedented access to information delivered instantaneously to the smartphones we carry in the palm of our hand. The leadership challenge is to infuse data and information with meaning and then to communicate and share this knowledge with others. This requires leaders to think and act in new ways as we will discover in this next section.

Daniel Pink makes a compelling case in his book *A Whole New Mind: Why Right-Brainers will Rule the Future* that old ways of thinking will not deliver the same results that were achieved in the past. He argues that we have shifted "from an economy and a society built on the logical, linear, computer like capabilities of the Information Age to an economy and a society built on the inventive, empathic, big-picture capabilities of what's rising in its place, the Conceptual Age" (Pink, 2006, pp. 1–2). Pink describes L-Directed Thinking as the valued attribute of the Information Age. This type of thinking emanates from the left hemisphere of the brain and is sequential, literal, functional, textual, and analytic. This type of thinking is emphasized in schools and has been the default way of thinking in most organizations. R-Directed Thinking is related to the right hemisphere of the brain and is the prized asset of tomorrow's world-class organizations and the key to career success. L-Directed Thinking is simultaneous, metaphorical, aesthetic, contextual, and focused on synthesis. To make the shift toward recognizing and valuing R-Directed Thinking, people—and leaders in particular—must possess the six "high-touch" senses of: Design, Story, Symphony, Empathy, Play, and Meaning. Pink recognizes that L and R-Directed Thinking are complimentary impulses. He defines the six "high-touch" senses and their relationship to L-Directed Thinking by saying we need:

1. Not just function but also DESIGN. It's no longer sufficient to create a product, a service, an experience, or a lifestyle that's merely functional. Today it's economically crucial and personally

① Forming or following in a logical order or sequence.
② Word for word ③ of or having a special activity, purpose.
④ relating to or using analysis or logical reasoning.
⑤ something characterized by a harmonious combination

rewarding to create something that is also beautiful, whimsical, or emotionally engaging.

2. Not just argument but also STORY. When our lives are brimming with information and data, it's not enough to marshal an effective argument. Someone somewhere will inevitably track down a counter point to rebut your point. The essence of persuasion, communication, and self-understanding has become the ability also to fashion a compelling narrative.

3. Not just focus but also SYMPHONY. Much of the Industrial and Information Ages required focus and specialization. But as white-collar work gets routed to Asia and reduced to software, there's a new premium on the opposite aptitude: putting the pieces together, or what I call Symphony. What's in greatest demand today isn't analysis but synthesis—seeing the big picture, crossing boundaries, and being able to combine disparate pieces into an arresting new whole.

4. Not just logic but also EMPATHY. The capacity for logical thought is one of the things that makes us human. But in a world of ubiquitous information and advanced analytic tools, logic alone won't do. What will distinguish those who thrive will be their ability to understand what makes their fellow woman or man tick, to forge relationships and to care for others.

5. Not just seriousness but also PLAY. Ample evidence points to the enormous health and professional benefits of laughter, lightheartedness, games, and humor. There is a time to be serious, of course. But too much sobriety can be bad for your career and worse for your general well-being. In the Conceptual Age, in work and in life, we all need play.

6. Not just accumulation but also MEANING. We live in a world of breathtaking material plenty. That has freed hundreds of millions of people from day-to-day struggles and liberated us to pursue more significant desires: purpose, transcendence, and spiritual fulfillment. (Pink, 2006, pp. 65–67)

Reprinted from *A Whole New Mind: Why RightBrainers Will Rule the Future* (2006), by permission of Penguin Group, Inc.

JANUSIAN AND PARADOXICAL THINKING

Daniel Pink's "high-touch" senses relate to earlier work by Albert Rothenberg. Rothenberg (1979) coined the term "janusian thinking" to describe the thought process of creative minds. According to Rothenberg, great scientific or artistic breakthroughs involve the ability to think in ways where seemingly contradictory or divergent viewpoints can be synthesized together. He says, "Janusian thinking consists of *actively conceiving two or more opposite or antithetical ideas, images, or concepts simultaneously*" (p. 55).

Commenting on Rothenberg's ideas, Lewis (2000) notes, "Mozart and Beethoven linked harmony *and* discord to fuel their musical inspiration. Artists such as Picasso and van Gogh used jarring juxtapositions to portray the ambiguity, diversity, and complexity of perceptions. And Einstein envisioned a man falling off a building at rest relative to things falling beside him *and* moving relative to sights he passed on the way down, forever altering understandings of physics" (pp. 764–765). Isaacson (2007) picks up on the idea of Einstein as a janusian thinker by observing, "He retained the ability to hold two thoughts in his mind simultaneously, to be puzzled when they conflicted, and to marvel when he could smell an underlying unity" (pp. 14–15).

This is a bit like F. Scott Fitzgerald's claim that the sign of a first-rate intelligence is the ability to hold two contradictory ideas in one's mind at the same time and still retain the ability to function. Janusian thinking is miles away from the *black* or *white, all* or *nothing, with me* or *against me*, thinking that Parker Palmer calls "the dullness of death." Writing to teachers, Palmer says:

> Paradoxical thinking requires that we embrace a view of the world in which opposites are joined, so that we can see the world clearly and see it whole. Such a view is characterized by neither flinty-eyed realism nor dewy-eyed romanticism but rather by a creative synthesis of the two.
>
> The result is a world more complex and confusing than the one made simple by either-or-thought—but that simplicity is merely the dullness of death. When we think things together, we reclaim the life force in the world, in our students, in ourselves.
>
> (Palmer, 1998, p. 66)

This way of thinking recognizes the complexity in human beings, relationships, experience, and existence. Simplistic ideas don't work in the globalized, interconnected world of today. Leaders are called to synthesize and construct from disparate, contradictory, and competing perspectives a new way forward for organizations, communities, and countries. Modern workplaces are challenged to take janusian and paradoxical approaches. For example, great companies are seen as places where work *and* play coexist; where order *and* chaos thrive. Organizations must also adapt and respond to market forces *and* not violate the core values that made the company successful in the first place. Finally, leaders are called to be visionary *and* realistic, tough *and* kind, forceful *and* democratic. Collins and Porras (1994) call this the "Genius of the AND" instead of the "Tyranny of the OR." Leaders don't always have to feel boxed-in by "either/or" decisions. Perhaps a story will help illustrate this point.

Merck, the worldwide medical and pharmaceutical company, developed a drug called Mectizan to cure "river blindness" which infected over a million people in poverty stricken Third World countries. This extremely painful disease results when parasitic worms enter body tissue finally resting in one's eyes causing blindness. Merck had a cure, but the people who needed the drug couldn't afford it. What would you do if you were the CEO of Merck? Give millions of doses away at a huge financial loss? Protect profits and not give the drug away? Merck tried to find a third party or governmental agency to purchase the drug and distribute it but they didn't find any takers. So, what to do? Well, Merck decided to give the drug away for free to anyone who needed it. When the CEO, P. Roy Vagelos, was asked why they made this decision, he said that "failure to go forward with the product could have demoralized Merck scientists—scientists working for a company that explicitly viewed itself as 'in the business of preserving and improving human life'" (Collins & Porras, 1994, p. 47). Vagelos went on to say:

> When I first went to Japan fifteen years ago, I was told by Japanese business people that it was Merck that brought streptomycin to Japan after World War II, to eliminate tuberculosis which was eating up their society. We did that. We didn't make any money. But it's no accident that Merck is the largest American pharmaceutical company in Japan today. The long-term consequences of [such actions] are not always clear, but somehow I think they always pay off. (Collins & Porras, 1994, p. 47)

Was the decision to give the drug away for free to millions of people pure altruism? Or, are these savvy business leaders who understand that it is possible to do good works *and* make a profit? I believe it was the latter. Additionally, even though the decision was risky from a short-term perspective, the public relations benefits were enormous and the integrity of the organization was on the line. After all, as the CEO astutely points out, the long-term consequences of such actions are not always clear but seem to "pay off" in the end.

① unselfish regard for.

THE INTERPLAY BETWEEN TECHNOLOGY AND THE MIND

What about the role of technology on how we think and process information? Electronic and Web-based technologies are accelerating the pace of work and play at an astonishing pace. For many people, this has created a tug-of-war between buckling down to complete work and surfing the Internet to watch a video on YouTube or respond to text messages from friends. Studies are beginning to emerge that take into account the daily use of Internet and smart phone technologies. Carr (2010) reports the following findings:

- People who read text studded with links comprehend less than those who read traditional linear text.

- People who watch busy multimedia presentations remember less than those who take in information in a more sedate and focused manner.

- People who are continually distracted by emails, alerts and other messages understand less than those who are able to concentrate.

- Research at Stanford University's Communication Between Humans and Interactive Media Lab, found that people who do a lot of media multitasking perform poorly on cognitive tests compared with those who multitask much less frequently. Researchers were surprised because they expected that the high multitaskers would have gained some unique mental advantages from all the on-screen juggling. However, they were considerably less adept at switching between tasks than the more infrequent multitaskers. Clifford Nass, the professor who heads the Stanford lab concluded, "Everything distracts them."

The fact that people (especially young people) are experiencing more distractions because of technology isn't surprising; however, at the same time, our schools and universities are working to incorporate more Internet applications and mobile devices into the classroom to connect with learners. While computer technology can play a useful role in education, we also need to think critically about how, when, and why it is used.

Richtel (2010) reports on an experiment at the German Sport University in Cologne in 2007. This study included boys from 12 to 14 that spent an hour each night playing video games after they finished homework. On alternate nights, the boys spent an hour watching an exciting movie rather than playing video games. The boys' brainwave patterns were then recorded while they were sleeping and their memory and homework performance was measured. Findings revealed that "playing video games led to markedly lower sleep quality than watching TV, and also led to a 'significant decline' in the boys' ability to remember vocabulary words . . . these brain studies suggest to researchers that periods of rest are critical in allowing the brain to synthesize information, make connections between ideas and even develop the sense of self." Michael Rich, associate professor at Harvard Medical School, says, "Downtime to the brain is what sleep is to the body. But kids are in a constant mode of stimulation." Dr. Rich doesn't advocate that young people should get rid of all their technology devices; however, they should find more balance between stimulation and reflection. This is good advice for leaders young and old.

INNOVATION AND CREATIVITY

change

Every organization is looking for creative people. But, how does one select for creativity during a job interview? One approach is to ask questions that elicit divergent thinking skills and creative problem solving aptitudes. Here's one example:

It is a dark, stormy night when you see three people waiting at a bus stop.

1. An old woman who looks as if she is about to die.
2. A friend who once saved your life.
3. The perfect partner that you have been dreaming about.

If you can only have one passenger in your car, who would you give a ride to? The old women in need of medical attention, the friend who saved your life, or the perfect partner of your dreams?

Take a moment to come up with a response. Well, the creative solution is to give the keys to the friend who once saved your life, that person takes the old lady to the hospital while you wait at the bus stop with the partner of your dreams. Was this the solution you came up with? I didn't when first posed with this dilemma! Let's explore innovation and creativity a little further in this next section.

In 2008, when Rich Lyons, dean of University of California, Berkeley's Haas School of Business, took the job, he sought feedback from company executives and recruiters on how Berkeley could better prepare the next generation of business leaders. One bit of feedback that stood out was that graduates weren't innovative or creative enough. To remedy this, the Haas School of Business added a new course required for all first-year students called "Problem Finding, Problem Solving." The class has no textbook or traditional problem sets and focuses on out-of-the-box thinking. One executive told Lyons, "I think MBA's tendency has been to see quick financial gain by pleasing the boss and harvesting cash, but they don't spend enough time just thinking" (Middleton, 2011, B9).

Birkinshaw, Bouquet, and Barsoux (2011) make the case that there has been a shift in who "owns" innovation in today's organizations. Innovation used to be the territory of designers, engineers and scientists; however, today it is the responsibility of everyone at every level of the organization. These researchers go on to list five "Myths of Innovation" based on research conducted over a three-year period with a number of companies from a variety of sectors:

Myth #1. The Eureka Moment

Rather than innovation coming from a flash of insight (like the story of Newton beneath the apple tree), the reality is more deliberate and pedestrian. In fact, most companies are pretty good at generating fresh, creative ideas; but they struggle further down the line with the implementation process. Companies like IBM have taken to hosting elaborate brainstorming activities such as their 2006 Innovation Jam. While a concerted effort to draw attention to innovation certainly draws awareness, most companies fail to think through the amount of work that is needed after such an event. For example, the IBM online event required a team of 60 researchers to sort through the 30,000 posts received over a 72-hour period. The second problem with such events according to the researchers "is that they can actually be disempowering if the organization lacks the capacity to act on the ideas generated" (p. 45). Many individuals involved in these types of company initiatives report that they don't see any action after the initial energy of a brainstorming event and some report never even receiving an acknowledgement that their ideas and suggestions were received.

Takeaway: "Most innovation efforts fail not because of a lack of bright ideas, but because of a lack of careful and thoughtful follow-up" (p. 45). Thus, there are structural implications involved with facilitating and implementing a successful innovation workshop.

Myth #2. Build It and They Will Come

The Internet provides countless opportunities for companies to develop tools and instruments to solicit feedback and generate ideas. However, simply creating a site for others to share information does not guarantee substantive and sustained involvement. First, after the initial novelty of logging on to a site once or twice wears off, there needs to be a hook that draws people back. Also, many times thousands of ideas are posted but managers spend a lot of time "separating the wheat from the chaff" because volumes of ideas can be "off-topic, half-baked, or irrelevant" (p. 46).

Takeaway: "Online forums are good for capturing and filtering large numbers of existing ideas; in-person forums are good for generating and building on new ideas. Smart companies are selective in their use of online forums and innovations" (p. 46).

Myth #3. Open Innovation Is the Future

Open innovation is defined as "the idea that companies should look for ways of tapping into and harnessing the ideas that lie beyond their formal boundaries" (p. 46). LEGO has been soliciting ideas for new products from kids and fans with great success and has even featured many of these products under the moniker "created by LEGO fans." Proctor and Gamble held a competition for people to make homemade videos spoofing their "Talking Stain" TV ad and post them on YouTube. They received over 200 submissions and some were even featured by the company in TV advertisements. Downsides or limitations to open innovation include intellectual property issues associated with collaboration outside the company and how the insights from external sources are used. In addition, open innovation can be very time consuming.

Takeaway: "External innovation forums have access to a broad range of expertise that makes them effective for solving narrow technological problems; internal innovation forums have less breadth but more understanding of context. Smart companies use their external and internal experts for very different types of problems" (p. 48).

Myth #4. Pay Is Paramount

Many companies struggle with the idea that the only way to get employees engaged and excited about innovation is to provide financial incentives. While pay has a place in the motivational process, people are also motivated by social factors such as recognition, and by intrinsic factors such as finding meaning and fulfillment in one's work.

Takeaway: "Rewarding people for their innovation efforts misses the point. The process of innovating—of taking the initiative to come up with new solutions—is its own reward. Smart companies emphasize the social and personal drivers of discretionary effort, rather than the material drivers" (p. 49).

Myth #5. Bottom-Up Innovation Is Best

The thinking here is that senior executives are too far removed from the day-to-day operations so innovation should be driven from the bottom up. Companies like 3M, Google, and W.L. Gore subscribe to the mantra, "Let 1,000 flowers bloom." While bottom-up ideas are important and responsible for such breakthroughs as Ericsson's mobile handset business, Sony's PlayStation, and HP's printer business, successful innovations need both bottom-up *and* top-down effort. "Broad-based innovation actually implies saying no to a lot of people, sometimes repeatedly. How their contributions are acknowledged, the transparency of the decision-making process and how the news is communicated are crucial factors in keeping the ideas coming" (p. 49).

Takeaway: "Bottom-up innovation efforts benefit from high levels of employee engagement; top-down innovation efforts benefit from direct alignment with the company's goals. Smart companies use both approaches, and are adept at helping bottom-up innovation projects get the sponsorship they need to survive" (p. 50).

COPING WITH FAILURE

"They sharpen their knives on my mistakes."

Tom Waits

Innovation and creativity require people to stretch and take risks. When risks pay off, there is celebration and relief. But what about the times when we make mistakes or experience outright failure? There is a wonderful story about a boy who asked his father, "Why are you so wise?" The father thought for a second and responded, "It is because of good judgment." The little boy thought more and asked, "How do you get good judgment?" The father replied, "Through experience, my son." The inquisitive little boy pressed on, "How do you get experience?" The father smiled and said, "Oh, my son that is through bad judgment." Failure certainly brings feelings of disappointment, remorse, and anxiety; but it is also a common experience among many successful people. For example,

- Babe Ruth struck out 1,330 times. In between his strikeouts, he hit 714 home runs.
- Martina Navratilova lost 21 of her first 24 matches against arch-rival Chris Evert. She resolved to hit more freely on the big points and beat Evert 39 out of their next 57 matches. No woman tennis pro has ever

won as many matches or tournaments, including a record non-Wimbledon singles titles, as Navratilova.

- R.H. Macy failed in retailing seven times before his store in New York became a success.

- Abraham Lincoln failed twice in business and was defeated in six state and national elections before being elected president of the United States.

- Theodor S. Geisel wrote a children's book that was rejected by 23 publishers. The 24th publisher sold six million copies of it—the first "Dr. Seuss" book—and that book and its successors are still staples of every children's library.

- Fred Astaire's first screen test assessment: "Losing hair. Can't sing. Can dance a little." RKO's head of production, David O. Selznick, also admitted to doubts about Astaire's "enormous ears and bad chin."

- Paul Cezanne, now recognized as the father of modern painting, was refused admission to the all-powerful Paris art school, the Ecole des Beaux-Arts.

(Source: Kouzes, J. & Posner, B. (2002). *The Leadership Challenge.* Jossey-Bass, CA, p. 214–216)

Writer and newspaper columnist Jon Carroll beautifully captures the positive aspects of failure in his article *Failure is a Good Thing*. He says:

> Last week, my granddaughter started kindergarten, and, as is conventional, I wished her success. I was lying. What I actually wish for her is failure. I believe in the power of failure.
>
> Success is boring. Success is proving that you can do something that you already know you can do, or doing something correctly the first time, which can often be a problematical victory. First-time success is usually a fluke. First-time failure, by contrast, is expected; it is the natural order of things.
>
> Failure is how we learn. I have been told of an African phrase describing a good cook as "she who has broken many pots." If you've spent enough time in the kitchen to have broken a lot of pots, probably you know a fair amount about cooking. I once had a late dinner with a group of chefs, and they spent time comparing knife wounds and burn scars. They knew how much credibility their failures gave them.

I earn my living by writing a daily newspaper column. Each week I am aware that one column is going to be the worst column of the week. I don't set out to write it; I try my best every day. Still, every week, one column is inferior to the others, sometimes spectacularly so.

I have learned to cherish that column. A successful column usually means that I am treading on familiar ground, going with the tricks that work, preaching to the choir or dressing up popular sentiments in fancy words. Often in my inferior columns, I am trying to pull off something I've never done before, something I'm not even sure can be done.

My younger daughter is a trapeze artist. She spent three years putting together an act. She did it successfully for years with the Cirque du Soleil. There was no reason for her to change the act — but she did anyway. She said she was no longer learning anything new and she was bored; and if she was bored, there was no point in subjecting her body to all that stress. So she changed the act. She risked failure and profound public embarrassment in order to feed her soul. And if she can do that 15 feet in the air, we all should be able to do it.

My granddaughter is a perfectionist, probably too much of one. She will feel her failures, and I will want to comfort her. But I will also, I hope, remind her of what she learned, and how she can do whatever it is better next time. I probably won't tell her that failure is a good thing, because that's not a lesson you can learn when you're five. I hope I can tell her, though, that it's not the end of the world. Indeed, with luck, it is the beginning.

Reprinted from http://www.npr.org, October 9, 2006, This I Believe, Inc.

While no one wants to fail, our failures can be reframed to develop psychological hardiness, persistence, and powerful learning opportunities. As the examples of famous people who have overcome disappointments and set-backs attest, we are in good company when we fail. As Jon Carroll points out, failure is "the natural order of things." Failure becomes a negative when we give up, adopt a defeatist attitude, or close ourselves off from the important—albeit painful—opportunity to learn and improve. In fact, paradoxically, past success doesn't always guarantee future success.

SUCCESS DOESN'T ALWAYS BREED SUCCESS

accidental success sometimes gives no lessons.

Gino and Pisano (2011) assert that "success can breed failure by hindering learning at both the individual and the organizational level" (p.69). They report three impediments to learning:

1. *Fundamental attribution errors*: When we succeed, we're likely to conclude that our talents and our current model or strategy are the reasons. We also give short shrift to the part that environmental factors and random events may have played.

2. *Overconfidence bias*: Success increases our self-assurance. Faith in ourselves is a good thing, of course, but too much of it can make us believe we don't need to change anything.

3. *Failure-to-ask-why syndrome*: The tendency not to investigate the causes of good performance systematically. For example, when executives and their teams suffer from this syndrome, they don't ask the tough questions that would help them expand their knowledge or alter their assumptions about how the world works.

Gino and Pisano offer five ways to avoid success induced traps and maximize organizational learning:

Celebrate success but examine it. After a success, organizational leaders should realistically assess why the victory happened. It could be because of the skill and ingenuity [1] of organizational members, or the success could have been the result of luck. In either case, it is a missed opportunity if learning doesn't accompany celebration.

Institute systematic project reviews. The military holds "after-action reviews" (AARs) of combat encounters and training exercises, regardless of whether or not the mission was a success. AAR participants meet after an important event or activity to discuss four key questions: What did we set out to do? What actually happened? Why did it happen? What are we going to do next time? Pixar has had a string of successful animated films and the company has built into the culture a rigorous evaluation of the process used to make each of its films. After a successful film release, leaders ask team members the top five things they would do and the top five things they would not do again. Leaders also collect copious notes along the way on all aspects of the production and use the data to ask questions and engage participants in the conversation. Pixar also conducts a review across several productions and tries to get an outsider's perspective—such as a new or recently hired manager—to lead the review.

[1] The quality of being clever, original, and inventive.

Use the right time horizons. In industries like pharmaceuticals and aerospace, the outcomes of some decisions will not be apparent for a decade or more. It is easy to decipher cause and effect when the time horizons are short, but when the horizons are long, leaders must build in an appropriate time frame to effectively evaluate performance.

Recognize that replication is not learning. If the conclusion of a performance analysis is a list of actions to replicate the same way the next time, there is a gap in learning. While best practices are important and tools like Six Sigma and total quality management have taught us to dig into the root causes of problems, the same approach should be used to understand the root causes of success. Every factor that contributed to the success should be classified into two areas: "something we can directly control" and "something that is affected by external factors." Factors under your control can remain part of your winning formula. But you need to understand how external factors interact with them.

If it ain't broke, experiment. Organizational experiments test theories and assumptions about what is needed to achieve high levels of performance. Experimentation can also push boundaries and lead to breakthroughs; however, they need to be managed carefully to avoid severe financial consequences or harming customers. The right question for leaders in learning organizations is not "What are we doing well?" but rather "What experiments are we running?"

REFRAMING: A TOOL TO MANAGE PARADOX AND AMBIGUITY - uncertainty

High levels of ambiguity and paradox exist in today's organizations. This creates a variety of practical challenges for managers and leaders. Westenholz (1993) has studied these dynamics in organizations and concludes:

> "... reality is chaotic and unstable to such an extent that it cannot be represented by unambiguous pictures. It also indicates that our way of constructing our pictures (frames of reference) of the world is decisive of our world view. As social beings, we are creating these pictures to defend our identity against a chaotic world. Without this defense we would be unable to deal with the world. At the same time, however, the pictures become a prison into which we are locked, so that we cannot view the world 'afresh'" (p. 39).

According to Westenholz, when our current frames of reference are no longer valid, there is a corresponding loss of stability and meaning. In order to remedy this state and find more effective solutions to complex problems, leaders must first realize that previous frames of reference are no longer valid (known as *deframing*) and then begin to *reframe* the situation. Westenholz says, "*Deframing* describes a situation in which previous frames of reference are no longer experienced as creating meaning, and hence become futile. *Reframing* describes the situation in which the individual creates a new reference which can be used to infuse situations with meaning" (p. 41). It is important to note that reframing is a *conscious choice*. As leaders we can choose to rely on outmoded and ineffective frames of reference that fail to appropriately assess and diagnose situations or we can choose to *reframe* in order to truly understand the situation and corresponding behaviors and actions that are needed. In her study of employee behaviors associated with deframing and reframing, Westenholz (1993, pp. 55–57) came to the following conclusions:

Reframing is challenging. Some employees may relapse into their old frames of reference before they get the time to construct a new understanding of the situation.

Reframing can create fear and anxiety. When certainty is lost through the process of deframing, the individual may experience being left in a void so frightening that he or she returns to the known frame. This fear may be emphasized if there is nobody with whom one can share this feeling or if one is subject to pressure from one's previous fellow partisans to return to the old ways of thinking.

If reframing replaces deframing, employees may be afraid to express new attitudes for fear of retribution. It is almost as if he or she has committed some kind of treason when viewed from the perspective of the old reference group.

Even those who successfully get through this new reframing process and who dare to take action, may experience being isolated from the old reference group or others.

Paradoxical thinking is the prerequisite to deframing and reframing. Through paradoxical thinking, one establishes a new relationship with the situation they are in. To establish a new relationship with the situation means to realize that one does not know in advance what the situation is about. One has no fixed model of the reality of one's own identity in this context.

Paradoxical thinking is both a cognitive process and an emotional experience. It is a cognitive process in that one comes to a conscious recognition that old frames of reference are no longer valid. It is an emotional experience because the person feels "something incompre-hensible happening." There is the feeling of "floating", of "letting go" and the excitement of being part of it!

Finally, just because people experience paradoxical thinking, deframing, and reframing, there is no guarantee that organizational change will ensue.

FOUR-FRAME LEADERSHIP: NEW WAYS OF THINKING AND ACTING AS A LEADER

Bolman and Deal (2008) offer four distinct frames as lenses to view the world of management, leadership, and organizational behavior (See Table 6-1).

Structural

Organizations can be seen as factories or complex machines. The structural frame involves an overall view of leaders and organizations that relies on rationality and logic. From this perspective, leaders are architects and analysts who research, design, build, and implement systems that get the job done in the most efficient manner. With its focus on data and quantitative analysis, the structural frame assists leaders in identifying root causes of organizational challenges. For example, the United States Postal Service reached a $9.2 billion deficit in 2011. Data indicate that mail volume is decreasing (due to email and online bill paying), the number of households receiving mail has steadily increased, labor represents 80 percent of the agency's expenses (compared with 53 percent at United Parcel Service and 32 percent at FedEx), and postal workers receive more generous health benefits than other federal employees (Greenhouse, 2011). To erase this budget deficit, the postmaster general is recommending a number of structural changes including eliminating Saturday mail, closing up to 3,700 postal locations and laying off 120,000 workers—nearly one-fifth of the agency's workforce—despite a no-layoffs clause in the unions' contract.

Human Resource

This frame emanates from the psychology and social psychology literature. Organizations are seen as extended families and leaders are focused on employee empowerment, engagement, need fulfillment, skill building, teamwork, and relationships. At a basic level, organizations need talented and productive employees; and workers need job security and fair wages.

TABLE 6-1 Overview of the Four-Frame Model.

	Frame			
	Structural	**Human Resource**	**Political**	**Symbolic**
Metaphor for organization	Factory or machine	Family	Jungle	Carnival, temple, theatre
Central concepts	Rules, roles, goals, policies, technology, environment	Needs, skills, relationships	Power, conflict, competition, organizational politics	Culture, meaning, metaphor, ritual, ceremony, stories, heroes
Image of leadership	Social architecture	Empower-ment	Advocacy	Inspiration
Basic leadership challenge	Attune structure to task, technology, environment	Align organizational and human needs	Develop agenda and power base	Create faith, beauty, meaning

Reprinted from *Reframing Organizations* (2008), by permission of John Wiley & Sons, Inc.

However, if the organization's needs dominate, there is the danger of exploitation and when employees' financial needs are exclusively emphasized there is the danger of financial insolvency. The central leadership challenge from the human resource perspective is to satisfy the interests of both people and the organization.

Political

Building on the political science literature, the dominant metaphor for organizational life is a jungle. Organizations can also be viewed from this perspective as an ecosystem where a variety of species live together—sometimes in harmony, other times in conflict. Organizations are also arenas where contests take place. Just like in an athletic contest, there are winners and losers. The dominant contest in organizational life is a competition over scarce resources. This view of leadership involves power, conflict, and organizational politics. The key to effectiveness lies in being politically savvy, advocating a compelling message, networking, building a power base, dealing with conflict, and competing to win (we'll look more closely at this process in Chapter 8).

Symbolic

Organizational life can feel a bit like theater; everyone seems to be playing a specific role (e.g., villain, hero, victim, neophyte, old-timer, etc.). Leaders "play" to different audiences (usually through storytelling) to impart their message or respond to a dilemma. From the symbolic perspective, organizations are viewed as temples where people derive meaning and significance from their workplace and the type of work they do. Members participate in rituals and ceremonies where what the event means is more important than the event itself. Symbolic leaders know that *activity* and *meaning* are loosely coupled. For example, a group of employees may all participate in the same meeting yet afterward there is tremendous variability in what people took away and how they interpreted the meeting. The symbolic leader is an ethical prophet, poet, and source of inspiration. The central challenge is to create faith, beauty, meaning, and significance.

Once again the ability to reframe emerges as a critical leadership practice. This is because while each of the four-frames contains valuable insights and tools, Bolman and Deal advise that the key to getting results "requires an ability to think about situations in more than one way" (Bolman & Deal, 2008, p. 6). Just as a carpenter must know what tool to use and how to use it, managers must be astute and nimble enough to assess organizational challenges from multiple perspectives and have a variety of tools at their disposal. Let's look at the use of performance appraisals to see how great managers and leaders rely on "multiframe thinking" to achieve organizational goals. Performance appraisals are a clearly delineated, systematic process (structural frame) but they are also theater (symbolic frame) signaling to people inside and outside of the organization that they care about performance and quality. For individual employees, performance appraisals also have promotion implications (political frame) and provide the opportunity for skill building and training (human resource frame). As Table 6-2 indicates, Bolman and Deal argue that managers need to expand their thinking to include more accurate and holistic assessments, an array of options to deal with leadership challenges successfully, and unwavering commitment to principle combined with flexibility in understanding and responding to nuanced events.

Measure your dominant leadership orientation using the following self-assessment.

TABLE 6-2 Expanding Managerial Thinking.

How Managers Think	How Managers Might Think
They often have a limited view of organizations (for example, attributing almost all problems to individuals' flaws and errors).	They need a holistic framework that encourages inquiry into a range of significant issues: people, power, structure, and symbols.
Regardless of a problem's source, managers often choose rational and structural solutions: facts, logic, restructuring.	They need a palette that offers an array of options: bargaining as well as training, celebration as well as reorganization.
Managers often value certainty, rationality, and control while fearing ambiguity, paradox, and "going with the flow."	They need to develop creativity, risk taking, and playfulness in responses to life's dilemmas and paradoxes, focusing as much on finding the right question as the right answer, on finding meaning and faith amid clutter and confusion.
Leaders often rely on the "one right answer" and the "one best way"; they are stunned at the turmoil and resistance they generate.	Leaders need passionate, unwavering commitment to principle, combined with flexibility in understanding and responding to events.

Reprinted from *Reframing Organizations* (2008), by permission of John Wiley & Sons, Inc.

Self-Assessment: Leadership Orientations

This questionnaire asks you to describe yourself as a manager and leader. For each item, give the number "4" to the phrase that best describes you, "3" to the item that is next best, and on down to "1" for the item that is least like you. Use the scoring key to add up your totals in the blanks that follow the questionnaire.

1. My strongest skills are:

    _____ a. *Analytic skills*

    _____ b. *Interpersonal skills*

    _____ c. *Political skills*

    _____ d. *Flair for drama*

2. The best way to describe me is:

    _____ a. *Technical expert*

    _____ b. *Good listener*

      c. *Skilled negotiator*

      d. *Inspirational leader*

3. What has helped me the most to be successful is my ability to:

      a. *Make good decisions*

      b. *Coach and develop people*

      c. *Build strong alliances and a power base*

      d. *Inspire and excite others*

4. What people are most likely to notice about me is my:

      a. *Attention to detail*

      b. *Concern for people*

      c. *Ability to succeed in the face of conflict and opposition*

      d. *Charisma*

5. My most important leadership trait is:

      a. *Clear, logical thinking*

      b. *Caring and support for others*

      c. *Toughness and aggressiveness*

      d. *Imagination and creativity*

6. I am best described as:

      a. *An analyst*

      b. *A humanist*

      c. *A politician*

      d. *A visionary*

_____ ST   _____ HR   _____ PL   _____ SY   _____ Total

Compute your scores as follows:

ST = 1a + 2a + 3a + 4a + 5a + 6a
HR = 1b + 2b + 3b + 4b + 5b + 6b
PL = 1c + 2c + 3c +4c + 5c + 6c
SY = 1d + 2d + 3d + 4d + 5d + 6d

High Score(s) indicate your dominat frame. Read the following descriptions of each frame.

Reprinted from *Reframing Organizations Instructor's Guide*, by Joan Gallos (2003), by permission of John Wiley & Sons, Inc.

1. **Structural** leaders emphasize rationality, analysis, logic, facts, and data. They are likely to believe strongly in the importance of clear structure and well-developed management systems. A good leader is someone who thinks clearly, makes the right decisions, has good analytic skills, and can design structures and systems that get the job done. *Like Frank at Sharper Image helping me.*

2. **Human resource** leaders emphasize the importance of people. They endorse the view that the central task of management is to develop a good fit between people and organizations. They believe in the importance of coaching, participation, motivation, teamwork, and good interpersonal relations. A good leader is a facilitator and participative manager who supports and empowers others.

3. **Political** leaders believe that managers and leaders live in a world of conflict and scarce resources. *insufficient* The central task of management is to *assemble* mobilize the resources needed to advocate and fight for the unit's or the organization's goals and objectives. Political leaders emphasize the importance of building a power base: allies, networks, coalitions. A good leader is an advocate and negotiator who understands politics and is comfortable with conflict.

4. **Symbolic** leaders believe that the essential task of management is to provide vision and inspiration. They rely on personal charisma and a flair for drama to get people excited and committed to the organizational mission. A good leader is a prophet and visionary who uses symbols, tells stories, and frames experience in ways that give people hope and meaning.

HAPPINESS AND THE GOOD LIFE

Recently, an entire industry has cropped up around the subject of happiness. Pop-psychologists, motivational speakers, and "life coaches" have published books and conducted countless seminars claiming to teach people how to be happy. The happiness movement is an outgrowth of an emerging academic discipline known as positive psychology. The traditional psychology literature is full of studies focused on depression, anxiety, insecurity, and other human dysfunctions. Positive psychology claims that the pendulum has swung too far in a deficiency based direction and that more research needs to be conducted in a positive direction, such as studies that identify the root causes and factors associated with happiness, joy, and fulfillment. Today, a growing number of colleges and universities offer positive psychology courses and even undergraduate and graduate degrees in positive psychology.

All of this modern day talk about happiness actually has ancient roots. In the 3rd century BC, Aristotle developed a systematic model of happiness in his *Nicomachean Ethics*. This book is not an exploration of ethics and morals in our modern sense of the term; rather, as Pakaluk (2005) points out, the book gets its name because of the manner in which Aristotle searches for the ultimate end—which is to realize the good life by acting in alignment with traits of character. The Greek word which means "pertaining to traits of character" is *ethike*, the source of our word "ethics" (Pakaluk, 2005, p. 4). Aristotle believed that most of the time people act purposefully and seek various means in order to achieve some specific end goal. For example, if a student wants to secure a career developing video games, he or she would consider getting a college degree, taking an internship at a software or gaming company, and making various sacrifices in their social life in order to study and network with professionals in the field. These actions could all be described as *means* to the *end* of getting a job developing video games. In this example, the student has engaged in purposeful activities (means) to achieve a distinct goal (or, end). We all work toward various ends; however, Aristotle believes that there is one correct end that we should all pursue and he calls this: living well, or living a good life. The Greek word Aristotle uses for living well is translated into English as "happiness" and Aristotle believes that this is the ultimate goal for everyone.

We need a plan to achieve happiness and Aristotle says there is one correct plan that we all should follow. In this plan we achieve happiness by *seeking and obtaining things that are truly good for us to have*. Fair enough. However, the next question is: what is good for us to have? This brings up the distinction between *wants* and *needs*. People differ in what they desire or want and, consequently, this is why it is common to believe that happiness varies from person to person based on one's own unique tastes. One person may define happiness as acquiring large amounts of material wealth while another defines happiness as being free from material pursuits. So, to extend this line of thinking: when people obtain what they want then they must be happy, right? Not so fast! We have to remember that what we want is not always what we need and sometimes what we want is actually bad for us. For example, we have all experienced times when we wanted more dessert, food, or drink and after getting more of what we wanted we immediately realize that desire has led us to an undesirable situation. The important point is that "in contrast to the things you want, which appear good at the time you want them but may turn out to be the opposite of good at a later time, the things you need are *always* good for you" (Adler, 1978, p. 87).

In addition to "wants" and "needs," Stoic philosophers beginning in the 2nd century BC argued that happiness involves being grateful for those things we already have. It is not uncommon that once we have the things we need—job, home, car, etc. —we begin to take these things for granted and want a better job, bigger home, and more luxurious car. Since gratitude leads to happiness, the Stoics recommended that "we spend time imagining that we have lost the things we value—that our wife has left us, our car was stolen, or we lost our job. Doing this, the Stoics thought, will make us value our wife, our car, and our job more than we otherwise would" (Irvine, 2009, p. 68). So, we are back to Aristotle's one correct plan for everyone to achieve happiness. As previously noted, this plan requires that we focus on obtaining what is good for us to have. Since we have already seen that what we want is not always good for us and that what is good for us is always good, Aristotle describes two types of goods that we should focus on and then he outlines how to achieve these goods. First, let's look at the two types of goods.

The first type Aristotle calls *external goods*. These include bodily goods such as food, clothing, and shelter. Wealth is also a bodily good because money is a means to providing for our basic needs. Aristotle makes the point that we need a certain amount of bodily goods, for example: pleasure, wealth, rest, food, and drink. He calls these *limited goods* because obtaining more is not always better (more pleasure, wealth, rest, food, or drink is not *always* good). This brings us to the second kind of goods: *goods of the soul*. These goods are related to our intellectual and social relationships. Activities of the mind—such as thinking, gaining knowledge, and refining our skills—are *unlimited goods*. These pursuits are always good because learning more and developing more skills will always benefit our life. We are also social animals, so part of a good life can be found in cultivating and maintaining quality relationships with others. These goods of the soul also include friendship, love, self-esteem, and honor. Current research has found that the happiest people do not necessarily have the most "external goods," rather happy people have fulfilling relationships with others—family and friends—and it is the strength of these bonds that creates a network of social support throughout one's life (Gilbert, 2012). On the subject of honor as a good of the soul, Aristotle notes that "being honored is not a real good unless it is for the right reason—unless we really deserve the honor we receive. Some individuals seek fame instead of honor. They are satisfied with having a good reputation even if they do not deserve it" (Adler, 1978, p. 98).

To review, there are both external goods and goods of the soul and we should seek to obtain these types of goods. External goods satisfy basic, physiological needs while goods of the soul nourish the good life by focusing on activities of the mind such as learning new things, developing skills we can put into practice, and experiencing meaningful relationships with others. Achieving these goods leads to a life well-lived or happiness. Now that we have classified these two categories of goods we have to answer an even more difficult, yet critical, question: How do we go about *achieving* these goods?

Mortimer Adler, the noted Aristotle scholar, says that to achieve the good life, "there is one more class of goods we need—good habits; more specifically, good habits of choice" (Adler, 1978, p. 98). Adler notes that the name Aristotle gives to all good habits has been translated into English from the Greek as "excellence." However, we know this term more from its Latin translation as the word "virtue." Thus, Aristotle concludes that good habits of choice become second nature and part of a person's character, so he calls these good habits: moral virtues. Moral virtue is the most important means to achieving happiness. Aristotle lists a collection of virtues—including the cardinal virtues of *prudence, justice, fortitude, temperance*—as essential habits that everyone should utilize when making decisions. Each of the cardinal virtues is discussed more fully in the final chapter of this book.

In addition to moral virtue as the primary means to achieve happiness, Aristotle astutely notes that circumstances are not always under our control. In other words, even if we consistently practice good decision making habits and live a life aligned with the cardinal virtues, chance and luck play a significant role. Adler (1978) concludes: "Good luck is as necessary as good habits" (p. 106). However, even when luck and good fortune are on our side, we need good habits of choice—moral virtue—so as not to lose or squander the goods that have been provided to us. We maximize and sustain good luck by instilling the virtues of prudence, justice, fortitude, and temperance in all that we do. Happiness is not the same as experiencing a life free from misfortune, pain, and suffering. Instead, the good life equips us with the necessary habits to respond constructively to good *and* bad fortune. Consequently, when individuals pursue Aristotle's vision of the good life the larger society also benefits. Aristotle's ideas point to goods that we need; goods that are desirable "ends" in themselves. Thus, undesirable wants and reckless actions are minimized. This is far from easy; but, the cardinal virtues bring forth good habits of choice and, in particular, the virtue of justice considers the good of others, friend and enemy alike. Therefore, our individual pursuit of happiness is not a selfish act because when individuals act with moral virtue they don't harm others and, in the highest sense, actually contribute to the greater good of society. Complete the What Do You Think? activity before moving on to the next section.

Why This Activity?

This activity is important for a number of reasons. First, as indicated in the research, followers have clear beliefs and expectations regarding the type of leader they want to follow. This doesn't mean that your style and

(1) Strength of mind that allows one to endure pain or adversity with courage.

(2) Moderation and self-restraint; as in behavior or expression-

What Do You Think?

We've covered a lot of ground in the personal leadership section of this book. Let's revisit your earlier leadership definition from the beginning of Chapter 2. Reflecting on the ideas you have read so far, has anything changed? Take another opportunity to articulate a concise, yet inclusive statement about great leadership. Remember, you can use words, phrases, complete sentences, or even draw a picture.

Great leaders . . .

_____

_____

_____

_____

_____

_____

_____

_____

_____

approach will resonate with each follower; however, clarifying the type of leadership others can expect from you elicits clarity and begins the process of developing constructive relationships. This can be especially timely when you are a new manager meeting your staff for the first time.

Second, this exercise helps to establish not only one's unique leadership message, but it also reminds us of the type of leader we are striving to become. By crafting a personal leadership philosophy, we can avoid becoming tongue-tied when trying to capture the essence of leadership and instead act authentically with focus and resolve. Our personal leadership message becomes our mantra.

Finally, when applying for a management position, a common interview question is to share your thoughts on leadership or to describe your leadership style. If you are preparing now or in the future for a career change, it is worth the time to reflect on the unique gifts you will offer others, and create your "elevator speech" that will clearly and concisely communicate—in just a few minutes—why you are the right leader for the job.

Questions for Review

1. What is L-Directed and R-Directed thinking? How is this idea related to leadership?

2. What is janusian and paradoxical thinking? How is this idea related to leadership?

3. How does the Internet, multitasking, and media impact the way people think?

4. What skills and practices foster creativity and innovation? What are the "Five Myths of Innovation"?

5. How can failure be a good thing? What role has failure played in the lives of many famous and successful people? Does success always breed success?

6. What is reframing? How can reframing help leaders manage paradox and ambiguity in modern organizations?

7. What are the main features of the structural, human resource, political, and symbolic frames? How does the four-frame model relate to leadership and organizational performance?

LEADING OTHERS

There will be a time when you retire or leave one leadership role for a different one. What will be your legacy? How will you be remembered? Ultimately, leaders are stewards of the organizations they lead. A steward holds something in trust for future generations. This means that when it is your time to lead, you must care for the long-term viability and health of the organization. When a great leader exits, the organization is better off than when he or she first arrived and in a position to thrive well into the future. Leaders become good stewards by navigating a variety of organizational dynamics discussed in this next section.

Specifically, this section focuses on politics, vision, exercising power, coalition building, conflict, change, motivation, employee engagement, job satisfaction, and the effective use of teams.

CHAPTER 7:
Political Philosophy and Leadership: Systems of Governance and Human Nature

LEARNING OBJECTIVES

After studying this chapter, you should be able to:

1. Demonstrate the role of political philosophy on leadership.
2. Summarize the contributions of Plato, Machiavelli, Hobbes, and Locke on political philosophy.
3. Compare and contrast the impact of political philosophers with the leadership literature.

One aim of political philosophy is to investigate human nature in search of the best way to organize systems of governance. While the scope of this book doesn't lend itself to a full discussion of political philosophy, let's turn to four brief sketches of political philosophers whose ideas continue to resonate in leadership circles today.

PLATO 427–347 B.C.

Plato represents the classical age of philosophy whose aim was investigating what it meant to live a good and virtuous life. Plato was a student of Socrates and because Socrates never wrote anything down, much of Plato's writing reflects the teaching of Socrates. Classical political thought focuses on replacing opinions with knowledge. This endeavor is threatening because it challenges orthodoxy and risks speaking truth to power. In fact, Socrates ended up being executed for precisely these reasons.

In the *Republic,* Plato recounts a variety of conversations between Socrates and others concerning the nature of justice. Socrates offers three types of cities: the healthy city, the luxurious city, and the just city. The healthy city consists of each member doing what he or she is most fit to do. That is to say, nature provides each person with talents and gifts and when we exercise our natural talents for cooking, working with our hands, producing goods, and so on, people are happy and the essential needs of the city are met. The healthy city needs no laws or ruler because it is operating in accordance with nature and the basic necessities are provided for everyone. However, this first city doesn't account for people's passions and desires. People aren't satisfied with basic necessities, they always want more. For this reason, the luxurious city emerges. Socrates claims that the soul consists of three parts: reason, passion, and spiritedness. The luxurious city is the city of passion and spiritedness. People fight over scarce natural resources to satisfy their desires and education emerges to teach character and calm our natural passions. Beyond the luxurious city lies the just city. Three virtues are expressed in the just city: wisdom, courage, and moderation. Wisdom is found in the ruling class, courage in the military class, and everyone in the just city must practice moderation. Socrates is then asked how this city can come about. He hesitates in answering (for fear of being ridiculed), and says:

> Until philosophers rule as kings or those now called kings and chiefs genuinely and adequately philosophize, and political power and philosophy coincide in the same place ... there is no rest from ills for the cities ... nor I think for human kind, nor will the regime we have now described in

speech ever come forth from nature, insofar as possible, and see the light of the sun. This is what for so long was causing my hesitation to speak: seeing how very paradoxical it would be to say. For it is hard to see that in no other city would there be private or public happiness. (Bloom, 1991, p. 153)

The philosopher-king is the ultimate unification of wisdom and power, the highest pinnacle of leadership. However, Socrates acknowledges that combining the ethos of "philosophers" and "kings" is paradoxical and highly unlikely because philosophers seek wisdom and kings seek power, rarely are the two aspirations compatible. The philosophical life demands leisure and reflection while the political life demands action. By presenting the philosopher-king as a leadership archetype, Socrates reminds us of the importance of both reflection *and* action. A leader's effectiveness requires contemplating complex ideas beyond simplistic sound bites, in addition to the simultaneous forward momentum of putting good ideas into action. The just city with its focus on virtue, wisdom-centered leadership, and call for human beings to aspire toward realizing their full potential—even if never achieved—is uniquely Greek and captures the essence of classical philosophy.

NICCOLO MACHIAVELLI 1469–1527

Machiavelli's reaction to classical thought is best summed up in Laurence Berns's statement, "the classics failed, according to Machiavelli, because they aimed too high. Because they based their political doctrines on considerations of man's highest aspirations, the life of virtue and the society dedicated to the promotion of virtue, they rendered themselves ineffective; as Bacon said, they made 'imaginary laws for imaginary commonwealths'" (Berns, 1987, p. 396). Machiavelli saw human beings as fickle, ungrateful, disloyal, and self-motivated. Therefore, leaders must learn how not to be good in order to understand human nature. He says, "For a man who wants to make a profession of good in all regards must come to ruin among so many who are not good" (Mansfield, 1985, p. 61). This fundamental idea ushers in modern political thought and breaks from the classical approach to training leaders. The fixed values of the classical world no longer guide the leader; instead leaders prosper by adapting to ever-changing times and circumstances. To the ancients, virtue was an end; to Machiavelli virtue affords glories and riches. It is important to note that Machiavelli uses the word "virtue" in a different way compared to classical political philosophers. To classical thinkers, politics was subordinate to moral, and above all, intellectual virtue. Machiavelli sees virtue as successfully using politics to achieve one's goals, consequently subordinating morality in the pursuit of glory (see Tarcov and Pangle, 1987, p. 917).

In his most famous work, *The Prince*, Machiavelli provides a summary of his reflections on the actions of "great men." He dedicates the book to Lorenzo de Medici, the duke of Urbino, in hopes that he will also achieve greatness and benefit from Machiavelli's leadership lessons. Machiavelli begins by advising leaders to imitate great men such as Moses, Cyrus, Romulus, and Theseus. In this way if a leader doesn't have much virtue, at least he will benefit from the "odor" of greatness in others. Machiavelli advocates the use of persuasion, but since human beings are unpredictable, the leader should also use force. In this respect, Machiavelli provides the example of Cesare Borgia. Borgia places Messer Remirro de Orco, one of his ministers, in charge of an unruly province. Remirro brings order to the province but he also generates hatred among many in the city. In order to distance himself from the acts of Remirro and gain the allegiance of the people, Borgia has Remirro killed and his body placed on display in the piazza for all to see. Machiavelli says, "The ferocity of this spectacle left the people at once satisfied and stupefied" (Mansfield, 1985, p. 30).

This brings us to Machiavelli's famous discussion of whether it is better to be loved or feared. He begins by saying:

> Each prince should desire to be held merciful and not cruel; nonetheless he should take care not to use this mercy badly. Cesare Borgia was held to be cruel; nonetheless his cruelty restored the Romagna, united it, and reduced it to peace and to faith (Mansfield, 1985, p. 65).

Thus, the ends justify the means. Machiavelli claims that prior to Borgia, lawlessness, factions, and riots ruled the day because leaders avoided forceful action. Regarding the question of fear and love, Machiavelli says that one would want to be both feared *and* loved but this is difficult to achieve, so it is safer to be feared than loved; this is because people love at their own convenience, but fear at the convenience of the leader. However, Machiavelli cautions that leaders, even if they are feared, must avoid being hated. He adds that the key to avoid being hated in politics is to abstain from taking the property of others.

In *The Prince*, Machiavelli goes on to offer a number of other provocative ideas. Briefly, these include taking advantage of opportunities through one's own virtue (Ch. VI), lessons from those who have achieved power through crimes (Ch. VIII), use of hope and fear (Ch. X), laws and arms (Ch. XII), avoiding being neutral (Ch. XXI), and receiving wise counsel from others but ultimately trusting only oneself (Ch. XXIII). Machiavelli even proposes some overly simplistic conclusions, such as "One who becomes prince through the support of the people should keep them friendly to him, which should be easy for him because they ask of him only that they not be oppressed" (Mansfield, 1985, p. 40). Ultimately, Machiavelli advances a very different view of leadership that rests on opportunism, cleverness, and power. Instead of moral virtue, we have political virtue necessitated by the chaos of human nature and the leader's obligation to bring order and stability.

THOMAS HOBBES 1588–1679

In many ways, Hobbes advances a similar trend away from classical thought. While Machiavelli breaks from classical philosophers and substitutes political gain for morality and virtue, Hobbes places human reason as the most important end. Philosophy becomes "the knowledge acquired by reasoning" and, according to Hobbes, "[reason] can never conclude an error" (Hobbes, 1962, p. 478). Hobbes advocates that each person has within him or herself the ability to arrive at a place of wisdom through his or her own senses and individual powers of reason. Hobbes cautions against imitating the Greeks, Romans, or other spiritual authorities because other people's knowledge cannot be trusted. Instead, mankind is in a natural state of war and must use reason to construct appropriate laws.

In Chapter 13 of Hobbes' most influential work, *Leviathan*, he articulates the war-like state of "natural man" and identifies three causes for such quarrels: competition, diffidence, and glory. In such a state:

> The first, maketh men invade for gain; the second, for safety; and the third, for reputation. The first use violence, to make themselves masters of other men's persons, wives, children, and cattle; the second, to defend them; the third, for trifles, as a word, a smile, a different opinion, and any other sign of undervalue, either direct in their persons, or by reflection in their kindred, their friends, their nation, their profession, or their name. (Hobbes, 1962, pp. 99–100)

Mankind lives in this condition because there isn't a leader to provide order, stability, or security. Instead, pre-political man lives in a state of perpetual war of "everyone against everyone" (Hobbes, 1962, p. 100). This is because self-preservation is the primary motive in the state of nature. Hobbes says "every man has a right to everything" because anything not under a man's own power can be regarded as a danger to his preservation. Hence, man has a right to everything (see Berns, 1987, p. 402). What is lacking in the state of nature is civil society. There is the absence of industry, commerce, business, art, culture, leisure, and the thirst for knowledge. In this natural state human beings have been reduced to "continual fear, and danger of violent death; and the life of man, solitary, poor, nasty, brutish, and short" (Hobbes, 1962, p.100).

To remedy this condition, a strong central government must be introduced so that mankind does not fall back into the state of nature. Government must acknowledge mankind's natural rights and construct a system of laws based on reason. However, the absolute ruler is not subject to these rules because living under the sovereign is always superior to the warlike state of pre-political man. Because the fundamental motive of human beings is self-preservation, mankind's nature is such that people act in accordance with their own judgment primarily to preserve their own interests and consequently their life. This helps to explain why more often than not people will act in their own self-interests no matter what they may publically proclaim. Hobbes then lists a series of laws to restrict behavior because human beings are now bound to the government that they set up. Hobbes' ideas contrast with classical philosophy because justice is now defined as obeying covenants and contracts to promulgate civil society while for Plato justice was realized by every citizen acting in accordance with their natural talents.

JOHN LOCKE 1632–1704

Locke picks up on many of the same themes as Hobbes. However, for Locke the state of nature is not equated with a state of war. Locke claims that in the state of nature human beings are perfectly free to act as they see fit; however, this natural state is governed by the Law of Nature: reason. More to the point, Locke says "being all equal and independent, no one ought to harm another in his Life, Health, Liberty, or Possessions" (Locke, 1988, p. 271). Sound familiar? Thomas Jefferson breathed Locke's ideas into the Declaration of Independence. While Locke proposes a more amiable state of nature compared to Hobbes, he still acknowledges that conflicts will develop. However, war is seen as more deliberate and premeditated than Hobbes' all out "war of everyone against everyone." For Locke, "The state of war is a state of enmity and destruction; and therefore declaring by word or action, not a passionate and hasty, but a sedate settled design" (Locke, 1988, p. 278). War emerges when others try to take by force what isn't rightfully their own (namely: life, health, liberty, or possessions). Civil society is primarily driven by the need for people to protect their property and even increase their possessions.

Like Hobbes, Locke advances civil society as a means to provide stability and security by which all members of the community must consent to fundamental rights and laws. However, there is a major distinction between Locke and Hobbes that goes back to the idea of self-preservation. While Locke agrees that self-preservation is a primary motive, he goes one step further than Hobbes. Locke says, "Every one as he is *bound to preserve himself*, and not to quit his station willfully: so by like reason when his own preservation comes not in competition, ought he, as much as he can, *to preserve the rest of mankind*" (Locke, 1988, p. 271). For Locke, if you are in a good place, then you have a duty to help others. The leadership implications are immense because the governed are the ultimate judges as to whether or not leaders fulfill their trust. Leaders may become tyrants and act with destructive intent contrary to the Law of Nature. Consequently, "the people have a right to act as supreme, and continue the legislative in themselves, or erect a new form, or under the old form place it in new hands, as they think good" (Locke, 1988, p. 428). We could go on and investigate Aristotle, Rousseau, De Tocqueville, Marx and others, but the scope of this book requires only this general introduction. I would encourage the reader to continue his or her own investigation; Leo Strauss and Joseph Cropsey's *History of Political Philosophy* is an excellent starting point.

Why the quick overview of political philosophy? Leadership involves cultivating and sustaining constructive relationships with others; therefore, leaders must understand the well-spring from which human behavior emanates and the best structures and systems to nurture one's natural longing for freedom and the necessary sacrifices that must be made for the sake of the community or organization as a whole. The next chapter expands on these ideas and explores the impact of politics on leadership.

Questions for Review

1. How does political philosophy relate to leadership?
2. In your own words, what are the contributions of Plato, Machiavelli, Hobbes, and Locke on political philosophy? Briefly discuss the main ideas from each writer.
3. What similarities exist in the writings of Plato, Machiavelli, Hobbes, and Locke? How does each writer differ in what they believe and advocate?

CHAPTER 8:
Political Intelligence: Vision, Power, and Conflict

LEARNING OBJECTIVES

After studying this chapter, you should be able to:

1. Define political intelligence.
2. Discuss the attributes of an effective vision.
3. Show how power is critical to leadership.
4. Identify and discuss multiple sources of power.
5. Identify and discuss the five conflict-handling modes.

"[Professional basketball players] make a lot of money, but they also spend a lot of money."

> Patrick Ewing, advocating for increased salaries when he was president of the National Basketball Association players union during the 1998 lockout.

"Man is by nature a political animal."

> Aristotle from *The Politics*, Book 1, Chapter 2

During a California State University Board of Trustees meeting in July 2011, the board approved a $100,000 raise to the new San Diego State president *and* raised annual student tuition 12% at the same meeting. This decision came after years of steady tuition increases and cuts to course offerings. Following the meeting, the board created a new committee to explore compensation models in an effort to defuse the controversy over raising executive salaries during tough economic times (Rivera, 2011). The actions by the CSU Board, and the statement above by Patrick Ewing, are perfect examples of what Lee Bolman and Terry Deal call the "curse of cluelessness" among managers and leaders. These actions can also be seen as politically *un*intelligent behavior. Anyone looking for an extended tenure in their leadership role must be politically intelligent. For example, leaders can possess the virtues of honesty, compassion, and integrity but be moved out of leadership roles quickly due to a lack of political acumen and the requisite skills necessary to survive and advance one's vision. Conversely, a manager that has been promoted beyond his skill set can be protected for a long time because of his political alliances.

Political leadership is more about *interests* than *personalities*. Parties spar over competing interests and the goal of the leader is to advocate for "her people" in a compelling and strategic manner focused on delivering results. This goes beyond personalities because many times enemies will rally together around a shared interest then go back to being enemies after the issue has played out. Effective leaders don't make the mistake of only working with people they like. If you want to get results, you will work with anyone that can help you achieve your objectives. Often the most powerful tactic of politically intelligent leaders is to appeal to others' self-interests. People want to know how they will personally benefit from a decision or new initiative, so the politically intelligent leader will frame proposals and change initiatives from this perspective. As the previous overview of political philosophy makes clear, self-interest and self-preservation are two of the most powerful forces of human nature. Adam Smith, the 18th century philosopher, professor, and government administrator who ushered in modern economic thought, famously declared: "It is not from the benevolence of the butcher, the brewer, or the baker, that we expect our dinner, but from their regard to their own interest. We address ourselves, not to their humanity but to their self-love, and never talk to them of our own necessities but of their advantages" (Smith, 1976, p. 18).

From a leadership and organizational context, politics can be defined as a *conflict over scarce resources*. When managers compete over a limited budget pie, political dynamics emerge and influence who wins and who loses. Additionally, politics can be viewed as the *unseen forces that propel or derail one's career*. The word "politics" evokes images of backstabbing, unfair competition, and dirty tactics; however, being politically intelligent does not require one to engage in sordid behavior or compromise one's principles. Instead, political intelligence requires the understanding and skillful application of *vision setting, power, coalition building*, and *dealing with conflict*.

VISION SETTING

When Ronald Reagan assumed the presidency he quickly expressed his vision. It consisted of reducing the size of government, lowering taxes, and strengthening the military. We can debate the merits of his vision, but it was clear where he stood and how he intended to transform the country. Followers want to know your vision and the shared role they play in turning the vision into reality. The key is to frame the vision in a way that resonates with people's minds *and* hearts. Bennis and Nanus (2003) say, "Vision *grabs*. Initially it grabs the leader, and management of attention enables others also to get on the bandwagon" (p. 26). For example, we all know Dr. Martin Luther King's vision: racial equality, justice, and equal opportunity. One key to Dr. King's success was his ability to articulate his vision in an inspiring way that connected the civil rights struggle with the country's national identity. His "I Have a Dream" speech still evokes passion, emotion, and action today. Take a moment to imagine listening to Dr. King's famous speech. Hear the cadence of his words, the poetry and musical quality of his delivery. Now, imagine if instead of saying "I have a dream," Dr King said: "*I have a list of measurable objectives.*" Big difference. How many times in our organizational life do we crave "I have a dream" from our leaders, but instead get "I have a list of measurable objectives"? Daniel Pink, in his book *Drive: The Surprising Truth about What Motivates Us*, shares a story about Clare Boothe Luce, a member of the U. S. Congress, who offered some advice to President John F. Kennedy in 1962.

> "A great man," she told him, "is one sentence." Abraham Lincoln's sentence was: "He preserved the union and freed the slaves." Franklin Roosevelt's was: "He lifted us out of a great depression and helped us win a world war." Luce feared that Kennedy's attention was so splintered among different priorities that his sentence risked becoming a muddled paragraph. (Pink, 2009, p. 154)

While Ronald Reagan and Martin Luther King, Jr. both excelled at public speaking, David Gergen notes that leaders need to do more than speak well. Gergen cites Reagan's farewell address as president, where Reagan said, "I won a nickname, the Great Communicator. But I never thought it was my style or the words I used that made a difference: It was the content. I wasn't a great communicator, but I communicated great things" (Gergen, 2003 p. 20). Gergen goes on to say, "King's 'I have a dream' speech in 1963 wasn't historic because he was so lyrical, though he was certainly that. It was the best of modern American speeches because he beautifully gave voice to people's own dreams . . . the leader and followers must unite around a shared vision" (Gergen, 2003, p. 20).

Leaders also use a certain amount of theater or "stagecraft" to inspire and motivate followers around a vision. As Gergen notes, President Franklin D. Roosevelt told Orson Welles that the two of them were the best actors in America. Reagan also commented, "There have been times when I've wondered in this office how you could do this job if you hadn't been an actor." Gergen provides the following story and advice on "authentic" and "phony" stagecraft:

> When the Revolutionary War ended, the British didn't just pick up and go home, so American troops couldn't either. When Congress wouldn't pay them, officers in Newburgh, New York, stirred up a near rebellion. In a famous incident, General Washington strode before the officers, started to read a statement, then fumbled in his pockets and pulled out reading glasses. The men had never seen him wear glasses before. Washington said, "I have already grown gray in the service of my country, and now I am going blind." The officers were so moved by his speech that they rallied around him and abandoned the rebellion. Some historians will tell you that Washington didn't really need those glasses—he was acting. And it was very effective theater.
>
> Washington's stagecraft worked because it came from an authentic core. Similarly, when Reagan pulled letters written by ordinary people out of his pocket and read them on television, it was theatrics, but it was honest. He really did share the writer's concerns, and the audience sensed that. On the other hand, phony stagecraft, which isn't tied to truth or to an uplifting vision, will nearly always backfire, especially in today's media-savvy world. When the Monica Lewinsky story broke, Clinton regrettably asked Dick Morris to take a poll about what he should say, and Harry Thomason rushed in from Hollywood to coach the president on wagging his finger into the camera, denying it all. It blew up in Clinton's face, and one of the most gifted presidents in recent times paid a huge price (Gergen, 2003, p. 21).

One of the most moving visions in history was expressed during an impromptu speech by Robert Kennedy on April 4, 1968, the day Martin Luther King Jr. was assassinated. Kennedy, on a routine campaign stop during his bid for the Democratic Party nomination for president, arrived in a poor section of Indianapolis to address a largely black crowd that had waited an hour to hear him speak. Kennedy had been warned by the city's police chief not to go, and when his car entered the neighborhood, his police escort left him. Kennedy, standing on the back of a flatbed truck, turned to an aide and asked, "Do they know about Martin Luther King?" The audience hadn't heard the news, so it was left to Kennedy to tell them that King had been shot and killed that night in Memphis, Tennessee. The crowd gasped in horror. In other towns riots were breaking out in response to King's assassination, but the crowd in Indianapolis remained calm. Kennedy never looked at his prepared speech and instead looked directly at the audience and spoke from his heart about the need for compassion, understanding, and his own life experiences having a brother assassinated by a white man. The following transcript of Kennedy's speech captures the power of an inspiring vision in the midst of a national tragedy.

Ladies and Gentlemen,

I'm only going to talk to you just for a minute or so this evening, because I have some—some very sad news for all of you—Could you lower those signs, please?—I have some very sad news for all of you, and, I think, sad news for all of our fellow citizens, and people who love peace all over the world; and that is that Martin Luther King was shot and was killed tonight in Memphis, Tennessee.

Martin Luther King dedicated his life to love and to justice between fellow human beings. He died in the cause of that effort. In this difficult day, in this difficult time for the United States, it's perhaps well to ask what kind of a nation we are and what direction we want to move in. For those of you who are black—considering the evidence evidently is that there were white people who were responsible—you can be filled with bitterness, and with hatred, and a desire for revenge.

We can move in that direction as a country, in greater polarization—black people amongst blacks, and white amongst whites, filled with hatred toward one another. Or we can make an effort, as Martin Luther King did, to understand, and to comprehend, and replace that violence, that stain of bloodshed that has spread across our land, with an effort to understand, compassion, and love.

For those of you who are black and are tempted to fill with—be filled with hatred and mistrust of the injustice of such an act, against all white people, I would only say that I can also feel in my own heart the same kind of feeling.

I had a member of my family killed, but he was killed by a white man.

But we have to make an effort in the United States. We have to make an effort to understand, to get beyond, or go beyond these rather difficult times.

My favorite poem, my favorite poet was Aeschylus. And he once wrote:

> Even in our sleep, pain which cannot forget
> falls drop by drop upon the heart,
> until, in our own despair,
> against our will,
> comes wisdom
> through the awful grace of God.

What we need in the United States is not division; what we need in the United States is not hatred; what we need in the United States is not violence and lawlessness, but is love, and wisdom, and compassion toward one another, and a feeling of justice toward those who still suffer within our country, whether they be white or whether they be black. So I ask you tonight to return home, to say a prayer for the family of Martin Luther King but more importantly to say a prayer for our own country, which all of us love—a prayer for understanding and that compassion of which I spoke.

We can do well in this country. We will have difficult times. We've had difficult times in the past, but we—and we will have difficult times in the future. It is not the end of violence; it is not the end of lawlessness; and it's not the end of disorder.

But the vast majority of white people and the vast majority of black people in this country want to live together, want to improve the quality of our life, and want justice for all human beings that abide in our land.

And let's dedicate ourselves to what the Greeks wrote so many years ago: to tame the savageness of man and make gentle the life of this world. Let us dedicate ourselves to that, and say a prayer for our country and for our people.

Thank you very much.

Kennedy's speech gave the audience another way forward. He reinforced the need to act in alignment with King's vision, and fight against the raw

---

💡 *What Do You Think?*

1. Think about a message you are trying to communicate to followers.

2. How are you currently communicating this message? What is working? What isn't resonating?

3. What changes can you make to get better results? Remember, an uplifting vision is concise, memorable, focused on shared aspirations, and uses authentic stagecraft. Also, visions are less about data (opponents will always counter your data with their data!) and more about persuasion and mobilizing others to take action.

---

emotions of vengeance and hatred. Under these tense, painful, and unpredictable circumstances it is astonishing to note that Kennedy successfully shifted the audience—in just a few minutes—from the shock of King's death toward a vision of gentleness, love, and forgiveness. Kennedy's leadership message was exactly what Indianapolis and the country needed at that moment. Tragically, only two months later Robert Kennedy was also killed by an assassin's bullet.

POWER

> "One day the lion will lie down with the lamb, but the lamb won't get much sleep."
>
> Woody Allen

Gene Sperling has spent a career in Washington D.C. earning a reputation as someone who can effectively influence others. He served as director of the National Economic Council during Bill Clinton's second term and was appointed to the same position by President Obama. He is praised as someone who can meld policy *and* politics when many people in government can only do one or the other. Shery Sandberg, chief operating officer at Facebook and a Treasury official in the Clinton administration says, "The N.E.C. director job is uniquely well suited for Gene because this is a job which is about figuring out what the economic policy should be, building consensus among policy makers and making sure that the policies are going to have the right impact in the real world." Most important, she added, "He gets things done" (Calmes, 2011). This assessment of Sperling's ability to design a solution, build consensus around an idea, and get results that impact the real world, perfectly describes the process of exercising power.

Renowned expert on managerial power and professor at the Stanford University Graduate School of Business, Jeffrey Pfeffer believes that the essential ingredient for a leader to get results is power. While qualities like emotional intelligence have their place, Pfeffer argues that we need to be more honest and direct in training leaders. In short, the ability to understand and effectively use power is the key to leadership success. He concisely defines power as "the ability to have things your way" (Pfeffer, 2010, p. 87). Pfeffer highlights the story of Zia Yusuf, a manager at SAP software, who found success building and running a strategy team within the company. Quoting Yusuf, Pfeffer says, "You need two things to succeed: substantive business knowledge, so you know *what* to do, and organizational or political skills, so you can *get it done*" (Pfeffer, 2010, p. 86). Pfeffer credits Yusuf's success in three areas: first, hiring exceptionally talented people and holding them to high standards; second, impeccable data and analysis to focus discussions on process rather than people; and, finally, Yusuf's ability not to become defensive or take things personally when others disagree with him.

Pfeffer discusses three barriers that hold leaders back from actualizing their potential power bases:

The Belief that the World Is a Just Place. Those subscribing to this belief figure that as long as they work hard, do a good job, and behave appropriately, others will notice and they will be rewarded accordingly. As they watch others engage in self-aggrandizing behavior, people holding on to this belief figure that those engaging in such behavior may be successful at the moment but in the end will be found out and brought down. In organizations, these beliefs usually don't play out and potential power players miss out while they sit on the sidelines and watch others increase and consolidate their own power. Pfeffer says that this belief limits ones "willingness to learn from all situations and all people, even those they don't like or respect" (Pfeffer, 2010, p. 88). This belief also "anesthetizes them to the need to proactively build a power base. People who believe the world is a fair place typically fail to see the land mines that can damage their careers" (Pfeffer, 2010, p. 88).

The Leadership Literature. Pfeffer believes that most of the leadership literature is well meaning but misses the mark. He claims that most leaders when they reach the executive suite and write books advising others about the leadership skills necessary to make it, "gloss over the power plays they used to get to the top" (Pfeffer, 2010, p. 88). Pfeffer says, "The teaching on leadership is filled with prescriptions about following your inner compass, being truthful, letting your feelings show, being modest and self-effacing, not behaving in bullying or abusive ways—in short, prescriptions that reflect how people *wish* those in positions of power behaved. There is no doubt that the world would be a much better place if people were always authentic, modest, truthful, and concerned about others, instead of simply pursuing their own aims. But wishing that's how people behaved won't make it so" (Pfeffer, 2010, p. 88).

Your Delicate Self-Esteem. Pfeffer notes that people are often their own worst enemies because in an effort to maintain their positive self image, people may intentionally put up obstacles to explain away failures or poor results. The research in this area is known as "self-handicapping" behavior. With regard to power, leaders can refrain from expanding their power and consequently when they don't obtain more influence in the workplace, they don't see it as a personal failure thus protecting their self-image.

McClelland and Burnham (2003) studied managerial effectiveness by identifying the factors that motivate managers. Their research reveals three motivational profiles that drive managerial behavior: achievement needs, affiliation needs, and power needs. Managers rating strong in achievement are driven to do things better and more efficiently than they have been done in the past. They focus on personal improvement and many times want to do things themselves which is unrealistic when one is leading a large organization and has to rely on the coordination and performance of many people. Managers with strong affiliative needs are primarily motivated by wanting to be liked by their subordinates. Finally, power-oriented managers want to be perceived as strong and influential. So, the question is: Which motivation profile produces the best manager? McClelland and Burnham conclude "that the top manager of a company must possess a high need for power—that is, a concern for influencing people. However, this need must be disciplined and controlled so that it is directed toward the benefit of the institution as a whole and not toward the manager's personal aggrandizement. Moreover, the top managers need for power ought to be greater than his or her need to be liked" (McClelland & Burnham, 2003, p. 118).

A primary finding indicates that the determining factor of high morale among employees rested on the manager's need for power outranking their need to be liked. This is because managers with a high affiliative need want to stay on good terms with everybody and consequently make what are viewed by most employees as capricious decisions to make individuals happy. McClelland and Burnham state bluntly, "Sociological theory and our findings both argue . . . the person whose need for affiliation is high does not make a good manager" (McClelland & Burnham, 2003, p. 120). While this doesn't mean that good managers are detached from the needs and feelings of their employees, it simply means that the strongest motivation of good managers is toward using their power and influence to serve the larger goals of the organization they are leading. McClelland and Burnham also investigated the role of management style on employee morale. They found that 63% of the best managers scored high on democratic or coaching styles in contrast to only 22% of the poorest managers. They go on to report that managers with low employee morale "scored higher on authoritative or coercive management styles. Since the better managers were also higher in power motivation, it seems that in action they express their power motivation in a democratic way, which is more likely to be effective" (McClelland & Burnham, 2003, p. 122).

An Important Note about the Motivation for Power

With an emphasis on hiring, developing, and promoting managers with a strong power motive, McClelland and Burnham caution that the exercise of power can sometimes lead to authoritarianism if taken to the extreme. Therefore, the manager's pursuit of power should be "socialized" or "regulated" so that the institution as a whole benefits, not just individual people. They offer two characteristics that serve as regulators, "a greater emotional maturity, where there is little egotism, and a democratic, coaching managerial style" (McClelland & Burnham, 2003, p. 126). Thus, effective power-oriented managers avoid aggressive, egotistical outbursts through emotional intelligence and seek the wise counsel of others through a relationship oriented management style.

Sources of Power

Many people only equate power with their job title or rank in the organizational hierarchy. Power is more nuanced and there are three sources from which power generates:

> **Where you are located.** This form of power is directly related to your job title. It is the exercise of power through authority. *Authority* is the right to command; *Power* is the ability to influence. If you are the boss,

then you have a legitimate right to tell people what to do. However, if you have held a management position, you know that relying on your job title to generate lasting commitment is a limited form of power. The ability to influence is the key, not authority.

Who you are. What personal qualities attract people toward you? Are you generous, thoughtful, a good listener, skilled at resolving conflict or synthesizing complex ideas? Every organization has *perceived leaders* and *actual leaders*. Those at the top of the hierarchy are the perceived leaders, but do people actually follow, respect, and admire them? Maybe, maybe not. There could be influential people at other levels of the organization who are the actual leaders. These people are the ones that organizational members really follow; they have the personal qualities and relationships to get things done. This is why personal power is much more fluid and dynamic than simply relying on one's positional authority to influence others.

What you have. When I share this idea with my students I always start by asking them, "Who has the power in this classroom?" They inevitably say, "You, because you are the teacher." "Good answer!" I say with a grin. Then I ask, "What do you have that I don't have?" They sit puzzled for a moment and then someone usually calls out, "There are more of us." Precisely. I keep pressing, "What happens to the power dynamics if you all decide to walk out right now?" Of course, power would instantly shift from the teacher to the students. Keep in mind, this example is a coercive form of power. The students could exercise a newly realized power source and make their point, but there would be fallout. Leaders can get into trouble when they overestimate their own power and underestimate the power of the opposition. During the early years of the labor movement, workers discovered that strikes were the only form of power they had to get authority figures to listen. Relationships and trust get damaged, but negotiation, compromise, and newly established roles and responsibilities emerge. For example, New York Catholic school teachers max out on their salary schedule at about $60,000 with a pension of $20,000 compared with New York public school teachers at $100,000 and $60,000 respectively. The Federation of Catholic Teachers has been unable to negotiate a contract with representatives from the New York archdiocese. The union proposed raises of 2 percent each year for three years while the church offered no raises the first year and 1 percent the second. However, teachers have precedent as a guide. In 2008 after going months without a contract, teachers at 23 archdiocesan schools held a surprise strike. Three days later, they had a 15 percent raise spread over four years.

FRENCH AND RAVEN'S (1959) FIVE SOURCES OF POWER IN LEADERSHIP

Referent power: Followers are attracted to the leader and want to be identified with the leader or what she represents. Followers feel a desire to join groups associated with the leader; if followers are already a member of the group they want to maintain their relationship with the leader.

"I admire her personal qualities and want to act in a way that gains her respect and admiration."

Expert power: Followers' perception of the leader's competence and knowledge.

"I comply with my supervisor's directives because I respect his experience and knowledge of the industry."

Reward power: Based on the leader's ability to reward followers. The strength of reward power increases with the magnitude of the reward and the perceived ability of the leader to actually deliver rewards.

"She influences what I do because of the special help and benefits she delivers to those who cooperate with her."

Legitimate power: The leader's authority and legitimate right to influence others and the obligation of followers to accept this influence.

"I comply with my supervisor's directives because he has a right, considering his position, to expect employees to do what he wants."

Coercive power: Stems from the expectation that followers will be punished by the leader if they fail to conform to the influence attempt.

"If I don't cooperate she can apply pressure or penalize me in some way."

Michael Winerip notes: "There are times when people in power will not listen until confronted by people with power" (Winerip, 2011, A14). Other examples of "what you have" sources of power include money, access to key decisions makers, networks, alliances, and relationships with influential people.

The classic and much referenced study by French and Raven (1959) defines five sources of power. They are: reward power, coercive power, legitimate power, referent power, and expert power.

The researchers set out to investigate two things: first, the factors that determine the behavior of the person exerting power and, second, the reactions of the recipient of this behavior. They conclude that *referent* power has the broadest range of influence. Referent power is based on attraction toward the leader and a desire to be associated with that person individually or to be associated with the group that person represents. Followers will subscribe to the attitudes and beliefs of a leader strong in referent power and gain satisfaction through such conformity. *Coercive* power results in decreased attraction of followers toward the leader and high resistance; however, the more legitimate the coercion, the less it will produce resistance and decreased attraction. French and Raven (1959) say, "Legitimate power in a formal organization is largely a relationship between offices rather than between persons. And the acceptance of an office as *right* is a basis for legitimate power—a judge has a right to levy fines, a foreman should assign work, a priest is justified in prescribing religious beliefs, and it is the management's prerogative to make certain decisions. However, legitimate power also involves the perceived right of the person to hold the office" (p. 160). Finally, French and Raven conclude that *reward* power results in increased attraction toward the leader and low resistance from followers. This attraction is strongly dependent on the leader's ability to actually deliver the rewards rather than make promises.

Influence Tactics that Work

Cialdini and Rhoads (2001) report six basic psychological principles that underlie successful influence tactics. These six principles serve as a framework to help individuals and work teams become more persuasive in their personal and business endeavors. While each of the six principles has been proven to get results, the authors note the ethical implications when employing any or all of the six principals.

Reciprocity

Simply put, people are much more inclined to help you if you have helped them. Cialdini and Rhodes state, "Societies worldwide abide by the norm of reciprocity, which obligates people to return in kind what they've received from others" (Cialdini & Rhodes, 2001, p. 10). Research points to results from simple acts such as including a few dollars in mailers to induce higher response rates to survey questionnaires or providing gifts to individuals in exchange for their support. Interestingly, people also reciprocate concessions. This means that when making large requests of others, if the initial request is turned down, a more modest follow-up request is usually reciprocated with a concession on the part of the other person. For example, Robert Cialdini supervised researchers on the streets of Tempe, Arizona as they asked people to help the County Youth Counseling Program by chaperoning a group of juvenile delinquents on a day trip to the zoo. Not surprisingly, only 17% agreed. However, when this request was preceded by a much larger request (asking if they would be willing to spend two hours a week as a counselor for juvenile delinquents for a minimum of two years), there was a dramatic improvement in results as 50% agreed to the more modest request.

Scarcity

We've all seen ads that claim "limited supply" or "for a limited time only." These tactics are commonplace because they work. Cialdini and Rhodes note that when an item or opportunity is perceived as scarce, it consequently becomes more attractive. For example, college students at Florida State University rated their cafeteria food as unsatisfactory; however, nine days later students rated the cafeteria food as much more desirable after learning that part of the cafeteria had been burned and they would not be able to eat there for several weeks. This principle also applies to the classic case from the mid-1980s when Coca-Cola changed its formula and introduced New Coke which was largely rejected by consumers. Because Old Coke was now scarce, it became more desirable even though many people couldn't distinguish the taste between the old product and new one in blind taste tests. Cialdini and Rhodes note, "Even Gay Mullins, the founder of the Old Cola Drinkers of America society—who worked tirelessly to get the traditional formula back into the marketplace by any civil, judicial, or legislative means possible—preferred the New Coke to the old in two separate blind taste tests. It's noteworthy that the thing Mullins liked more was less valuable to him than the thing he was being denied" (Cialdini & Rhodes, 2001, p. 11).

Authority

Credibility is the key to maximizing influence as an authority figure. Credibility derives from being seen as both an *expert* and *trustworthy*. Cialdini and Rhodes say, "Expertise refers to a communicator's knowledge and experience while trustworthiness refers to the communicator's honesty and lack of bias" (Cialdini & Rhodes, 2001, p. 11). Trustworthiness is the most important attribute because expertise only goes so far. If one is an expert on a subject but perceived as biased or dishonest, he will fail to persuade others because of a lack of trustworthiness. People can dramatically increase their trustworthiness by communicating both sides of an argument. This gives the impression of fairness and impartiality.

Cialdini and Rhodes conclude, "Researchers have long known that communicators who present two-sided arguments can gain the trust of their audiences and thereby achieve the goal of becoming influential, credible sources. This two-sided approach is especially effective when the audience initially disagrees with the commentator" (Cialdini & Rhodes, 2001, p. 11).

Consistency

People tend to behave in a manner consistent with public commitments or declarations. For example, a Chicago restaurant was struggling with the associated costs of customers that make reservations yet no-show without calling to cancel the reservation. This restaurant made huge strides in getting customers to change their behavior by adding two words in the host's telephone script. Instead of saying, "Please call if you have to change your plans," the host asked, "*Will you* please call if you have to change your plans?" and then politely waited for a response. This caused the customer to make a public commitment to call if he needed to cancel the reservation. As a result, the no-show rate dropped from 30% to 10% immediately. Building on the principle of consistency, Cialdini and Rhodes offer the example of Joseph Schwarzwald of Bar-Ilan University in Israel. Schwarzwald and his co-workers were seeking to increase contributions to causes for the disabled. They first canvassed neighborhoods asking residents to sign a petition supporting the disabled. A few weeks later, they visited those same homes and asked for financial contributions, thus giving residents a chance to act in alignment with their previous public commitment. Schwarzwald and his colleagues found that people were much more generous when given an opportunity to remain consistent with their initial commitment.

Liking

Likability is defined by three characteristics: physical attractiveness, cooperation, and similarity. Research shows that good-looking fundraisers generate more donations, attractive political candidates fare better at the polls, well-groomed job candidates have an advantage in interviews, and economists studying wages of U.S. and Canadian workers found that attractive individuals get paid an average of 12% to 14% more than their colleagues. People also tend to like those that display cooperative behaviors and attitudes. For example, when salespeople present themselves as advocates for the customer in order to find the best deal on their behalf, they are more likely to generate positive feelings and behaviors on the part of the customer. Finally, when one feels that another person is "like them," he or she is more likely to follow through on a request. Cialdini and Rhodes note that salespeople are trained to "mirror and match" the customer's body posture, mood, and verbal styles because these techniques achieve results.

Consensus

When making decisions about a product or service to purchase, people tend to trust the conclusions of friends and associates—especially if those people are like us. Cialdini and Rhodes say, "If all our friends are raving about a new best-selling book, travel agent, or piece of software, we will probably like those things, too. We can use the actions of others to locate and validate correct choices" (Cialdini & Rhodes, 2001, p. 13). For example, research has shown that fundraisers canvassing a neighborhood are more likely to increase contributions if they share the names of neighbors that have already donated to the cause. No matter how independent we think we are, the behaviors of others we like and admire affect our own judgments and conclusions.

Influence Options for Managers

Falbe and Yukl (1992) found a lack of empirical studies that demonstrate the effectiveness of different influence tactics on subordinates, peers, and superiors. In their own study, Falbe and Yukl identified nine influence tactics and measured the effectiveness of each tactic when used alone or in combination with other tactics. When change agents employ these influence tactics, three outcomes emerge: commitment, compliance, and resistance. The researchers note:

> Commitment occurs when a target person agrees internally with an action or decision, is enthusiastic about it, and is likely to exercise initiative and demonstrate unusual effort and persistence in order to carry out the request successfully. Compliance occurs when the target person carries out the requested action but is apathetic about it rather than enthusiastic, makes only minimal or average effort, and does not show any initiative. Resistance occurs when the target person is opposed to the requested action and tries to avoid doing it by refusing, arguing, delaying, or seeking to have the request nullified (Falbe & Yukl, 1992, pp. 639–640).

It is important to recognize that while commitment is ideal, many times all a manager desires is compliance with an initiative.

Nine Influence Tactics Defined

Tactic	Description
Personal Appeal	Appeals to the follower's feelings of loyalty and friendship to influence the follower to do something extra as a favor.
Exchange Tactics	Explicit or implicit offers to provide some benefit in return for doing what the leader requests.
Pressure Tactics	Demands, threats, frequent checking, or persistent reminders in an attempt to get others to carry out a request.
Legitimating Tactics	Establishes the legitimacy of a request by claiming one's authority.
Coalition Tactics	Enlists the aid or endorsement of other people to influence behaviors of others.
Inspirational Appeal	Request or proposal that arouses enthusiasm by appealing to values and aspirations or by increasing follower's confidence that he or she can do the requested task. Inspirational vision—transformational.
Consultation	Seeks participation in planning a strategy, activity, or change. Leader is willing to modify a proposal based on follower's concerns or suggestions.
Rational Persuasion	Uses logical arguments and factual evidence to persuade others.
Ingratiation	Seeks to increase cooperation by increasing the follower's feelings of positive regard toward him or her.

(Adapted from Falbe, C., & Yukl, G. (1992). Consequences for managers of using single influence tactics and combinations of tactics. *Academy of Management Journal*, 35 (3), 640–643.)

Findings suggest that the most effective tactics were inspirational appeals and consultation. The least effective were pressure, legitimating, and coalition tactics. Intermediate effectiveness occurred with rational persuasion, ingratiation, personal appeals, and exchange tactics. Rational persuasion was found to be much more effective when used in combination with soft tactics such as consultation, inspirational appeals, or ingratiation. Falbe and Yukl also examined the outcomes associated with combining hard tactics, soft tactics, and rational persuasion. Hard tactics are those associated with pressure, legitimating, coalition, and exchange, while soft tactics correspond with ingratiation, consultation, inspiration, and personal appeals. Overall, influence attempts had a more favorable outcome when a leader used a pair of tactics rather than a single tactic. However, effectiveness was determined by the types of tactics that were combined. Falbe and Yukl note, "A combination of two hard tactics was no better than a single hard tactic, and a soft-hard combination was no better than a single soft tactic. Thus, when managers use tactic combinations, they should pay careful attention to the selection of component tactics" (Falbe & Yukl, 1992, p. 650).

Coalition Building

In the workplace, friends, enemies, heated disagreements, and differing opinions are the norm. Coalitions form around shared interests. Furthermore, coalitions are fluid and often short lived. Leaders form coalitions and partnerships with anyone that can help them achieve their objectives. The key—as was mentioned earlier in this section—is to develop a compelling agenda, network, and build a power base. Alliances and coalitions are always more powerful than lone wolves.

Psychologist Dacher Keltner says, "We've done a good job documenting how harshly humans treat their enemies throughout evolution but we also have evidence of an early shift in human evolution to hypersociality—a

Outcomes of Influence Tactics Used Alone

Influence Tactics	Resistance	Compliance	Commitment
Inspiration	0%	10%	90%
Consultation	18	27	55
Personal appeals	25	33	42
Exchange	24	41	35
Ingratiation	41	28	31
Rational Persuasion	47	30	23
Legitimating	44	56	0
Coalition	53	44	3
Pressure	56	41	3

Outcomes of Influence Tactics Used in Combination

Influence Tactics	Resistance	Compliance	Commitment
Soft with soft	14%	12%	74%
Soft with rational	14	31	55
Soft alone	27	28	45
Hard with rational	28	46	26
Soft with hard	33	35	32
Rational alone	47	30	23
Hard with hard	45	47	8
Hard alone	47	43	10

(Adapted from Falbe, C., & Yukl, G. (1992). Consequences for managers of using single influence tactics and combinations of tactics. *Academy of Management Journal*, 35 (3), 647, 649.)

default orientation toward trust, toward sharing resources, toward forgiveness" (Carey, 2010, p. 6). One key to building a coalition is focusing on shared values that supersede the immediate source of controversy or argument. This is especially effective one-on-one because in groups (especially in the company of fellow partisans) individuals tend to exaggerate their positions and the most defiant rise above others as the de-facto leaders. For example, when President Jimmy Carter was facilitating negotiations between Israel and Egypt in 1978, Israeli Prime Minister Menachem Begin threatened to walk away from the negotiating table. Carter visited Menachem and personally delivered autographed photos of the meeting addressed to the prime minister's eight grandchildren. Reflecting on this event in 1994, Carter reminisced, "That was it. He looked at those eight photographs, and tears began to run down his cheeks—and mine—as he read the names. In just a few minutes he sent his attorney general to tell me he was going to look at the negotiations again" (Carey, 2010, p. 6).

The use of social media tools such as Facebook and Twitter has revolutionized the way coalitions are built. During 2010 and 2011, these tools were used to rally people in Iran and Cairo to demonstrate for government reform. In the early months of 2011, the government in Tunisia dissolved in response to massive demonstrations in the streets that were

⚡ Power Map Activity

1. Think of an objective or goal you are trying to accomplish.

2. Develop a compelling message why others should get on board with your idea. Think about others' interests in the endeavor and the influence tactics mentioned in this chapter.

3. Use the map below to chart your allies, fence-sitters, and opponents and their corres-

ponding levels of power. (The X's below are just examples of categories people may fall into, remove these X's and chart the names of people in your own organization.)

4. What was revealed? Using the influence tactics you've learned, how can you increase your allies and deal with opponents?

	Allies	Fence-sitters	Opponents
High Power	X	X X	X
	X X X	X X X X	X X
Low Power	X X	X	X

organized in large part through the rapid sharing of information and coordination efforts made easier by social media tools. Interestingly, Navid Hassanpour argues that social media also complicated the uprisings in Egypt. He studied how the decision by the government of Hosni Mubarak to completely shut down the Internet and cellphone service on January 28, 2011—in the middle of the crucial protests in Tahrir Square—affected revolutionary forces. Hassanpour concludes that, "full connectivity in a social network sometimes can hinder collective action" (Cohen, 2011, B3).

This is because instant communications can spread a message of caution, delay, confusion, or people are simply more distracted because of access to the Internet. Hassanpour says, "The disruption of cellphone coverage and Internet on the 28th exacerbated the unrest in at least three major ways. It implicated many apolitical citizens unaware or uninterested in the unrest; it forced more face-to-face communication, i.e., more physical presence in streets; and finally it effectively decentralized the rebellion on the 28th through new hybrid communication tactics, producing a quagmire much harder to control and repress than one massive gathering in Tahrir" (Cohen, 2011, B3).

Building coalitions also requires strategic thinking. Using a Power Map to identify allies, fence-sitters, and opponents (and corresponding levels of power) can help clarify the political terrain. Strategically, the goal is to get to high power fence-sitters before your opponents and use the influence tactics mentioned earlier to move fence-sitters to your side.

DEALING WITH CONFLICT

Organizations can have too much conflict or too little. The key is having the right type of conflict. There are two types of conflict: affective and cognitive. *Affective conflict* is personality based and fueled by jealousy, insecurity, and petty gripes. *Cognitive conflict* focuses on challenging others' ideas and ways of thinking in order to accomplish organizational objectives in the most efficient and effective way possible. When chairing an emotional meeting where there is the danger of affective conflict, it is helpful for the leader to say, "I know this is a controversial subject, so before we get started, let me be clear: it is okay to attack ideas, but not okay to attack people." Leaders set the tone and norms for the group. They must frame contentious discussions by neutralizing any attempt to engage in the destructive elements of affective conflict and move the group toward cognitive conflict. Since there will always be some form of conflict in any social endeavor, leaders can benefit from best practices to effectively manage and breakthrough conflicts. The Thomas-Kilman Conflict Mode Instrument (TKI) provides one of the best tools to understanding conflict and the variety of options available to leaders and managers.

The TKI instrument identifies five conflict-handling modes: *competing, collaborating, compromising, avoiding,* and *accommodating*. Each conflict-handling mode reflects two independent dimensions of behavior. The first dimension is *cooperativeness*. This is defined as the degree to which a person attempts to satisfy the other person's concern. The second is *assertiveness*. Assertiveness is defined as attempting to satisfy one's own concerns (Kilmann & Thomas, 1977, p. 310).

Let's look more closely at each the modes individuals and groups kick into when conflicts erupt. Thomas (1992) describes each of the five conflict-handling modes as having a distinct strategic intention:

Competing intention (uncooperative, assertive). This behavior represents an attempt to prevail or win one's position at the others' expense. This can also take the form of attempts to convince the other that one's conclusion is correct and the other's is mistaken or when one tries to make another party accept blame for some perceived transgression and accept any responsibilities attached to the blame (guilt, punishment, restitution, etc.). Other terms for competing include forcing, win-lose, dominating, and contending.

Accommodating intention (cooperative, unassertive). This is the opposite of competing. Accommodating is an attempt to satisfy the other's concerns at the neglect of one's own. There is an element of self-sacrifice in this mode where an individual may support the other's opinion despite one's own reservations. Other terms for accommodating include smoothing over, obliging, and yielding.

Compromising intention (intermediate in both cooperativeness and assertiveness). This is midway between competing and accommodating. Compromising is an attempt to attain moderate but incomplete satisfaction of both parties' concerns—giving up something but also holding out for something. Other terms for compromising include splitting the difference and sharing.

Collaborating intention (cooperative, assertive). In contrast to compromise, this mode represents an attempt to fully satisfy the concerns of the two parties to achieve an integrative settlement. This is seen as a win-win solution where seemingly divergent perspectives are synthesized to create a new solution that may not have been realized in the initial stages of the conflict. Other terms for collaborating are problem solving, synergy, integrating, and confronting (in the sense of confronting the conflict to work it through).

Avoiding intention (uncooperative, unassertive). This behavior reflects a desire to ignore or neglect the concerns of both self and other. One seeks to avoid involvement in the issue, allowing events to take their own course without attempting to steer the outcome toward the concern of either party. Other terms for avoiding are withdrawing and inaction.

(Adapted from Thomas, K. (1992). Conflict and negotiation process in organizations. In M. Dunnette, & L. Hough, *Handbook of industrial & organizational psychology* (2nd ed., Vol. III, pp. 651–717). Palo Alto: Consulting Psychological Press, Inc. Pages 668–669)

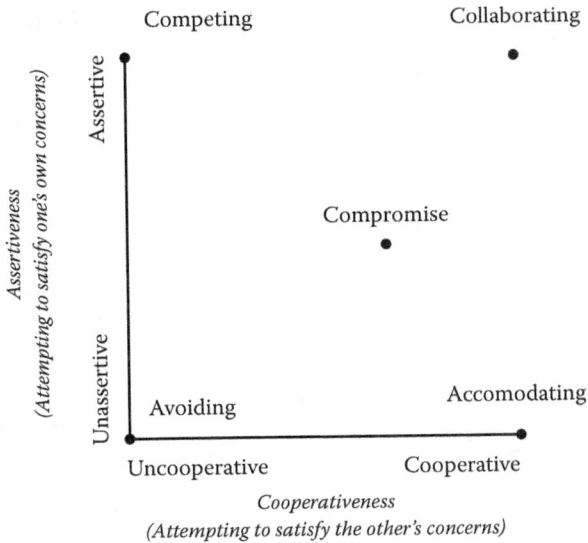

FIGURE 8-1 Two-dimensional Taxonomy of Strategic Intentions

From "Conflict" by K. W. Thomas, 1979, in S. Kerr (Ed.), *Organizational Behavior* (p.154). Grid Publications. Copyright 1979 by S. Kerr. Adapted by permission.

Reprinted from "Conflict," by Kenneth W. Thomas, *Organizational Behavior*, edited by S. Kerr (1979), by permission of John Wiley & Sons, Inc.

The TKI instrument allows participants to identify their dominant conflict handling mode(s). Like most self-assessments, there is not one "correct" mode for dealing with conflict. Rather, effective conflict management involves both strategic intent and response to situational variables. Thomas (1992) notes, "These strategic intentions provide a way of describing a party's general aims during a conflict. Without such steering mechanisms, the party's conflict behavior would merely be reactive or wandering. Nevertheless, there is a danger in viewing these strategic intentions in an oversimplified manner—in identifying them as "cast in concrete." A strategic intention need not remain fixed during the course of a conflict and may change with a party's reconceptualizations and emotions. Likewise, there are times when a party may in fact lack a clear strategic intention and simply react to unfolding events" (pp. 669–670).

Thomas (1977) reports on the situational nature of each conflict-handling mode. In his research, 28 chief executives furnished lists of managerial situations where each of the conflict-handling modes would provide unique tools in alleviating or resolving conflicts. Thomas provides this list as evidence that experienced managers, "(a) see the usefulness of conflict modes as depending upon a complex set of situational circumstances, and (b) see all five modes as useful skills in appropriate situations" (p. 487). See Table 8-1 for a list of conflict-handling modes and situational variables.

TABLE 8-1 Situations in Which to Use the Five Conflict-Handling Modes, as Reported by 28 Chief Executives of Organizations

Conflict Mode	Situation	Conflict Mode	Situation

Competing

1. When quick., decisive action is vital— e.g., emergencies.
2. On important issues where unpopular action need implementing — e.g., cost cutting, enforcing unpopular rules, discipline.
3. On issues vital to company welfare when you know you're right.
4. Against people who take advantage of non-competitive behavior.

Collaborating

1. To find an integrative solution when both sets of concerns are too important to be compromised.
2. When your objective is to learn.
3. To merge insights from people with different perspectives.
4. To gain commitment by incorporating concerns into a consensus.
5. To work through feelings which have interfered with a relationship.

Compromising

1. When goals are important, but not worth the effort or potential disruption of more assertive modes.
2. When opponents with equal power are committed to mutually exclusive goals.
3. To achieve temporary settlements to complex issues.
4. To arrive at expedient solutions under time pressure.
5. As a backup when collaboration or competition is unsuccessful.

Avoiding

1. When an issue is trivial, or more important issues are pressing.
2. When you perceive no chance of satisfying your concerns.
3. When potential disruption outweighs the benefits of resolution.
4. To let people cool down and regain perspective.
5. When gathering information supercedes immediate decision.
6. When others can resolve the conflict more effectively.
7. When issues seem tangential or symptomatic of other issues.

Accommodating

1. When you find you are wrong — to allow a better position to be heard, to learn, and to show your reasonableness.
2. When issues are more important to others than yourself — to satisfy other; and maintain cooperation.
3. To build social credits for later issues.
4. To minimize loss when you are outmatched and losing.
5. When harmony and stability are especially important.
6. To allow subordinates to develop by learning from mistakes.

(Source: Kenneth W. Thomas, *Toward multi-dimensional values in teaching: The example of conflict behaviors*, Academy of Management Review, July 1977, p. 487)

Reprinted from "Toward Multi-dimensional Values in Teaching: The Example of Conflict Behavior, *Academy of Management Review* (1977), by permission from the Academy of Management Review.

? *What Do You Think?*

Where might I/we improve in these areas? Think about: Clarifying the vision, mission or goals to the team, communicating the vision, networking and building coalitions to get others on board, influence tactics, competing to win, dealing with conflict, creating arenas for issues to be discussed, etc.

_____
_____
_____
_____
_____
_____
_____
_____

Are power, politics, and/or conflict getting in the way of our performance? Think about: dysfunctional political dynamics, too much emotional conflict, lack of influence on others, lack of clarity on strategy and objectives, not seen as an advocate, etc.

_____
_____
_____
_____
_____
_____
_____
_____

Questions for Review

1. What does it mean to be politically intelligent?

2. What are the characteristics of an effective vision?

3. How is power related to leadership? According to Pfeffer (2010), what three barriers hold leaders back from actualizing their potential power bases?

4. What sources of power can leaders use to influence people and situations?

5. What are the five conflict-handling modes? How can leaders use each mode to effectively handle conflict?

CHAPTER 9:
Leading Change

LEARNING OBJECTIVES

After studying this chapter, you should be able to:

1. Define and discuss three types of change.
2. Demonstrate strategies to successfully lead change.
3. Identify approaches leaders can take to decrease resistance to change.
4. Compare and contrast change with transition.

THOMAS PAINE AND EDMUND BURKE ON CHANGE

Thomas Paine and Edmund Burke both supported the American Revolution; however, they viewed the nature of change very differently. Paine believed in radical change. In fact, he suggested that laws should expire after 30 years to give each new generation a fresh start. Paine saw the American Revolution as an articulation of universal ideals and the necessary dismantling and restructuring of an entire system of government to support these truths. Burke also supported the American Revolution but he believed that the best type of change is measured and gradual. Burke argued for continuous, systematic change that retains what is working and adjusts what isn't working. History contains atrocity but it also harbors wisdom. Too much change risks losing this wisdom and entering a dangerous cycle of continual chaos (see Brooks, 2010). Leaders must reconcile "out-with-the-old-in-with-the-new" impulses with an approach that recognizes the accumulated wisdom that has served the organization well and must be passed down—a little improved each time—to future generations. The first step in leading change is distinguishing between different types of change.

THREE TYPES OF CHANGE

There are three types of change in organizations: *developmental, transitional,* and *transformational*. Developmental change is the simplest. It seeks to improve upon existing practices without dramatically changing the organization's

Developmental Change

Old State — Transition State → New State

Transitional Change

Growth / Success plateau / Wake-up calls / Chaos / Death – forced to shift / Re-emergence through visioning and learning / Birth

Transformational Change

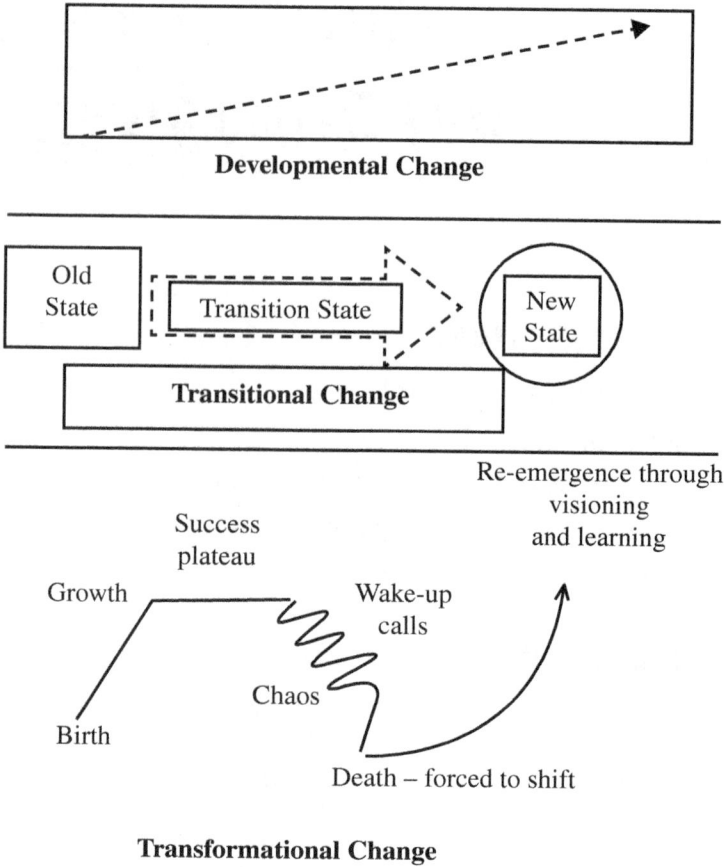

FIGURE 9-1 Three Types of Organizational Change

Reprinted from *Organization Development: The Human and Social Dynamics of Organizational Change* (1996), by permission of the University Press of America.

culture. Examples include opening up new business locations or updating policies and procedures. Transitional change is different. This type of change involves replacing an old practice with something new. There are psychological implications with this form of change because organizational members must let go of the old way of doing things, go through a transition state, and then enter something new. Shifting from one computer system to an entirely new system is a common example of transitional change in organizations. Other examples include reorganizations, implementing new products and services, or new policies and procedures that replace existing ones.

The third, and most complex, form of change is transformational change. This involves fundamentally changing core beliefs and practices. Jackson (2006) points out that transformational change stands out from other forms of change in two ways. First, the future is unknown at the start of the change process and can only be created and realized by forging ahead. Leaders enter uncharted waters with only their instincts as guide. Second, the future state is so radically different than the current state that a shift in mindset is required to invent, implement, and sustain the change. Essentially, the organization's culture changes as members must adapt to new ways of doing things, but more important, change the way they think. What causes transformational change? As noted in the figure 9-1, with transformational change, organizations tend to rely on past successes as a predictor of future success. They can operate almost on automatic pilot because what has worked in the past continues to work in the present. However, organizations then experience abrupt wake-up calls. Unfortunately, many leaders ignore early warning signs until it is late in the game and they are forced to change. Wake-up calls can be in the form of a competitor that threatens market share, shifts in customer demand, or new political realities in the form of governmental expectations and regulations. A few examples include Toyota's gain in market share against GM in the 1980s, Nokia's first mover advantage over Motorola at the start of the digital age in cellular technology, Netflix's transformation of how consumers watch and rent videos, and the Internet's impact on traditional newspapers and print publications. Jackson notes, "The true transformational moment occurs when the organizational leaders really listen to the wake-up calls, which catapults them into a breakthrough in their awareness and beliefs. They begin to formulate new intentions about what is possible and necessary for the organization to survive" (Jackson, 2006, p. 8).

STRATEGIES TO SUCCESSFULLY LEAD CHANGE EFFORTS

The literature has reflected a shift away from "top-down" leadership styles that impose change on others toward a more collaborative style where the leader serves as a facilitator of the change process. In short, *imposition* inevitably equals *opposition*. In other words, people don't necessarily resist change, they resist having change forced upon them. Today's organizations are comprised of knowledge workers with access to information and ideas on how to increase organizational performance. Likewise, leaders must create a transparent environment where people are invited to leverage their talents and expertise and discuss and debate the future direction of the organization and how best to get there. However, the leader still plays a vital role in this process. It is her job to listen and synthesize the disparate ideas into a coherent road map for the future then validate their conclusions against the beliefs of organizational members. Because transformational change involves uncertainty, confusion, and anxiety, it is critical for leaders to honestly acknowledge the current reality and articulate a vision for the future that reflects the shared aspirations of the entire organization. This is a tall order and it's no wonder so many change efforts fail or make the situation worse.

One of the leading researchers on the subject of change is John Kotter. The following is a summary of his eight reasons why change efforts fail. Being on the lookout for these eight roadblocks and proactively seeking remedies will give any change initiative a critical advantage.

Not establishing a great enough sense of urgency. To counter this, leaders must communicate why the need for change is critical to the advancement (or survival) of the organization. Many leaders underestimate how difficult it is to get others to shift away from their comfort zones. Also, leaders can rush this process believing that others are ready for change when, in actuality, they are not.

Not creating a powerful enough guiding coalition. In the early stages of any change effort, leaders must assemble a team of supporters to advocate and guide the change effort. While leadership from the top is critical, successful guiding coalitions must also include other influential members such as senior managers, board members, union leaders, and respected rank and file employees. A powerful guiding coalition is essential to counter other coalitions that will rise to resist the change.

Lacking a vision. It is the leader's job to initiate a clear and compelling vision. The leader doesn't have to have all the answers immediately, but he needs to get the process started. Too often leaders rely on volumes of data and reports without clearly expressing where the organization is heading and why. If you cannot communicate the vision to someone in less than five minutes and get a reaction that signifies both understanding and interest, this phase of the change process is not complete and you need to go back to the drawing board.

Undercommunicating the vision by a factor of ten. Effective leaders use every opportunity to draw things back to the vision. They do this during employee performance appraisals, board meetings, and informal conversation in the hallways. Many leaders try to inspire change by sending out a memo. This doesn't resonate. Kotter notes that successful leaders, "turn boring, unread company newsletters into lively articles about the vision. They take ritualistic, tedious quarterly management meetings and turn them into exciting discussions of the transformation. They throw out much of the company's generic management education and replace it with courses that focus on business problems and the new vision. The guiding principle is simple: Use every possible channel, especially those that are being wasted on nonessential information."

Not removing obstacles to the new vision. Communication isn't enough. After people become committed to the change, they will report obstacles that impede the change from happening. These could be deficiencies in the organizational structure, compensation methods, or bosses that pay lip service to the change but in reality put up roadblocks. Leaders must listen to the reports on what is getting in the way and work to keep things moving forward.

Not systematically planning for and creating short-term wins. Transformational change takes time. Managers and leaders need to actively search for and create opportunities to achieve and celebrate small victories along the way. Urgency levels can drop when it looks like the change is going to take a long time. This makes it critical for progress to be demonstrated through short-term wins.

Declaring victory too soon. In May 2003, President George W. Bush gave a speech aboard an aircraft carrier while standing under a banner that read "Mission Accomplished." He declared that major combat operations in Iraq had ended. In fact, the mission was not completed that month and intense fighting continued for many more years. During the final news conference of his presidency in January 2009, Bush said, "Clearly, putting 'Mission Accomplished' on an aircraft carrier was a mistake. It sent the wrong message" (Stolberg, 2009). Kotter suggests, "Instead of declaring victory, leaders of successful efforts use the credibility afforded by short-term wins to tackle even bigger problems." Kotter reports that in one study of a seven-year change effort, peak accomplishments didn't occur until year five. This was a full 36 months after the first signs of progress were noticed.

Not anchoring changes in the corporation's culture. No transformational change effort is complete until it becomes integrated into the culture of the organization. Two factors institutionalize the change into the culture. First, leaders must show people how the new approaches, behaviors, and attitudes have lifted performance. Organizational members need to be shown how *their own* changes have led to increases in productivity, service, and results. Second, future top management hiring decisions must reflect the new culture. Boards of directors must understand the change effort in order to hire senior managers that embody the change. This is especially a risk if the main champion for change is a retiring CEO that is leaving the company. Kotter notes that one bad hire can set back decades of hard work.

(List adapted from Kotter, J. (1997, January). Leading change: Why transformation efforts fail. *Harvard Business Review*, 96–103.)

EIGHT STEPS TO TRANSFORMING YOUR ORGANIZATION

1 Establishing a Sense of Urgency
- Examining market and competitive realities
- Identifying and discussing crises, potential crises, or major opportunites

2 Forming a Powerful Guiding Coalition
- Assembling a group with enough power to lead the change effort
- Encouraging the group to work together as a team

3 Creating a Vision
- Creating a vision to help direct the change effort
- Developing strategies for achieving that vision

4 Communicating the Vision
- Using every vehicle possible to communicate the new vision and strategies
- Teaching new behaviors by the example of the guiding coalition

5 Empowering Others to Act on the Vision
- Getting rid of obstacles to change
- Changing systems or structutes that seriously undermine the vision
- Encouraging risk taking and nontraditional ideas, activities, and actions

6 Planning for and Creating Short Term Wins
- Planning for visible performance improvements
- Creating those improvements
- Recognizing and rewarding employees involved in the improvements

7 Consolidating Improvements and Producing Still More Change
- Using increased credibility to change systems, structures, and policies that don't fit the vision
- Hiring, promoting, and developing employees who can implement the vision
- Reinvigorating the process with new projects, themes, and change agents

8 Institutionalizing New Approaches
- Articulating the connections between the new behaviors and corporate success
- Developing the means to ensure leadership development and succession

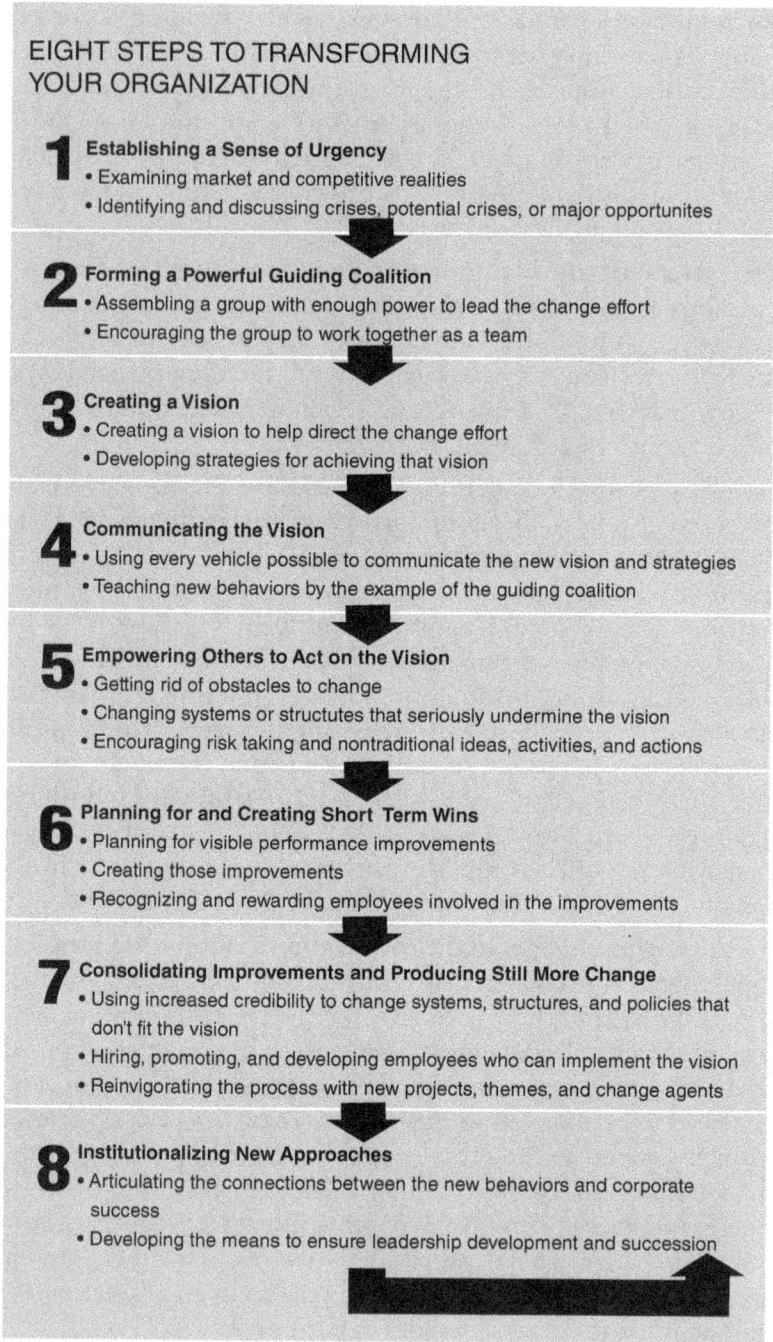

Reprinted from *Leading Change: Why Transformation Efforts Fail* (2007), by permission of Harvard Business School Publishing.

Resistance to change is inevitable. Kotter and Schlesinger (1979) suggest that successful change efforts involve using the right strategy in response to the nature of resistance. Leaders should realistically appraise the virtues and drawbacks of each strategy and use a variety of approaches. This may require a leader to engage in behaviors that he wouldn't normally use. For example, some leaders always rely on coercion when another option would be more effective. Figure 9-2 offers five approaches leaders can take to decrease resistance to change.

DIFFERENCES BETWEEN CHANGE AND TRANSITION

There is a distinction between change and transition. Change happens externally; something new is thrust upon us such as a new boss, office location, or company policy. Transition is an internal, psychological process that requires us to come to terms with the new situation, let go of the old, and embrace the new. Bridges (2004), in his research on transitions, states, "*Change* is situational. *Transition*, on the other hand, is psychological. It is not those events, but rather the inner reorientation and self-definition that you have to go through in order to incorporate any of those changes into your life" (p. xii). This distinction is important because too many leaders focus only on change and neglect the personal process of transition. Most employees feel a deep connection to their work and workplace. A significant amount of our identity is related to our work. When things change—abruptly or over a period of time—skilled leaders recognize that people will experience a period of disorientation before reorienting to the new reality. Leaders tend to force and rush this process expecting others to adapt overnight. Transition requires time and—of course—time is a precious commodity in today's workplace. However, transformational change is necessary for organizations to stay competitive and this requires a deliberate period of transition for each member of the organization to truly incorporate and support the change.

Bridges offers three stages associated with the process of transitions. Transitions begin with (1) an ending, followed by (2) a neutral zone marked by a period of confusion and distress, which leads to (3) a new beginning (see Figure 9-3). Common transition periods all people experience include: youth, adolescence, school, living on our own, careers, marriage, parenting, aging, and death. Of course, this is just a brief list and each of us could add our own unique experiences. The point is that we are more resilient and familiar with transition than we think. Many transitions involve difficulty and suffering; however, if we are open to it, with these experiences also comes insight, growth, heightened awareness, and the opportunity for increased effectiveness. Because few of us enjoy suffering,

Approach	Idea in brief	Commonly used in situations	Advantages	Drawbacks
Education and communication	People need information in order to better understand the need for change.	Where there is a lack of information or inaccurate information that needs clarification.	Once persuaded of the need for change, people will be more likely to support and even advocate for the change.	Can be very time consuming in large organizations with numerous stakeholders.
Participation and involvement	Those that are going to be most affected by the change should participate in the change initiative early.	Where the initiators do not have all the information they need to design the change and where others have considerable power to resist.	People who participate will be committed to implementing the change and any relevant information they have will be integrated into the plan.	Can be very time consuming if participators design an inappropriate change.
Facilitation and support	Managers should provide training for employees to develop new skills, listen, and offer emotional support when necessary.	Where people are resisting because of adjustment problems.	No other approach works as well with adjustment problems.	Can be time consuming, expensive, and still fail.
Negotiation and agreement	Change creates winners and losers. Negotiation around mutual benefits can reduce resistance to the change.	Where someone or some group will clearly lose out in the change, and where that group has considerable power to resist.	Sometimes it is a relatively easy way to avoid major resistance.	Can be too expensive in many cases if it alerts others to negotiate in order to comply.
Explicit and implicit coercion	Forcing others to change or threatening to fire, transfer, or withhold promotion opportunities.	Where speed is essential, changes are necessary yet unpopular, and the change initiators posses considerable power.	It is speedy and can overcome resistance.	Can be risky if it leaves a majority of people angry at the initiators.

FIGURE 9-2

Adapted from Kotter, J., & Schlesinger, L. (1979). Choosing strategies for change. *Harvard Business Review, 57*(2), p. 111. Reprinted from *Choosing Strategies for Change* (1979), by permission of Harvard Business School Publishing.

"Transition is a natural process that marks the turning points of the path of growth."

Stage 3: **Beginning**
"The New"

Stage 2: **The Neutral Zone**
"The In-Between"

Stage 1: **Ending "The Old"**
Letting Go

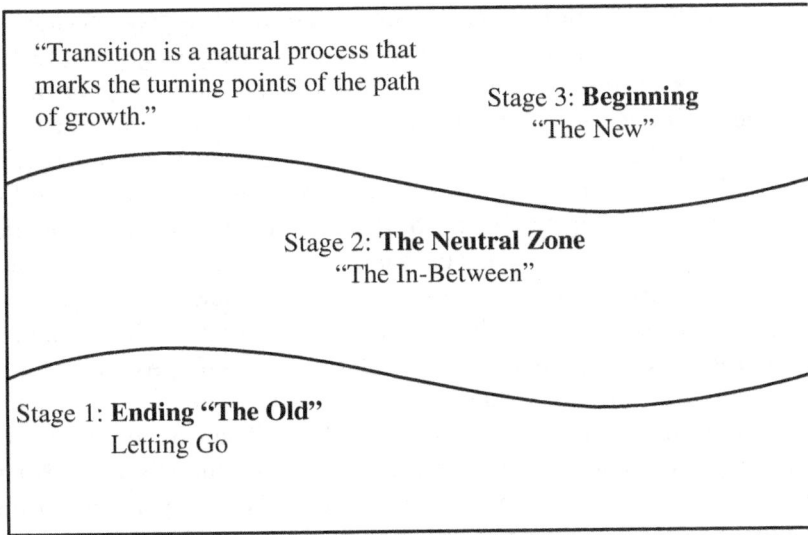

FIGURE 9-3 Stages of Transition
Reprinted from *Organization Development: The Human and Social Dynamics of Organizational Change* (2006), by permission of the University Press of America.

it can be tempting to resist this process and seek the predictable comfort of the familiar. Yet, it is worth remembering that ships weren't meant to stay docked in safe harbors; they were meant to be taken into the open, unpredictable sea. Leaders need to remind their followers of this from time to time.

Endings, Neutral Zone, New Beginning

Endings are the first stage in the transition process. Before rushing into the new beginning, we need to acknowledge and let go of the past. Cultural anthropology is filled with rite of passage ceremonies marking the end of youth and the beginning of adulthood. These ceremonies are replete with ritual and symbolism allowing recognition of the past and marking the transition into a new state of life. There is a symbolic "death" which bids farewell to old behaviors and anticipates the transition to a new way of thinking and being. These dramatic and powerful ceremonies make clear that change is happening. In modern organizations we have lost the impact and significance of these types of experiences.

Bridges explains five stages associated with endings: disengagement, dismantling, disidentification, disenchantment, and disorientation. With *disengagement,* we consciously break from the familiar. Sometimes we initiate this stage but more often we are forced into this stage because of changes in our personal or professional life. In the early stages of endings, the experiences are too raw for much reflection and reframing: we simply must experience each stage trusting that clarity will follow. Once we break from the past we begin to dismantle it. *Dismantling* involves deconstructing the old and preparing to make sense of one's relationship to what was lost or one's own loss of identity. During *disidentification* the old way we defined our self doesn't work anymore. There is a feeling of not being quite sure who one is anymore as our identity becomes clouded. This leads to *disenchantment.* Bridges says that our lifetime "contains a long chain of disenchantments, many small and a few large: lovers who prove unfaithful, leaders who are corrupt, idols who turn out to be petty and dull, organizations that betray your trust" (p. 119). There is an important difference between disenchantment and disillusionment. Disenchantment signals that there is more to learn while the disillusioned person becomes closed off to any true learning or progress. Bridges says, "The disenchanted person moves on, but the disillusioned person stops and goes through the play again with new actors. Such a person is on a perpetual quest for a *real* friend, a true mate, and a *trustworthy* leader. The quest only goes around in circles, and real movement and real development are arrested" (p. 121). The final stage of endings, *disorientation,* is marked by confusion and emptiness. We feel stuck and lose motivation in old goals that used to provide certainty and direction. Bridges explains that "some of our resistance to going into transition comes from our fear of this emptiness. The problem is not that we don't want to give up a job or a relationship, or that we can't let go of our reality. The problem is that before we can find something, we must deal with a time of nothingness" (p. 123).

After passing through the various stages of endings, we enter the neutral zone. This stage requires us to surrender to uncertainty while at the same time actively discovering what we truly want. Bridges states that "the neutral zone is a time when the real business of transition takes place. It is a time when an inner reorientation and realignment are occurring" (p. 154). To find clarity and meaning in this stage requires work. Strategies include: journaling our thoughts and experiences, writing an autobiography of our life outlining our hopes and aspirations, going on a retreat, seeking the wise counsel of others, or taking time to reflect and find order amidst the confusion. It is important not to rush the process. This is a wonderful opportunity to practice what Stephen Covey, bestselling author of *The 7 Habits of Highly Effective People,* calls "Putting First Things First." This practice demands that we clarify what is truly important, the "First Things" in our life, and give priority to them. Common first things are quality time with family and friends, living a healthy lifestyle, spiritual or religious devotions, intellectual activities, or professional growth. After clarifying what is important (there isn't a right set of answers to this question, it is a matter of how we want to live our life and be remembered) we then have to look at where we spend our time and energies. Do we put "First Things First" or do we need to make some hard choices and say "no" in areas of our life to make room for what is truly important? When I cover this concept in my leadership classes, I have students start by clarifying their "First Things" and then track where they spend their time for one week. Inevitably this activity becomes a wake-up call for many when they realize the disconnect between what they say is important and where they actually spend their time.

Only by acknowledging endings and progressing through the wilderness of the neutral zone are we are ready to embrace the new beginning. There comes a time in any journey when we have to stop deliberating and take action. While we can't rush the process of the neutral zone, as the saying goes, we must also avoid "paralysis by over analysis." Human beings and organizations experience a continuous cycle of endings and beginnings. Transition keeps us vibrant and always moving forward in a quest to realize our full potential. Alfred Lord Tennyson captures this sentiment in the closing lines of his poem *Ulysses*:

> We are not now that strength which in old days
> Moved earth and heaven, that which we are, we are,
> One equal temper of heroic hearts,
> Made weak by time and fate, but strong in will
> To strive, to seek, to find, and not to yield.

Questions for Review

1. What are three types of change? What is the most complex type of change? How can leaders anticipate and respond to this type of change?

2. What strategies can leaders employ to successfully lead change? According to John Kotter, what are the eight reasons why change efforts fail?

3. What approaches can leaders take to decrease resistance to change?

4. How is change different from transition? According to Bridges (2004), what are the three stages associated with the process of transitions? Briefly summarize each stage.

CHAPTER 10:
Motivation

LEARNING OBJECTIVES

After studying this chapter, you should be able to:

1. Identify what workers want from their jobs.
2. Discuss the role of money as a motivator.
3. Identify motivation strategies.
4. Discuss needs theory and its impact on motivation.
5. Distinguish between motivators and hygiene factors in the workplace.

> "If you're after getting the honey, then you don't go killing
> all the bees."
>
> Joe Strummer

Every manager has contemplated how best to motivate his or her employees. This is no easy task, in part, because people are motivated by a variety of workplace and psychological factors. Take a moment to find out what you want from your job using the instrument below. Rank the following job qualities from 1–10 with one being the most important quality you are looking for in a job down to number ten for the least important quality.

This survey instrument has been used for decades to measure what employees are looking for in their job. See the chart below for a comparison of employee rankings.

What stands out from these results? Full appreciation for work done, interesting work, and good wages rank as the most important job characteristic during at least one time period. Feeling in on things, an understanding boss, and job security also rate as important job dimensions. Clearly employees are motivated by a variety of factors; however, this survey provides an opportunity for managers and employees to discuss trends in the research and use common language when identifying which factors

Job Qualities	Rank (1–10)
Job security	
Full appreciation for work done	
Promotion and growth	
Tactful disciplining	
Good wages	
Feeling in on things	
Interesting work	
Management loyalty	
Good working conditions	
Sympathetic understanding of personal problems	

influence certain employees. The year when employees completed the survey also points to the larger economic context that drives certain needs. For example, in 1992 wages jumped up to the number one spot. According to need theory, the strength of individual needs can change for an individual depending on circumstances. In the early 1990s, the American economy experienced a deep recession, consequently pay and job security were ranked in the top three qualities employees wanted from their job. (Bill Clinton was elected into office in 1992 using the famous slogan "It's the economy, stupid" to remind him of what was front-and-center in the minds of the American people.)

Coming out of the Great Recession of 2008, job security and basic level needs such as steady wages were once again predominant factors as unemployment rates and economic trends reflected the worst economy since the Great Depression. Of course, money is a significant motivating variable but the bigger question is: since individuals are motivated by a variety of needs and because people respond differently to various incentives, should money be used as the *primary* incentive to motivate? Furthermore, during economically challenging times there is never enough money to go around, so what are managers left to do? Financial bonuses can actually undercut motivation in an interesting way. For example, if an employee receives a large bonus one year and then a smaller bonus the next year, he or she can experience dissatisfaction even though financial incentives are in place. Also, there are lots of well compensated employees

COMPARISONS OF EMPLOYEE RESPONSES IN 1946, 1980, 1986 AND 1992

Qualities	1946	1980	1986	1992
Full appreciation for work done	1	2	2	2
Feeling of being in on things	2	3	3	9
Sympathetic help with personal problems	3	9	10	10
Job security	4	4	4	3
Good wages	5	5	5	1
Interesting work	6	1	1	5
Promotion and growth in the organization	7	6	6	4
Personal or company loyalty to employees	8	8	8	6
Good working conditions	9	7	7	7

(Source: Carolyn Wiley, 1997, What motivates employees according to over 40 years of motivation surveys, *International Journal of Manpower*, Vol. 18, No. 3, p. 263)

Reprinted from "What Motivates Employees According to Over 40 Years of Motivational Surveys," by Carolyn Wiley, International Journal of Manpower 18, no. 3 (1997), by permission of Emerald Journals.

who hate their jobs because of workplace dynamics unrelated to pay. Leaders and managers who are serious about getting the best from their team need to shift their perspective and realize that what motivates one person (or even themselves!) may be different for another. In short, leaders and managers need more tools in their toolbox when it comes to motivation. When looking at employee responses across the decades, "full appreciation for work done" was either the first or second factor across each time span—even during economic recessions. This is an important message for managers and leaders: employees are looking for more out of their work than just a paycheck.

Hersey and Blanchard (1993, pp. 50–51) note an important aspect regarding the 1946 study referenced above. In this study, supervisors were asked to *predict* what workers wanted from their jobs by ranking the

10 items from most important to least important. The supervisors were *not* to rank these items according to what they wanted, but instead were to guess how their employees would rank each item. Below are the employees' actual rankings beside the supervisors' predictions:

Job Qualities	Employees' Actual Answers	Supervisor Predictions of Employees' Answers
Job security	4	2
Full appreciation for work done	1	8
Promotion and growth	7	3
Tactful disciplining	10	7
Good wages	5	1
Feeling in on things	2	10
Interesting work	6	5
Management loyalty	8	6
Good working conditions	9	4
Sympathetic understanding of personal problems	3	9

Reprinted from *Management of Organizational Behavior: Utilizing Human Resources* (1993), by permission of the Center for Leadership Studies.

What can we learn from this study? First, there is a clear disconnect between supervisors' expectations and what employees actually want. This suggests a lack of communication and accurate need fulfillment between management and employees. Second, supervisors overemphasize the role of money and financial incentives in motivation. But, let's stick with the role of money on motivation a little longer.

MONEY MATTERS

Of course money and wages are significant factors in the workplace. Lazarus (2008) reports that real wages—the value of peoples' paychecks adjusted for inflation—have stagnated or eroded for most of the last 30 years except

DECEMBER 17, 2008 OC   **Los Angeles Times**

Everything is going up but your pay

While prices and productivity go up, real wages in the U.S. have declined. (Data prices and real wages are for October of each year, productivity date are for the third quarter of each year.)

Prices
(Consumer price index)

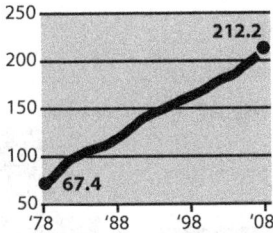

Productivity (Productivity index for business output)

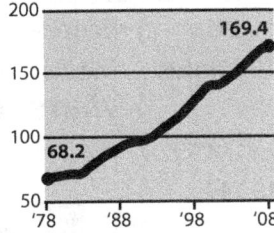

Real wages
(Per hour, inflation-adjusted)

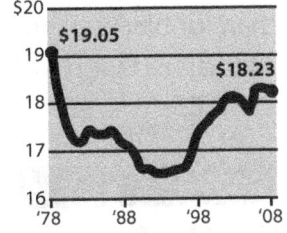

Source: Bureau of Labor Statistics

Los Angeles Times

for a period of modest gains from 1997 to 2003. At the same time, wage stagnation has been coupled with rises in the consumer price index and worker productivity.

There has also been a profound shift in wealth nationwide according to the Pew Research Center, an independent think tank. Wealth is defined as the sum of assets such as real estate, cars, stock portfolios, and bank and retirement accounts, minus the sum of one's debt. Wealth is a critical indicator because as senior Pew researcher, Rakesh Kochhar, says, "Wealth can establish the financial status of a family for generations" (Jordan, 2011). Data analyzed by the Pew Research Center showed a decline in wealth from 2005 to 2009 among white, Hispanic, and black households. Inflation-adjusted median wealth declined 16% for white households, but plunged two-thirds among Hispanic households and 53% among black households. This is the largest disparity among ethnic groups since the government began tracking such data over twenty-five years ago.

Several factors account for these findings. First, home ownership is the biggest contributor to net worth among all groups; however, declining home values affect minorities more than whites because Hispanics and blacks derive more than half of their net worth from home equity, whereas it accounts for 44% of a white household's net worth. Second, Hispanics were affected disproportionately by the housing meltdown because they are concentrated in some of the states that were most affected by declining home values such as Arizona, California, Florida, and Nevada. Third, the median value of directly held stock and mutual funds dropped the most for Hispanics and blacks. The value fell 32% for Hispanics and 71% for blacks. The value fell 9% for white households. Kochhar suggested this may be because blacks and Hispanics in financial distress sold stocks or stopped contributing to pension plans causing whites to benefit more from the stock-market rebounds since 2009 (see Jordan, 2011).

Growing Wealth Gap

The net worth of whites declined less percentagewise than for blacks or Hispanics during the recession.

Median net worth of households   Median wealth ratios

WHITES

| 2005 | $134,992 |
| 2009 | $113,149 |

HISPANICS

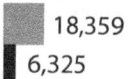

18,359

6,325

BLACKS

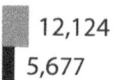

12,124

5,677

Note: Dollar figures for whites and blacks exclude Hispanics. Ratios for both whites and blacks inlcude Hispanics. The Survey of Income and Program Participation was redesigned in 1996, which may affect comparability of data before and after the change.
Source: Pew Research Center tabulations of SIPP and Census data

WHITE-TO-BLACK ·······································

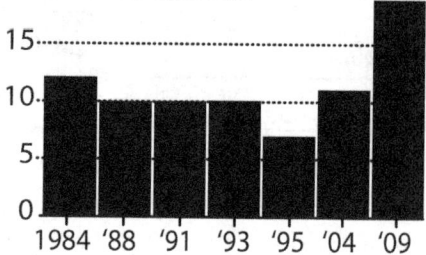

WHITE-TO-HISPANIC ·······························

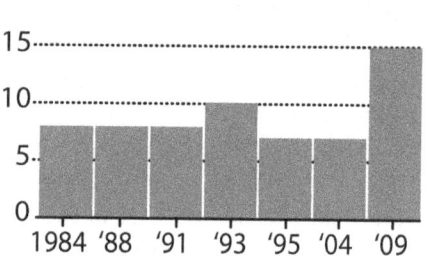

Reprinted from "White-Minority Gulf Widens," *The Wall Street Journal*, July, 26, 2011, by permission of the Dow Jones Company.

EDUCATIONAL ATTAINMENT AND EARNING POTENTIAL

More and more Americans are pursuing higher education. According to the Census Bureau, as of March 2011, 30.4% of people over age 25 in the United States held at least a bachelor's degree and 10.9% held a graduate degree. This is up from 26.2 percent and 8.7 percent 10 years earlier. College freshman are also pursuing higher education for different reasons today than in previous generations. UCLA's Higher Education Research Institute conducts an annual survey asking freshman to select reasons why they are seeking a college degree. For years the most popular response was "to learn more about things that interest me." However, results from the 2012 survey reveal that 85.9% of first-year students are attending college in order to secure a good job. Seeing college as a necessary path to good jobs is the strongest response in the 40 years since

2008 median earnings for full-time, year-round workers ages 25 and older by education level

Not a high school graduate	$24,300
High school graduate	33,800
Some college, no degree	39,700
Associate degree	42,000
Bachelor's degree	55,700
Master's degree	67,300
Doctoral degree	91,900
Professional degree	100,000

Source: U.S. Census Bureau, 2009.

Unemployment rate in 2011, reported by educational attainment

Doctoral degree	2.5%
Professional degree	2.4
Master's degree	3.6
Bachelor's degree	4.9
Associate degree	6.8
Some college, no degree	8.7
High school diploma	9.4
Less than a high school diploma	14.1

Average unemployment rate: 7.6%

Source: Bureau of Labor Statistics, 2012.

the survey has been conducted. This is up sharply from 2006 when 70.4% of students focused on jobs as the reason for attending college. This trend is due in part to the financial crisis of 2008 and subsequent recession where children saw their parents struggle with unemployment and a weak job market.

Data also indicates there is a clear relationship between education level and earning potential/unemployment.

Nelson (2002) points out that money matters; however, "for most of us, most of the time, once we are able to meet our monthly expenses, our attention turns to other factors that have much greater significance in our work lives" (Nelson, 2002, p. 2). According to Nelson, once we achieve a level of financial stability, we look to get other things out of work such as: feeling we are making a contribution, having a manger that tells us when we do a good job, having the respect of our peers and colleagues, being involved and informed about what is going on in the company, and having meaningful, interesting work. Nelson offers the following 10 ways that managers can motivate employees beyond a paycheck.

1. Personally thank employees for doing a good job—one on one, in writing, or both. Do it timely, often and sincerely.

2. Be willing to take the time to meet with and listen to employees— as much as they need or want.

3. Provide specific feedback about performance of the person, the department and the organization.

4. Strive to create a work environment that is open, trusting and fun. Encourage new ideas and initiative.

5. Provide information on how the company makes and loses money, upcoming products and strategies for competing in the marketplace, and how the person fits into the overall plan.

6. Involve employees in decisions, especially as those decisions affect them.

7. Recognize, reward and promote people based on their performance; deal with low and marginal performers so that they improve or leave.

8. Provide employees with a sense of ownership in their work and the work environment.

9. Give people a chance to grow and learn new skills; show them how you can help them meet their goals within the context of meeting the organization's goals. Create partnerships with each employee.

10. Celebrate successes—of the company, of the department and of individuals in it. Take time for team and morale-building meetings and activities.

Nelson concludes by saying, "For the best results, pay them [employees] fairly, but treat them superbly" (Nelson, 2002, p. 5). This is succinct and astute advice for anyone in a management or leadership role!

Reprinted from *Personnel Journal*, July 1, 1996.

NEEDS THEORY AND MOTIVATION

Psychologists have identified a variety of universal "needs" (e.g., achievement, power, safety, esteem, and meaning) where people seek fulfillment. Also, the strength of certain needs varies depending on circumstance. For example, if a person has a rewarding and fulfilling job and then is laid off, safety or security needs become stronger and dominate other needs. People can satisfy many of these needs through their work and the type of environment that leaders and managers create.

During the economic slowdown beginning in 2008, a unique trend surfaced. Unemployment spiked dramatically, yet corporate profits and worker productivity also increased. What was happening? Part of the answer is workers who remained employed were working twice as hard to cover the loss in output from employees that were let go. Also, corporations were able to save money by not having to rehire workers because output remained strong. While the primary needs of corporations were being satisfied (i.e., increased profits), there were tremendous human costs in being unemployed, underemployed, or unable to meet the basic needs of one's family. Conversely, if organizational leaders fulfill every wage and health care demand from labor unions, there is the potential for unsustainable financial commitments. Leaders are constantly challenged with meeting the needs of their employees *and* the needs of the organization. When the needs of one party are exaggerated at the expense of the other, a dangerous imbalance occurs.

MASLOW . . . AGAIN?

Abraham Maslow's ideas appear in numerous disciplines such as, psychology, leadership, marketing, organizational behavior, and sociology. In this section, we'll investigate his model and see how organizations and leaders contribute to the fulfillment of employee needs. Even though there is debate as to the empirical evidence for Maslow's ideas, his work continues to turn up in corporate training manuals and contemporary books on management, leadership, and organizational behavior. This is testament to the value of Maslow's conceptualization of human beings' universal longing for fulfillment in specific aspects of life.

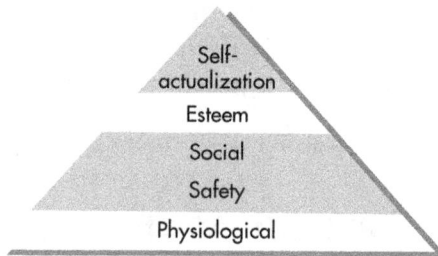

FIGURE 10-1   Maslow's Hierarchy of Needs

Source: A. H. Maslow, *Motivation and Personality*, 3rd ed., R. D. Frager and J. Fadiman (eds.), © 1997. Adapted by permission of Pearson Education, Inc., Upper Saddle River, New Jersey.

Physiological Needs
(For example: Food, water, sexual desire, sleep)

According to Maslow, these "are the most prepotent of all needs" (Maslow, 1954, p. 82). For example, if a person lacks food, safety, love and esteem, the need to satisfy hunger would rank stronger than anything else. However, "it is quite true that man lives by bread alone—when there is no bread" (Maslow, 1954, p. 83). In other words, when this basic need is satisfied, higher needs begin to emerge. The lack of satisfaction *and* the gratification of needs influence one's motivation. If one lacks the satisfaction of physiological needs, he or she will be motivated to satisfy other needs. Also, if one achieves gratification of a need, motivation to satisfy other needs commences. This concept of "need strength" helps to explain the dynamic nature of Maslow's hierarchy and why individuals can find themselves bouncing between multiple need categories depending on life circumstances.

Safety Needs
(For example: Freedom from fear or threat, health and well-being, security)

Similar to physiological needs, safety needs present basic and critical needs for both individuals and society. "The safety needs can become very urgent on the social scene whenever there are real threats to law, to order, to the authority of society" (Maslow, 1970, p. 43). Danger causes all human beings to regress to safety needs in order to defend themselves. This helps explain why societies may accept dictatorship or military rule when the alternative is chaos.

Belongingness and Love Needs (For example, social connections and relationships, affection, friendship)

Human beings are social beings. Even introverts who prize their alone time still crave human connections and social experiences. The Myers-Briggs Typology Indicator, measures introversion/extroversion by how one regains energy or "recharges their batteries." For example, on a Friday night after a long week of work, an extrovert will most likely meet up with friends and hit the town while an introvert would rather wind down a busy week with a quite night at home. Belongingness needs help to describe the popularity of social and political affiliations. Classic car enthusiasts will form clubs with others that share similar interests and Republicans, Democrats, Libertarians, and Green Party members will congregate together because shared values contribute to one's sense of identity. These types of affiliations demonstrate powerful human longings that help define one's identity within a group.

Maslow sees "love needs" as the universal craving for affection. "Practically all theorists of psychotherapy have stressed thwarting of the love needs as basic in the picture of maladjustment. Many clinical studies have therefore been made of this need, and we know more about it perhaps than any other needs except the physiological ones" (Maslow, 1970, p. 44). Deep feelings of fulfillment resound with the satisfaction of this need while the "pangs of loneliness, or ostracism, or rejection, of friendlessness, of rootlessness" abound in its absence. Maslow, notes that love is not synonymous with sex. He says, "not to be overlooked is the fact that the love needs involve both giving *and* receiving love" (Maslow, 1970, p. 45).

Esteem Needs (For example, the desire for self-respect and the esteem of others)

Maslow supposes two sets of esteem needs. First, the desire for strength, achievement, adequacy, mastery and competence, confidence, and in-dependence and freedom. Second, the desire for reputation or prestige, status, dominance, recognition, attention, importance, and appreciation. Satisfaction of esteem needs consequently leads to self-confidence, worth, strength, capability, adequacy, and a sense of usefulness in society. Lack of fulfillment leads to feelings of inferiority, weakness, and helplessness. Suffering from low self-esteem is debilitating until these esteem needs are met. Maslow cautions against basing one's self-esteem entirely on the opinions of others. Hence, "the most stable and therefore most healthy self-esteem is based on *deserved* respect from others rather than on external fame or celebrity and unwarranted adulation" (Maslow, 1954, p. 91).

Self-Actualization (For example, realizing and acting upon one's potential, doing what you were put on this earth to do)

"In one individual it may take the form of the desire to be an ideal mother, in another it may be expressed athletically, and in still another it may be expressed in painting pictures or in inventions. At this level, individual differences are greatest" (Maslow, 1970, p. 46).

Ultimately, when the previous four needs are fulfilled, the desire for self-actualization becomes paramount. Discovering one's natural talents and how best to express them takes time and focus. Consider this question: What is the most popular college major? Most people say psychology, business, or liberal arts. The correct answer: Undeclared. Part of the college experience (at any age) is discovering what you are good at *and* what you like to do. Many students change their major multiple times as they explore different subjects and reconcile what they think they are good at (or are told to major in by their parents) with their true talents and passions. Discovering what you were put on this earth to do, and then doing it, is the domain of self-actualization. See the chart for examples of how organizations can satisfy each of Maslow's need levels.

NEED FULFILLMENT AT THE MANAGERIAL LEVEL

Porter (1962) investigated need fulfillment at all levels of management from entry level supervisors to senior executives. In a questionnaire distributed to approximately 6,000 managers and executives, job characteristics were

How Can Organizations Satisfy Maslow's Needs Hierarchy?

Need	Organizational Contribution
Self-Actualization	Autonomy, Challenge and Support
Esteem	Recognition and demonstrations of appreciation
Belongingness and Love	Social opportunities, friendships, and demonstrations of appreciation
Safety	Wages/Health Benefits
Physiological	Wages

classified according to Maslow's need types. The figure below provides examples of management characteristics associated with Maslow's model.

MANAGEMENT CHARACTERISTICS ASSOCIATED WITH MASLOW'S NEED TYPES

Security needs

- The feeling of security in my management position.

Social needs

- The opportunity, in my management position, to give help to other people.
- The opportunity to develop close friendships in my management position.

Esteem needs

- The feeling of self-esteem a person gets from being in my management position.
- The prestige of my management position inside the company (that is, the regard received from others in the company).
- The prestige of my management position outside the company (that is, the regard received from others not in the company).

Autonomy needs

- The authority connected with my management position.
- The opportunity for independent thought and action in my management position.
- The opportunity, in my management position, for participation in the setting of goals.
- The opportunity, in my management position, for participation in the determination of methods and procedures.

Self-actualization needs

- The opportunity for personal growth and development in my management position.
- The feeling of self-fulfillment a person gets from being in my management position (that is, the feeling of being able to use one's own unique capabilities, realizing one's potentialities).

• The feeling of worthwhile accomplishment in my management position.

(Adapted from Porter (1962) *Job attitudes in management: Perceived deficiencies in need fulfillment as a function of job level*. Journal of Applied Psychology, (46)6, p. 375–384.)

Porter found that social and security needs were well-satisfied throughout management levels; however, the higher-order needs—esteem, autonomy, and self-actualization—were found to produce great discrepancies in need fulfillment depending on one's job. In other words, esteem, autonomy, and self-actualization produced the largest deficiencies among management positions. While this study did not show that lower and middle-level managers were highly dissatisfied, it did show them to be more dissatisfied than top-level managers. To remedy this disconnect, lower-level managers would have to change their expectations or upper-level managers would have to focus on providing more opportunities for satisfaction of higher-order needs at lower management levels. The study also revealed that "fairly large numbers of managers even at high levels of organizations are not satisfied with their opportunities to obtain the amount of self-actualization they think should be available from their jobs. The same conclusion would hold true for the Esteem and Autonomy need areas, although to a slightly reduced extent" (p. 384). Therefore, the assumption that senior and executive management positions provide greater satisfaction in the highest-order needs may not be reflected in practice. Consequently, through job design and leadership, a concerted effort should be made to satisfy esteem, autonomy, and self-actualization needs for managers at any level.

FREDERICK HERZBERG AND EMPLOYEE SATISFACTION

The human animal has two categories of needs. One set stems from his animal disposition, that side of him previously referred to as the Adam view of man; it is centered on the avoidance of loss of life, hunger, pain, sexual deprivation, and other primary drives, in addition to the infinite varieties of learned fears that become attached to these basic drives. The other segment of man's nature, according to the Abraham concept of the human being, is man's compelling urge to realize his own potentiality by continuous psychological growth.

Frederick Herzberg (1966)
Work and the Nature of Man, p. 56

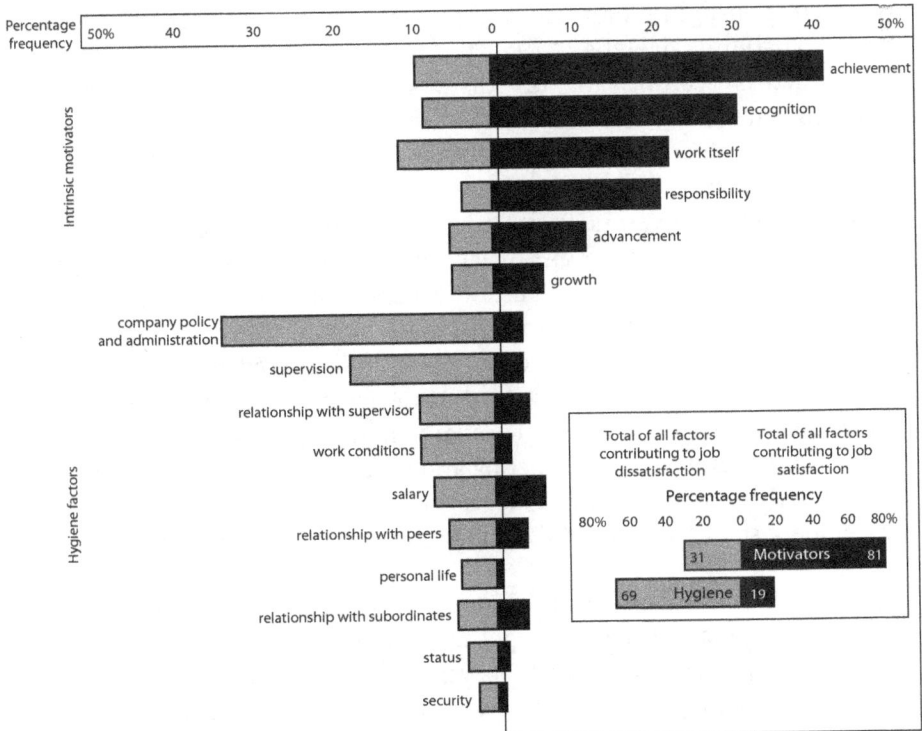

FIGURE 10-2 Factors affecting job attitudes as reported in 12 investigations

Reprinted from *One More Time: How Do You Motivate Employees?* (2003), by permission of Harvard Business School Publishing.

Frederick Herzberg expanded research on need fulfillment to employees in the workplace. Herzberg presents two classifications of workplace events that effect job satisfaction: hygiene factors and motivators.

Hygiene factors serve primarily to prevent job dissatisfaction and have little effect on positive job attitudes (the term hygiene refers to the medical use of the word as "preventative and environmental"). Examples include company policies, supervision, salary, interpersonal relations, and working conditions. On the right side of Figure 10-2, six factors stand out as strong predictors of job satisfaction: achievement, recognition, work itself, responsibility, advancement, and growth. These factors have the longest duration in changes of an employee's attitudes toward work. Herzberg notes that recognition for achievement—rather than general recognition as a management behavior—specifically leads to satisfaction. Job satisfiers describe an employee's direct relationship to work, such as, "job content, achievement on a task, recognition for task achievement, the nature of the task, responsibility for a task, and professional advancement or growth in task capability" (Herzberg, 1966, p. 74).

Factors leading to job dissatisfaction describe an employee's relationship to the work environment. "One cluster of factors relates to what the person does and the other to the situation in which he does it" (Herzberg, 1966, p. 74). In this framework, the factors that lead to satisfaction (motivators) contribute very little to job dissatisfaction while those factors that create dissatisfaction (hygiene factors) contribute very little to job satisfaction. Thus, "the factors involved in producing job satisfaction were *separate* and *distinct* from the factors that led to job dissatisfaction" (Herzberg, 1966, p. 75–76). The presence of hygiene factors does not necessarily motivate, but *when taken away*, they produce dissatisfaction (e.g., salary, company policies, up-to-date equipment, environmental factors like heating and air conditioning, etc.).

So, why are "motivators" such a positive force in employee satisfaction? Herzberg shares a wonderful analogy to answer this question:

> When a child learns to ride a bicycle, he is becoming more competent, increasing the repertory of his behavior, expanding his skills—psychologically growing. In the process of the child's learning to master a bicycle, the parents can love him with all the zeal and compassion of the most devoted mother and father. They can safeguard the child from injury by providing the safest and most hygienic area in which to practice; they can offer all kinds of incentives and rewards, and they can provide the most expert instructions. But the child will never, never, learn to ride the bicycle—unless he is given a bicycle! The hygiene factors are not a valid contributor to psychological growth. The substance of a task is required to achieve growth goals. Similarly, you cannot love an engineer into creativity, although by this approach you can avoid his dissatisfaction with the way you treat him. Creativity will require a potentially creative task to do. (Herzberg, 1966, p. 75)

Based on Herzberg's research, if you want to improve the motivation and engagement of employees, pay particular attention to the "motivator" factors and avoid job dissatisfaction through improvements in the workplace environment (hygiene factors) such as clear and effective policies and procedures, quality supervision, fair compensation, constructive management of interpersonal dynamics, and maintaining appropriate working conditions.

A NEW LOOK AT MOTIVATION

People are motivated to seek pleasure and avoid pain. If a student is offered $500 to memorize a list of mathematical formulas, he or she will instantly become motivated to do the work (even if the student dislikes math) because obtaining the financial reward is desirable. Conversely, if a student is told he or she will be punished if the list is not memorized, the student will become motivated in order to avoid the pain associated with not completing the task. The job may (or may not) get done under these simplistic conditions; however, many managers rely almost exclusively on punishment and rewards to motivate. Daniel Pink, in his bestselling book *Drive: The Surprising Truth about What Motivates Us*, argues that the old paradigm of using carrots and sticks (i.e., rewards and punishments) to get people to do things is outdated and often destructive. Using research-based examples, Pink offers three elements that encompass a more enlightened approach to motivation and achieving organizational results. The essential elements are: (1) *Autonomy*—the desire to direct our own lives; (2) *Mastery*—the urge to make progress and get better at something that matters; and (3) *Purpose*—the yearning to do what we do in the service of something larger than ourselves (Pink, 2009, p. 219).

Autonomy

Traditional managers focus on compliance and control—getting people to do things in an orderly, predictable, and routine manner. However, this approach comes into conflict with our natural yearning for a certain amount of freedom, space, and autonomy. It can be tense, oppressive, and unproductive to work for a manager or in an environment that zaps our enthusiasm with over-burdensome processes and unnecessary intrusions. Keep in mind: there is a time and a place for tight control measures around quality, safety, and standardization (e.g., maintaining airplane engines, building homes, manufacturing cars on an assembly line, or conducting performance appraisals in the workplace). However, managers who overplay the compliance and control elements of management risk a downward spiral in employee motivation, morale, and productivity. According to Pink (2009, p. 222), motivation comes from giving employees autonomy over *task* (what they do), *time* (when they do it), *team* (who they do it with), and *technique* (how they do it).

One way to provide autonomy is with a ROWE—a results-only work environment. In this type of workplace employees don't have schedules and they show up when they want. Pink (2009) reports, "They just have to get their work done. How they do it, when they do it, and where they do it is up to them" (p. 84). In a ROWE people still have specific deliverables, goals, and objectives to meet—and managers are there to assist—but employees are free to achieve these goals how they best see fit. The focus is on getting the job done; not how one does it. This approach was instituted at Meddius, a computer software and hardware company, and CEO Jeff Gunther credits the ROWE with increases in productivity and a marked decrease in workplace stress. Does a ROWE sound too radical? Other companies are approaching autonomy in different ways.

The software company Atlassian encourages creativity and continuous improvement with "FedEx Days" where programmers are given twenty-four hours to work on any problem or idea they want. The only requirement is that they deliver something overnight (hence the name FedEx Days) and present their ideas in a raucous all-staff meeting stocked with beer and chocolate cake. These activities have "produced an array of software fixes that might otherwise never have emerged" (Pink, 2009, p. 91). Because FedEx days only last for twenty-four hours and then employees don't have much time to follow up on their ideas, executives at Atlassian instituted "20 percent time" where people can work on projects of their choosing. This is a practice made famous at Google where employees have used their 20 percent time to create products such as Google News, Gmail, and Google Sky.

Mastery

Psychologist and professor at the Claremont Graduate University, Mihaly Csikszentmihalyi (his last name is pronounced "chick-sent-me-high"), has called the mental state where people experience peak levels of performance— when the task meshes perfectly with our skills—as moments of "flow." Csikszentmihalyi found that the "highest, most satisfying experiences in people's lives were when they were in flow" (Pink, 2009, 114). For example, a painter might experience flow when he or she is totally "in the moment" and the image the painter imagines in her head is almost automatically working through her fingers and onto the canvas. When a football player races down the field and catches a pass and scores a touchdown he doesn't consciously direct his arms and legs to move, instead he is operating in the flow zone where preparation and skill allow the athlete to respond instinctively to the challenge. Athletes describe feelings of time slowing down and events unfolding in slow motion during such moments. If you've ever delivered a speech or performance where every word you spoke and point you made effortlessly unfolded from one sentence to another, you have experienced flow.

Flow experiences require the presence of three elements: 1.) There must be a clear goal, 2.) Immediate feedback, and 3.) The challenge should be a little bit of a stretch beyond one's current abilities (i.e., the challenge isn't too easy or too difficult). The implications for leaders and managers are explicit. To motivate others and create the conditions for organizational members to experience flow, there must be clear, challenging goals and methods to deliver feedback on performance. Feedback can come from the job itself, customers, or supervisors. Mastery and continuous improvement stem from flow experiences. Finally, mastery also requires that one is engaged in his or her work (employee engagement is discussed further in the next chapter).

Purpose

The final element in Daniel Pink's model of motivation is purpose. He declares, "Autonomous people working toward mastery perform at very high levels. But those who do so in the service of some greater objective can achieve even more" (Pink, 2009, p. 133). Pink's "purpose motive" connects with modern organizations through the use of: goals, words, and policies. Pink offers Blake Mycoskie, founder of TOMS shoes, as an example of organizational goals driving a company's sense of purpose. For example, the TOMS business model is set up to turn customers into "benefactors" by giving away a new pair of shoes to a child in a developing country every time a customer buys a pair of their shoes. TOMS represents:

> [A] far cry from the 'socially responsible' businesses that have been all the rage for the last fifteen years . . . the aims of these Motivation 3.0 companies are not to chase profits while trying to stay ethical and law-abiding. Their goal is to pursue purpose—and to use profit as the catalyst rather than the objective" (Pink, 2009, p. 137).

Today's organizations also realize purpose through the power of words. Pink notes that after the financial crisis of 2008, a group of Harvard MBA students created the "MBA Oath" which articulates a code of conduct for business leaders. The idea is to get leaders (business students in particular) to supplement profit motives with an emphasis on purpose, serving a greater good, and sustainable business practices. As leaders, the words we use should appeal to the mind—and the heart—of followers, constituencies, and stakeholders. Infusing language with a sense of purpose helps to motivate others and inspire behaviors that reach beyond narrow self-interests and toward a sense of community. The final element of purpose is realized through organizational policies. Policies alone are a weak predictor of results. For example, over the last decade almost every major company has developed corporate ethics guidelines yet instances of unethical behavior still happen. The key to realizing purpose is to integrate policies with autonomy and mastery. For example, Pink notes that doctors experience pressures and demands that can lead to burnout. However, policies at the Mayo Clinic allow physicians to spend one day a week on any aspect of the job that they find most meaningful (e.g., patient care, research, or community service). Research found that this policy reduced physical and emotional exhaustion and doctors who participated in the policy had half the burnout of those who did not (Pink, 2009, p. 141).

In conclusion, punishment and rewards are limited ways of thinking about and practicing motivation. Autonomy, mastery, and purpose allow us to broaden the way we conceptualize motivation and provide managers with additional tools to get the best out of others and create dynamic workplaces. Shifting our focus toward autonomy, mastery, and purpose may allow leaders to foster better connections with individuals and inspire teams to achieve breakthrough performance.

Questions for Review

1. According to the research studies at the beginning of this chapter, what job qualities did employees rank highest? How do these rankings relate to what you want from your job?

2. What are the benefits of using money as a motivator? What are the limitations?

3. According to Nelson (2002), what techniques can managers use to motivate employees? What is your reaction to his suggestions?

4. What is the basic idea behind needs theory? What are some examples of universal human needs? How can organizations satisfy these needs?

5. What job characteristics are classified as motivators? What job characteristics are considered hygiene factors? How does this impact motivation in the workplace?

CHAPTER 11:
Employee Engagement and Job Satisfaction

LEARNING OBJECTIVES

After studying this chapter, you should be able to:

1. Define employee engagement.
2. Identify practices that lead to employee engagement and employee disengagement.
3. Discuss the role of job satisfaction on performance.
4. Distinguish between narrow engagement and full engagement.

EMPLOYEE ENGAGEMENT

A motivated employee isn't necessarily an engaged employee. Employee engagement is defined as an individual's *involvement, satisfaction*, and *enthusiasm* for work. Harter, Schmidt and Hayes (2002) studied the effects of employee engagement on customer satisfaction, productivity, profit, employee turnover, and safety. This study used the Gallup Workplace Audit (GWA) as a measure of engagement. The Gallup research indicates, "the importance of the supervisor or the manager and his or her influence over the engagement level of employees and their satisfaction with their company . . . the specific facet of satisfaction most highly related to performance has been satisfaction with the supervisor" (Harter, Schmidt and Hayes, 2002, p. 269). At the business-unit level (i.e., department, work-unit), overall satisfaction and employee engagement positively influenced customer satisfaction and loyalty, profitability, productivity, safety, and lower employee turnover rates. These bottom line results regarding employee engagement translate to millions of dollars in increased revenues. For example, productivity measures for top-scoring employee engagement business units revealed on average $80,000 to $120,000 higher monthly revenue for sales. The Gallup Organization concludes that managers and supervisors have tremendous influence over engagement levels of their employees and can improve employee engagement in a number of ways. For example:

- Supervisors can help people see how their work connects to a broader purpose, reminding them about and helping them see the larger context of their work.

- Supervisors can influence the extent to which employees respect one another by selecting conscientious employees, providing common quality-related goals and metrics, and increasing opportunities for employees to have interaction about these outcomes.

- While supervisors cannot force or mandate finding a "best friend" at work, they can provide opportunities for employees to get to know one another and connect in the context of regular business activities. Many supervisors encourage close friendships at work which they see as a factor in improved communication and trust.

(List Adapted from Harter et al. (2002). Business-unit-level relationship between employee satisfaction, employee engagement, and business outcomes: A meta-analysis. *Journal of Applied Psychology, 87*(2), 268-279.)

Marciano (2010) surveyed individuals from over 100 companies worldwide to determine the behaviors and characteristics associated with engaged employees. Review the list below and think about how many of these qualities are demonstrated by members of your work team.

1. Brings new ideas to work
2. Is passionate and enthusiastic about work
3. Takes initiative
4. Actively seeks to improve self, others, and business
5. Consistently exceeds goals and expectations
6. Is curious and interested; asks questions
7. Encourages and supports team members
8. Is optimistic and positive; smiles
9. Overcomes obstacles and stays focused on tasks; is persistent
10. Is committed to the organization

We all would love to fill our organizations with these types of people. The big question is: How? In order to find the answer, Marciano set out to uncover the factors that lead to employee engagement and disengagement. He asked people in the workforce, "What causes you to become engaged or disengaged in your work?" The following results provide specific behaviors managers should adopt to increase engagement, in addition to specific practices managers must stop to avoid disengagement.

Factors that Cause Employee Engagement

- When I respect my employer or supervisor, when I respect the goals of the organization or the project, and when other people at work treat me with respect
- Trust; feeling that my supervisor has my back
- Feeling connected to the end result
- Knowing that what I do matters and can make a difference to others and to the business
- Feeling proud of my work
- Feeling a sense of empowerment and trust from my supervisor
- A supervisor who believes in me and wants me to excel
- A team that enjoys working with me and respects me
- Freedom to do my job and awareness that my contribution makes a difference
- Honesty and trust in management
- When my manager recognizes me and gives me credit for my work
- Respect for my opinion and trust in my abilities
- When I understand how and why the work matters
- When I have the tools to do my job properly
- When I feel I have a say in setting my goals and receive regular feedback from my supervisor about my performance
- Having a supervisor who does not feel it necessary to look over my shoulder
- The opportunity to learn new things at work and being given interesting things to do
- Having clear goals and objectives
- Having opportunities for promotion within the organization

- When I feel as though I am part of and needed by the organization and that my work is genuinely valued
- When I have freedom to determine how I achieve my goals
- Mutual and contagious respect among co-workers

Factors that Cause Employee Disengagement

- When my manager takes credit for my work
- Unrealistic expectations
- Lack of coaching, feedback, and support
- Incompetent leaders whom people don't respect
- Constantly being underappreciated and devalued
- Lack of basic pleasantries such as "hello" or "thank you"
- Lack of support from my manager
- Having to do work that doesn't appear to add value
- Seeing managers who are not actively engaged
- When a manager asks for an employee's opinion and then makes him or her feel stupid
- When a manager holds a meeting to get employee feedback and suggestions and doesn't follow up
- When your boss never asks for your input
- Lack of appreciation or compliments for a job well done
- Criticism that isn't constructive
- When you have no idea what direction the organization is headed
- Not being respected
- When you go above and beyond but your efforts are never recognized
- When you have to keep climbing over or around barriers to get what you need to do your job
- Overburdensome processes

(Source: Marciano, P. (2010). *Carrots and Sticks Don't Work*, McGraw Hill, New York, pp. 46–50)

JOB SATISFACTION AND JOB PERFORMANCE

Hsu (2010) reports that job satisfaction has fallen to its lowest level in 22 years. Findings from the New York based nonprofit group, the Conference Board, revealed just 45% of employees are happy in their positions compared with 61% in 1987. Young workers, under age 25, were the least satisfied with their jobs at 35.7% compared with 55.7% in 1987. According to the survey, discontent ranged from wages and vacation policies to the nature of positions and quality of supervisors. The connection between workplace satisfaction and job performance has intrigued researchers for years. So, is there a connection between job satisfaction and performance? The short answer is yes; however, the strength of the relationship is debatable. Judge, Bono, Thoresen, and Patton (2001) argue that researchers have hastily discounted the link between job satisfaction and performance because narrow methodology has revealed a weak or slight relationship. Judge and his colleagues set out to conduct an "updated, and more comprehensive, meta-analysis of the relationship between job satisfaction and job performance" (Judge, Bono, Thoresen, & Patton, 2001, p. 383). They report that the "results of the present study indicate that the relationship between individual, overall job satisfaction and individual job performance is stronger and more consistent than that reported in previous reviews" (Judge, Bono, Thoresen, & Patton, 2001, p. 381). What accounts for this difference? Primarily, it is because prior studies only measured a single facet of job satisfaction rather than looking at *overall* job satisfaction in relation to job performance. Because multiple factors are at play in the satisfaction-performance dynamic, a more holistic and integrative model is needed. (See Figure 11-1 on the next page).

Based on an exhaustive literature review on the topic, this model accounts for other variables that can influence the relationship between job satisfaction and job performance.

Job Satisfaction Variables that Can Influence Performance

Personality Traits: Conscientious employees may be less willing to let job dissatisfaction interfere with their performance output.

Self-identity: If high levels of job performance are integral to one's self-concept or identity, then employees will behave in alignment with their self-concept.

Autonomy: Jobs with higher levels of autonomy tend to have a stronger satisfaction-performance relationship because there is greater opportunity for attitudes and motives to affect behavior.

Norms: When group norms indicate high performance standards, then dissatisfaction is less likely to result in reduced performance because pressure to act in alignment with the norms is great.

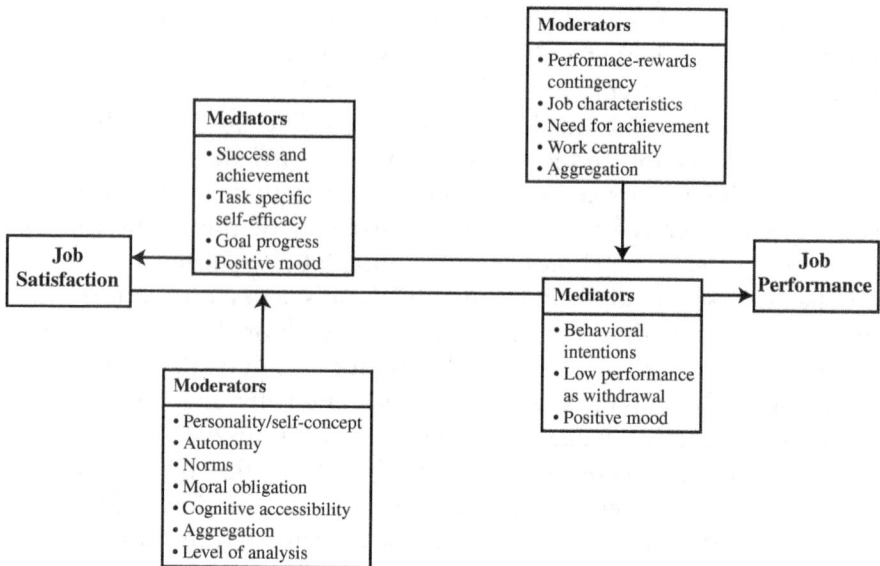

FIGURE 11-1 Integrative model of the relationship between job satisfaction and job performance

Moral Obligation: If one feels a responsibility to perform up to one's capabilities, then this moderating effect will influence performance regardless of satisfaction levels.

Cognitive Accessibility: Based on the literature correlating attitude to behavior, employees whose attitudes about job satisfaction (or dissatisfaction) are fresh in their mind may tend to behave in ways aligned with their most recent attitude.

Aggregation: The methodology researchers use to calculate the influence of attitudes on behavior can affect results.

Level of Analysis: The satisfaction-performance results can vary depending on whether or not the level of analysis is focused on the individual, group, or organization.

Job Performance Variables that Can Influence Satisfaction

Performance-Rewards Contingency: Jobs where rewards are contingent on performance may be more satisfying than jobs with less emphasis on rewards for performance.

Job Characteristics: Effective performance in complex jobs may fulfill many individuals' values for intrinsic fulfillment in their work.

Need for Achievement: Based on needs theory, performing a job well is likely to be more satisfying (and performing a job poorly more dissatisfying) to individuals with a high need for achievement because success is their primary motivation.

Aggregation: Like the satisfaction-performance relationship, the methodology researchers use to calculate the influence of job performance on satisfaction can affect results.

(Lists adapted from Judge, T., Bono, J, Thoresen, C., & Patton, G. (2001). The job satisfaction-job performance relationship: A qualitative and quantitative review. *Psychological Bulletin, 127*(3), 376–407.)

THE IMPACT OF FULL ENGAGEMENT ON JOB SATISFACTION AND JOB PERFORMANCE

Robertson and Cooper (2010) argue that definitions of employee engagement need to be expanded to encompass an employee's psychological well-being. Psychological well-being is defined as feeling positive emotions and deriving satisfaction from a life that has meaning and purpose. Robertson and Cooper believe that traditional conceptualizations of employee engagement include three core concepts: an employee's attachment to work, commitment to his job, and displaying organizational citizenship behaviors. These three concepts of engagement lead to "narrow engagement" because they focus on employee behaviors that are most likely to provide direct benefits to the organization. As the researchers report, typical questions in "narrow" engagement surveys include:

- The goals of my organization make me feel that my job is important.
- I am committed to this organization.
- My opinions are listened to by my bosses at work.
- I am enthusiastic about the job I do.
- At work, I am prepared to work hard, even when things do not go well.

Since these factors tend to focus on employees as production entities and lead to narrow engagement, "full engagement" would also include the well-being components of deriving pleasure and purpose from one's work. In this way, the "beneficial impact of narrow engagement is enhanced when psychological well-being is also high—and similarly the negative effects of low engagement would be exacerbated when psychological well-being is poor" (Robertson & Cooper, 2010, p. 328). Robertson and Cooper cite empirical evidence for this proposition from a sample of over 10,000 people across 12 different organizations where the inclusion of measures of psychological well-being enhanced the relationship between narrow engagement and job-related outcomes such as productivity. Three categories influence the types of interventions that can improve workplace well-being and engagement:

1. **Composition**: changing the composition of people in the work force, through selection processes, redeployment and job placement;

2. **Development**: developing the people who are already part of the workforce through training, coaching, feedback and other development activities; and,

3. **Situational engineering**: utilizing job and work redesign, employing changes in management and supervision and organizational change.

Overall, Robertson and Cooper warn that managers should avoid "consultation without action" where surveys, input, and various forms of data are collected but employees never see anything done with the information and, worst of all, fail to see on-the-ground improvements in their working lives.

What Do You Think?

1. Review the lists from Marciano on behaviors that cause employee *engagement* and *disengagement*. What behaviors should managers and leaders in your own organization change? What can you change to increase engagement and decrease disengagement?

2. What can you do to cultivate and sustain the "full engagement" of your employees? Remember this includes the well-being components of deriving pleasure and purpose from one's work.

THRIVING ORGANIZATIONS: SUSTAINING EMPLOYEE PERFORMANCE FOR THE LONG RUN

What leadership and organizational dynamics create high-performing workplaces? We've seen that engaged and satisfied employees add value to the workplace, but let's extend this discussion and introduce current research on *thriving* employees and organizations. A thriving workforce is "one in which employees are not just satisfied and productive but also engaged in creating the future" (Spreitzer & Porath, 2012, p. 94). Researchers from the University of Michigan's Ross School of Business identified two components of thriving: *vitality* and *learning*. Employees who experience vitality are highly energized and impact the energy levels of others. Employees that value learning are excited to gain new knowledge and skills. Why does this matter? It matters because in several studies involving more than 1,200 workers, thriving employees demonstrated 16% better overall performance (as reported by their managers) and 125% less burnout (self-reported) compared with their peers. They were 32% more committed to the organization and 46% more satisfied with their jobs. Additionally, they missed much less work and reported significantly fewer doctor visits, which meant health care savings and less lost time for the company (Spreitzer & Porath, 2012, p. 94). While some people naturally meet the criteria for a thriving employee, research points to four mechanisms—that managers can influence—to create the conditions for employees to thrive at work.

Provide Decision-Making Discretion

Employees thrive when they are given the opportunity to solve problems and make decisions affecting their work without having to navigate a lot of rigid bureaucratic structures. This can be achieved by creating forums where employees can offer creative solutions to organizational challenges. For example, in 2010 senior management at Alaska Airlines opened up communication channels to employees by soliciting input on how to improve service while maintaining timely departures. Many of the ideas and new business practices offered by employees at Alaska Airlines helped the company receive a number one rating for on-time performance and expand into new markets across the US. At Facebook the company's motto, "Move fast and break things," encourages employees to take initiative, make decisions, and act. Employees have tremendous leeway to solve problems on their own without excessive layers of hierarchical review by managers.

Share Information

Managers need to help employees see how what they do fits into the organization's mission and strategy; this is done by making information as transparent as possible. Sharing information goes beyond simply posting weekly sales figures and performance goals on a wall because these methods fail to engage employees in what the data means. At Zingerman's restaurants in Ann Arbor, Michigan, weekly meetings are held around a whiteboard where teams use data to track results and forecast the next week's numbers. Zingerman employees have also instituted "mini games" where short-term incentives are developed to solve a problem or capitalize on an opportunity. For example, staff at one restaurant used the greeter game to track how long it took for customers to be greeted. "Ungreeted" customers expressed less satisfaction and employees found themselves "comping" purchases to make up for service lapses. Other Zingerman businesses started similar games, with incentives for faster service, fewer knife injuries in the bakery (which would lower insurance costs), and neater kitchens. All of this effort at sharing information has increased frontline employees' sense of ownership and produced bottom-line results. From 2000 to 2010 revenue grew by almost 300% to more than $35 million.

Minimize Incivility

Many times the root cause of decreased performance is a lack of civility in the workplace. Research has discovered that 50% of employees who experienced uncivil behavior at work intentionally decreased their efforts. More than a third deliberately decreased the quality of their work. Two-thirds spent a lot of time avoiding the offender, and about the same number said their performance had declined. Leaders at Caiman Consulting, headquartered in Redmond, Washington, hire employees that have a demonstrated track record of treating people with respect. When there are instances of disrespectful behavior in the workplace, managers at Caiman swiftly act to pull the offender aside and make clear the company's policy on civil behavior. Management attributes the firm's 95% retention rate to its culture of respect and civility. Managers must model civility in the way they communicate and interact with others. The ripple effects of uncivil behavior by managers and colleagues quickly and powerfully infect the culture of an organization and inhibit the ability of employees to thrive. Creating a culture of civility is most directly influenced through hiring decisions. At Caiman, getting results matter, but the company passes up on highly qualified candidates that don't demonstrate strong interpersonal skills and emotional intelligence. Surprisingly, too few companies consider civility—or incivility—when evaluating candidates.

Offer Performance Feedback

Feedback creates opportunities for learning and the energy so critical for a culture of thriving. Feedback also helps people focus on individual and organizational goals. For feedback to be useful, it must be timely and direct. Quicken Loans, a mortgage finance company, continually updates performance feedback using two types of dashboards. The first dashboard displays group and individual metrics along with data feeds that show how likely an employee is to meet his or her daily goals. The second dashboard allows managers to track performance so they know when an employee or team needs some coaching or other type of assistance. Versions of these charts are displayed on monitors, with a rotating list of the top 15 salespeople for each metric. Instead of employees feeling overwhelmed and oppressed by so much data, Quicken has created strong norms for civility and respect and for giving employees a say in how they accomplish their work. This creates a context where feedback is energizing and promotes growth.

(Adapted from, Spreitzer, G. & Porath, C. (2012). Creating sustainable performance. *Harvard Business Review 90,* 1/2, p. 93-99.)

Questions for Review

1. How is employee engagement defined?
2. What practices lead to employee engagement? What practices lead to employee disengagement?
3. Is there a relationship between job satisfaction and performance? Discuss.
4. What are the differences between narrow engagement and full engagement?

CHAPTER 12:
Leading Teams

LEARNING OBJECTIVES

After studying this chapter, you should be able to:

1. Identify the qualities of an effective team.
2. Discuss how to get results from teams.
3. Identify the five dysfunctions of a team.
4. Discuss how to avoid the five dysfunctions of a team.
5. Define groupthink.
6. Discuss how to avoid groupthink in teams.

LEADING TEAMS

What is a team? According to Katzenbach and Smith (2003), there are specific practices that distinguish a team from a group of people with a common assignment. They define a team as a "small number of people with complementary skills who are committed to a common purpose, performance goals, and approach for which they hold themselves mutually accountable" (Katzenbach & Smith, 2003, p. 45). This is a comprehensive and enlightened definition because all the dimensions of effective teamwork are included: small, manageable number of people (size matters in team performance), recognition of unique individual talents that must complement and coexist with others, common purpose, performance standards, and finally the most important component of all, *accountability*. You can't talk about team performance without accountability. Individual team members must hold *one another* accountable and not always look to the manager or leader to do this for them. However, beyond individual contributions, ultimately all great teams recognize that success or failure is a collective effort. This level of deep responsibility, ownership, and shared accountability is the foundation of any successful team.

Getting Results with Teams

Richard Hackman is recognized as an expert in team performance and leadership. He opens his book *Leading Teams* with a pop quiz:

> When people work together to build a house, will the job probably (a) get done faster, (b) take longer to finish, or (c) not get done at all?

This question is actually taken from a fourth grade standardized test question in Ohio and the "correct" answer is (a) the work will get done faster. However, anyone with real world experience working on a team could make the case for all three answers being correct! Hackman offers the following advice to leaders looking to get the most out of their team:

What is the best size for a team? The general rule of thumb is no double digits. You don't want a team to be too small because it will lack diversity of opinion and expertise, but you don't want a team so big that it becomes unruly and too difficult to manage.

Importance of having team members know one another well. The National Transportation Safety Board found that 73% of the incidents in its database occurred on a crew's first day of flying together with 44% of those incidents occurring on a crew's very first flight. Also, a NASA study found that fatigued crews who had a history of working together made about half as many errors as crews composed of rested pilots who had not flown together before. Knowing your teammates well matters.

Teams that stay together for a long time need a "deviant." Deviants ask difficult and even uncomfortable questions to help the team avoid groupthink or too much homogeneity. When things are going well, a deviant will push back and ask questions like, "Wait a minute, why are we even doing this at all? What if we looked at the thing backwards or turned it inside out?" Many times a leader will see a deviant as rocking the boat and remove them from the team; however, according to Hackman, it's when you lose the deviant that the team can become mediocre.

The first meeting and even first few minutes of a meeting are critical. Hackman cites research suggesting, "The things that happen the first time a group meets strongly affect how the group operates throughout its entire life. Indeed, the first few minutes of the start of any social system are the most important because they establish not only where the group is going but also what the relationship will be between the team leader and the group, and what basic norms of conduct will be expected and enforced."

Teams must be real. People have to know who is on the team and who is not. Leaders must avoid politics when assigning team members and instead focus on the best people for the job.

Teams need a compelling direction. Members need to know, and agree on, what they're supposed to be doing together. Unless a leader articulates a clear direction, there is a real risk that different members will pursue different agendas.

Teams need enabling structure. Teams that have poorly designed tasks, the wrong number or wrong mix of members, or fuzzy and unenforced norms of conduct invariably get into trouble.

Teams need a supportive organization. The organizational context—including the reward system, the human resource system, and the information system—must facilitate teamwork.

Teams need expert coaching. Most executive coaches focus on individual performance, which does not significantly improve teamwork. Teams need coaching as a group in team processes—especially at the beginning, midpoint, and end of a team project.

(Adapted from: Why Teams Don't Work, *Harvard Business Review*, Interview with Richard Hackman conducted by Diane Coutu, May 2009, pages 98–105)

Patrick Lencioni has created a popular and useful model to assess team dynamics and remedy common pitfalls that prevent teams from achieving great results. His ideas have been used by professional athletic teams as well

FIGURE 12-1 The Five Dysfunctions of a Team

Reprinted from *The Five Dysfunctions of a Team* (2002), by permission of John Wiley & Sons, Inc.

as corporate and public sector organizations. Lencioni (2002) describes five dysfunctions that inhibit team performance.

Lencioni asserts that each dysfunction is not distinct and isolated, rather each is interrelated and feeds off each other ultimately destroying overall team performance. He describes the five dysfunctions this way:

1. The first dysfunction is an **absence of trust** among team members. Essentially, this stems from their unwillingness to be vulnerable within the group. Team members who are not genuinely open with one another about their mistakes and weaknesses make it impossible to build a foundation of trust.

2. The failure to build trust is damaging because it sets the tone for the second dysfunction: **fear of conflict**. Teams that lack trust are incapable of engaging in unfiltered and passionate debate of ideas. Instead, they resort to veiled discussions and guarded comments.

3. A lack of healthy conflict is a problem because it ensures the third dysfunction of a team: **lack of commitment**. Without having aired their opinions in the course of passionate and open debate, team members rarely, if ever, buy-in and commit to decisions, though they may feign agreement during meetings.

4. Because of this lack of real commitment and buy-in, team members develop an avoidance of **accountability**, the fourth dysfunction. Without committing to a clear plan of action, even the most focused and driven people often hesitate to call their peers on actions and behaviors that seen counterproductive to the good of the team.

5. Failure to hold one another accountable creates an environment where the fifth dysfunction can thrive. **Inattention to results** occurs when team members put their individual needs (such as ego, career development, or recognition) or even the needs of their divisions above the collective goals of the team. (Lencioni, 2002, pp. 188–189)

Lencioni suggests specific practices to overcome each of the five dysfunctions. The first involves what he calls **vulnerability-based trust**. This means that leaders and team members check their egos at the door and are comfortable enough with each other to admit weakness and mistakes and ask for help. Members of trusting teams accept questions and input about their areas of responsibility, give one another the benefit of the doubt before arriving at a negative conclusion, take risks in offering feedback and assistance, appreciate and tap into one another's skills and experiences, focus time and energy on important issues (not politics), offer and accept apologies without hesitation, and look forward to meetings and other opportunities to work together as a group (Lencioni, 2002, p. 197). To achieve these high levels of trust "requires shared experiences over time, multiple instances of follow-through and credibility, and an in-depth understanding of the unique attributes of team members" (Lencioni, 2002, p. 197). Leaders must genuinely model the behaviors associated with vulnerability-based trust and create an environment that doesn't punish such behaviors in others. To increase trust, Lencioni suggests the following exercises:

- *Personal Histories Exercise*: Have team members go around the table and share a short history of themselves. Questions don't need to be overly sensitive, and could include things like hometown, number of siblings, unique challenges of childhood, favorite hobbies, first job, and worst job. It is amazing to see how these simple prompts can elicit in-depth conversations and connections.

- *Team Effectiveness Exercise*: Team members identify the single most important contribution that each of their peers makes to the team as well as the one area that they must either improve upon or eliminate for the good of the team. All members then report their responses, focusing on one person at a time, usually beginning with the leader. Lencioni reports that this may seem intrusive and dangerous; however, the activity surfaces critical information and even dysfunctional teams often make it work with little tension.

- *Personality and Behavioral Preference Profiles*: Under the guidance of a licensed consultant, teams should consider profiling tools such as the Myers-Briggs Type Indicator (MBTI). The MBTI provides practical and scientifically valid behavioral descriptions of team members according to the diverse ways that they think, speak, and act. This heightened awareness of self and others is a powerful way to break down barriers by allowing people to better understand and empathize with others.

To overcome the second dysfunction, **fear of conflict**, teams must acknowledge that there are productive elements to conflict. Teams that engage in constructive conflict tend to have lively, interesting meetings, extract and exploit the ideas of all team members, solve real problems quickly, minimize politics, and put crucial topics on the table for discussion (Lencioni, 2002, p. 204). Lencioni suggest the following practices to increase positive conflict:

- *Mining*: Someone on the team must assume the role of "miner of conflict." This person (or persons) extracts buried disagreements within the team and brings them to the forefront of the conversation.

This requires courage and a degree of objectivity during meetings and a commitment to stay on task until the conflict is resolved.

- *Real-Time Permission*: While mining for conflict, some team members may become uncomfortable with the level of discord. In these moments, it is important for the leader to remind participants that what they are doing is necessary and, while uncomfortable in the short term, the exercise is good for the team in the long term.
- *Use of Personality and Behavioral Tools*: The Thomas-Kilmann Conflict Mode Instrument specifically assesses individual conflict profiles and suggests corresponding behaviors to deal with conflict effectively. (This instrument and the conflict handling modes are discussed in this book in Chapter 8.)

The two factors that perpetuate the third dysfunction, **lack of commitment**, are the desire for consensus and the need for certainty. Getting unanimous agreement from all team members is next to impossible. Great teams make sure that everyone's opinions are heard and genuinely considered and when there is impasse, the leader of the team is allowed to make the call. Regarding certainty, leaders and teams do not possess a crystal ball and can't predict with 100% accuracy the outcome of any decision. Instead, after everyone has voiced his or her opinions and perspectives, great teams confidently and boldly make their decision. If it turns out to be the wrong decision, then the team changes direction with equal boldness. This is always preferable to waffling. Lencioni provides the following suggestions to overcoming a lack of commitment:

- *Cascading Messaging*: At the end of a staff meeting or off-site, a team should explicitly review the key decisions made during the meeting and agree on what needs to be communicated to employees or other constituents about those decisions. This allows for clarity among team members on exactly what was discussed and provides opportunities to assure that everyone is on the same page. This allows for leaders to be clearly aligned with one another and send a powerful and welcomed message to employees that have grown accustomed to receiving conflicting messages from managers who attended the same meeting.
- *Deadlines*: A simple and effective tool to ensuring commitment is the use of deadlines for when decisions will be made and honoring those deadlines with discipline and rigidity. This allows teams to avoid ambiguity by sticking to clear deadlines for decisions.
- *Contingency and Worst-Case Scenario Analysis*: By coming up with contingency plans and clarifying the worst-case scenario up front, teams can reduce their fears by realizing that the costs of an incorrect decision are survivable.

Lencioini notes that the most effective and efficient means of combating the fourth dysfunction of a team, **avoidance of accountability**, is peer pressure. He states, "One of the benefits is the reduction of the need for excessive bureaucracy around performance management and corrective action. More than any policy or system, there is nothing like the fear of letting down respected teammates that motivates people to improve their performance" (Lencioni, 2002, p. 213). Strategies to increase accountability include:

- *Publication of Goals and Standards*: Teams should clarify publically what needs to be achieved and who needs to deliver what. This helps the team avoid ambiguity and makes agreements open so that no one can easily ignore them.
- *Simple and Regular Progress Reviews*: As Lencioni notes, "A little structure goes a long way toward helping people take action that they might not otherwise be inclined to do" (Lencioni, 2002, p. 214). Leaders should mandate that team members regularly communicate with one another, verbally or in writing, about how they feel teammates are progressing toward stated objectives and standards. When leaders assume that this will get done on its own, and don't provide any structure, they are inviting potential avoidance of accountability.
- *Team Rewards*: Rather than reward individual achievers, the entire team should be rewarded for achievement. This will motivate team members to deal with a peer who is not pulling his or her weight in the interest of overall team performance.

Teams that overcome the fifth dysfunction, **inattention to results**, retain achievement-oriented employees, minimize individualistic behavior, enjoy success and suffer failure acutely, benefit from individuals who subjugate their own goals/interests for the good of the team, and avoid distractions (Lencioni, 2002, p. 218). Getting results doesn't just mean financial performance; rather it refers to multiple outcome-based measures that organizations plan to achieve in a given period of time. To focus attention on results, Lencioni suggests the following actions:

- *Public Declaration of Results*: In contrast to an athletic team that is cautioned from publically guaranteeing a victory because it un-necessarily provokes the other team, most teams benefit from making public proclamations about intended success. Lencioni notes, "Teams that are willing to commit publicly to specific results are more likely to work with a passionate, even desperate desire to achieve those results. Teams that say, 'We'll do our best,' are subtly, if not purposefully, preparing themselves for failure" (Lencioni, 2002, p. 219).

- *Results-Based Rewards*: Tying rewards, especially compensation, to the achievement of specific outcomes keeps team members focused on results. While Lencioini acknowledges the limitations of financial incentives as a primary motivator, he states that letting people take home a bonus for merely "trying hard" sends a message that achieving specific results is not terribly important.

When teams honestly assess their own performance in light of the "Five Dysfunctions" outlined by Patrick Lencioni, they are sure to isolate performance gaps and take corrective actions to enhance results. This will inevitably reduce "groupthink" which we'll learn about in the next section.

GROUPTHINK

Groupthink is one of the most powerful and dysfunctional phenomena that can infect team dynamics. Irving Janis (1971) coined the term groupthink which he defines as a "mode of thinking that persons engage in when *concurrence-seeking* becomes so dominant in a cohesive in-group that it tends to override realistic appraisal of alternative courses of action . . . symptoms of groupthink arise when the members of decision-making groups become motivated to avoid being too harsh in their judgments of their leaders' or their colleagues ideas" (p. 43). Groupthink has been implicated in NASA's Space Shuttle *Challenger* and *Columbia* tragedies and a host of corporate scandals at organizations such as Enron, WorldCom, and Tyco.

Janis and Mann (1977) offer the following historical examples where groupthink has played a role in bad or irrational decisions:

- Neville Chamberlain's inner circle, whose members supported the policy of appeasement of Hitler during 1937 and 1938, despite repeated warnings and events indicating that it would have adverse consequences;
- President Truman's advisory group, whose members supported the decision to escalate the war in North Korea despite firm warnings from the Chinese Communist government that US entry into the war would be met with armed resistance from the Chinese;
- President Kennedy's inner circle, whose members supported the decision to launch the Bay of Pigs invasion of Cuba despite the availability of information that it would be an unsuccessful venture and damage US relations with other countries;
- President Johnson's close advisors, whose members supported the decision to escalate the Vietnam War despite intelligence reports and other information indicating that this course of action would not

defeat the Vietcong or the North Vietnamese and would entail unfavorable political consequences within the United States.

It is important to note that groupthink only occurs when cohesiveness among group members is high. It requires that members share a strong "we-feeling" of solidarity and desire to maintain relationships within the group at all costs. When colleagues operate in a groupthink mode, they automatically apply the "preserve group harmony" test to every decision they make. This results in a situation in which the group ultimately agrees on an action which each individual member might normally consider unwise. There are eight symptoms of groupthink:

1. An illusion of invulnerability, shared by most or all of the members, which creates excessive optimism and encourages taking extreme risks.

2. Collective efforts to rationalize in order to discount warnings which might lead the members to reconsider their assumptions before they recommit themselves to their past policy decisions.

3. An unquestioned belief in the group's inherent morality, inclining the members to ignore the ethical or moral consequences of their decisions.

4. Stereotyped views of rivals and enemies as too evil to warrant genuine attempts to negotiate, or as too weak or stupid to counter whatever risky attempts are made to defeat their purposes.

5. Direct pressure on any member who expresses strong arguments against any of the group's stereotypes, illusions, or commitments, making clear that such dissent is contrary to what is expected of all loyal members.

6. Self-censorship of deviations from the apparent group consensus, reflecting each member's inclination to minimize to himself the importance of his doubts and counterarguments.

7. A shared illusion of unanimity, partly resulting from this self-censorship and augmented by the false assumptions that silence implies consent.

8. The emergence of self-appointed "mindguards"—members who protect the group from adverse information that might shatter their shared complacency about the effectiveness and morality of their decisions.

(Janis, I. & Mann, L. (1977). *Decision Making: A psychological analysis of conflict, choice, and commitment*, The Free Press, New York, pp. 130–131)

Reprinted from *Decision Making: A Psychological Analysis of Conflict, Choice, and Commitment* (1977), by permission of Simon & Schuster, Inc.

The following figure represents the main conditions under which a strong concurrence-seeking tendency is likely to become dominant in a policy-making group, giving rise to the symptoms of groupthink and to defective decision making:

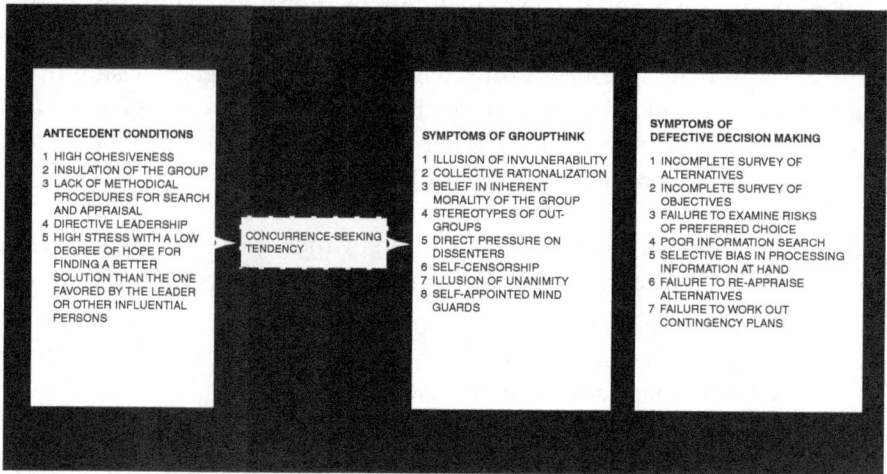

FIGURE 12-2 Analysis of groupthink, based on comparisons of high- and low-quality decisions by policy-making groups.

Reprinted from *Decision Making: A Psychological Analysis of Conflict, Choice, and Commitment* (1977), by permission of Simon & Schuster, Inc.

Janis concludes that two well-worked-out policy decisions by groups were the formulation of the Marshall Plan in the Truman Administration and the handling of the Cuban missile crisis by President Kennedy and his advisors. Incorporating the constructive practices of each of these groups, Janis offers the following recommendations to prevent groupthink:

1. The leader of a policy-forming group should assign the role of critical evaluator to each member, encouraging the group to give high priority to airing objections and doubts. This practice needs to be reinforced by the leader's acceptance of criticism of his own judgments in order to discourage members from soft-pedaling their disagreements.

2. When the key members of a hierarchy assign a policy-planning mission to any group within their organization, they should adopt an impartial stance instead of stating preferences and expectations at the beginning. This will encourage open inquiry and impartial probing of a wide range of policy alternatives.

3. The organization routinely should set up several outside policy-planning and evaluation groups to work on the same policy question, each deliberating under a different leader. This can prevent the insulation of an in-group.

4. At intervals before the group reaches a final consensus, the leader should require each member to discuss the group's deliberations with associates in his own unit of the organization—assuming that those associates can be trusted to adhere to the same security regulations that govern the policy makers—and then report back their reactions to the group.

5. The group should invite one or more outside experts to each meeting on a staggered basis and encourage the experts to challenge the views of the core members.

6. At every general meeting of the group, whenever the agenda calls for an evaluation of policy alternatives, at least one member should play devil's advocate, functioning as a good lawyer in challenging the testimony of those who advocate the majority position.

7. Whenever the policy issue involves relations with a rival nation or organization, the group should devote a sizable block of time, perhaps an entire session, to a survey of all warning signals from the rivals and should write alternative scenarios on the rivals' intentions.

8. When the group is surveying policy alternatives for feasibility and effectiveness, it should from time to time divide into two or more subgroups to meet separately, under different chairpersons, and then come back together to hammer out differences.

9. After reaching a preliminary consensus about what seems to be the best policy, the group should hold a "second-chance" meeting at which every member expresses as vividly as possible their residual doubts, and rethinks the entire issue before making a definitive choice.

(Janis, I (November, 1971). Groupthink: The desperate drive for consensus at any cost that suppresses dissent among the mighty in the corridors of power, *Psychology Today*, p. 76)

Reprinted from *Psychology Today*, November 1971, by permission of Sussex Publishers.

Janis readily acquiesces that there are certain disadvantages to following these standard operating procedures when teams are charged with making consequential decisions (e.g., prolonged and costly debates, rejection, anger, security leakages by setting up outside evaluation groups); however, creative leaders can figure out ways to avoid these pitfalls and the long-term benefits to quelling groupthink outweigh any short-term inconveniences.

What Do You Think?

Where might I/we improve in these areas? Think about: leading change, employee needs, mentoring/job shadowing, cultivating and sustaining teamwork, motivation, employee engagement, job satisfaction, hiring practices, orienting new employees, listening, service attitude, etc.

_____

_____

_____

_____

_____

_____

_____

_____

_____

Are change, motivation, engagement, job satisfaction, or teamwork issues getting in the way of our performance? Think about: Kotter's "Eight Steps" to leading change, attention to transitions and resistance to change, motivating employees beyond a paycheck, hiring practices to get the right people on board, job/skill fit among employees, increasing job satisfaction and engagement, dysfunctional team dynamics, etc.

_____

_____

_____

_____

_____

_____

_____

_____

Questions for Review

1. How do Katzenbach and Smith (2003) define a team? What qualities do you think are most important in effective teams?

2. How can leaders get better results from teams?

3. What are the five dysfunctions of a team? What strategies can leaders enact to avoid each of the five dysfunctions of a team?

4. What is groupthink? How does groupthink influence team performance?

5. What strategies help to reduce the risk of groupthink?

ORGANIZATIONAL CULTURE

Culture is the glue that binds together tribes, communities, civilizations, and organizations. Culture provides the signposts that impart meaning, significance, and direction to leaders, organizational members, and external audiences. Organizational culture consists of symbols, values, rituals and ceremonies, humor, and storytelling. There are also distinct profiles that define organizational cultures. This section also explores how information is communicated within cultures, the role of culture on performance, and strategies to shape and change cultures.

CHAPTER 13:
Organizational Culture

LEARNING OBJECTIVES

After studying this chapter, you should be able to:

1. Define organizational culture.
2. Identify the three cultures of management.
3. Discuss the hallmarks of organizational culture including: symbols, core ideology, rituals and ceremony, humor, and storytelling.
4. Identify and discuss four culture profiles.

ORGANIZATIONAL CULTURE AT APPLE

Apple Inc.'s retail stores have taken the country by storm. The layout, architecture and store furnishings reflect the hipster, modern vibe of Apple's fanatical customers. In 2010, more people visited Apple's 326 stores in a single quarter than the 60 million who visited Walt Disney

Co.'s four biggest theme parks. In 2009, when retail sales declined 2.4%, Apple's retail sales, excluding online, jumped 70% handily exceeding the overall retail industry's sales growth of 4.5%. Other companies such as Microsoft and Best Buy have tried to duplicate elements of Apple's approach, however, without the same success. Part of this is due to intense demand for Apple's products. What also drives customers to Apple retail stores is the level of service from employees and the overall shopping experience. Customers feel as though they are part of something special when they walk into a crowded Apple store. For example, when a new product is launched, customers are cheered as they enter and exit the store. Getting a job at an Apple store is a competitive process that usually requires multiple interviews where applicants are questioned about their leadership and problem-solving skills in addition to their enthusiasm for Apple products. Employees then receive extensive training where recruits are drilled in classes that apply Apple's principles of customer service. New hires also shadow more experienced colleagues and aren't allowed to interact with customers on their own until they're deemed ready which could be up to two weeks or even longer.

Apple knows what they want in an employee and hires hard to make sure that people fit the mold. If employees don't meet the high expectations, they are let go. For example, Apple employees who are six minutes late in their shifts three times in six months may be let go. Sales associates are taught not to sell, but rather to help customers solve problems. One training manual says, "Your job is to understand all of your customers' needs—some of which they may not even realize they have." Training manuals communicate the company's "steps of service" using the acronym APPLE. "Approach customers with a personalized warm welcome," "Probe politely to understand all the customer's needs," "Present a solution for the customer to take home today," "Listen for and resolve any issues or concerns," and "End with a fond farewell and an invitation to return." Apple even provides detailed training in communication and how to deal with emotional customers by suggesting: "Listen and limit your responses to simple reassurances that you are doing so. 'Uh-huh' 'I understand,' etc." Training in language extends also to technical support staff where they are told to say, "as it turns out" rather than "unfortunately" to sound less negative if they are unable to solve a technical problem. (see Holmes & Lublin, 2011)

ORGANIZATIONAL CULTURE DEFINED

Culture is defined as a "pattern of shared basic assumptions learned by a group as it solved its problems of external adaption and internal integration, which has worked well enough to be considered valid and, therefore, to be taught to new members as the correct way to perceive, think, and feel in relation to those problems" (Schein, 2010, p. 18). This is a comprehensive (perhaps overly academic) definition that gets to the heart of what culture is all about. However, I like a different definition of organizational culture: "The way we do things around here" (Deal & Kennedy, 1982, p. 4). This definition is concise, accurate, and memorable. For example, the *way* Apple does things is reflective of its culture. Similarly, Ford and GM, Nordstrom's and Macy's, Bank of America and Wells Fargo, and Target and Wal-Mart each compete in the same industry, but have different ways of going about business. Usually when companies merge or are acquired, they experience "culture clash" and struggle to define the dominant culture or redefine how the cultures of both organizations will coexist (an infamous example was the America Online Inc. merger with Time Warner in the year 2000). Even within the same organization, multiple cultures exist due to differences in norms, values, and assumptions. We'll explore this idea more in the next section.

Three Cultures of Management

Edgar Schein has been studying the role of culture on leadership and organizations for decades. Schein summarizes culture as shared norms, values, and assumptions among organizational members. He argues that years of research on leaders and organizational behavior have overlooked the role of culture. Schein contends that a leader's style can certainly influence productivity and employee satisfaction; however, the more powerful (and often undetected) systemic forces of an organization's culture—especially among senior level managers—is what really drives managerial behavior. For example, if the culture creates autocratic managers, then the organization will get autocratic managers. He says, "We did not grasp that norms held tacitly across large social units were much more likely to change leaders than to be changed by them. We failed to note that 'culture,' viewed as such taken-for-granted, shared, tacit ways of perceiving, thinking and reacting, was one of the most powerful and stable forces operating in organizations" (Schein, 1996, p. 231). Norms (i.e., the way people do things) are fairly visible in organizational life, but it is important to remember that behind the norms lies a deeper, taken-for-granted set of assumptions that members never question or examine until they encounter a different culture. Therefore, as organizations work to improve efficiency and effectiveness, three management cultures clash with one another because of different norms, values, and assumptions. Schein describes three cultures of management: operators, engineers, and executives.

1. The *operators* are the line managers and workers who make and deliver the products and services that fulfill the organization's basic mission. This group typically becomes the target of change programs and organizational learning efforts. This group is closest to the day-to-day action of the organization and discovers the interdependencies among work groups and learns to deal with them. Operators have a "people" focus.

2. The *engineers* have a "technical" focus. There are many types that fall into the "engineer" group including, designers, technocrats, or programmers. Every organization has a core technology that underlies what the organization does, and that technology is designed and monitored by the engineers. This group prefers solutions without people, that is, they prefer systems, machines, routines, and rules that are automatic and totally reliable. Operators, with their systemic insights and desires to work in effective teams, are often thwarted by the lack of support and enthusiasm of the engineers who keep proposing technical solutions that make operators very skeptical and feel threatened because they might lose their job as a result of the technical solution. The resolution of this tension often results in proposals for new machines or training programs that need the buy-in of the third culture group.

3. The *executives* focus on "financial results." The essence of this role is financial accountability to the owner shareholders or Board of Directors. Though lip service is paid to long-range strategy, to human resources, to balancing the needs of different stakeholders, the reality is driven by the capital markets and the need to remain financially viable. CEO's learn that they alone must make the tough financial decisions based on imperfect information because they become isolated and find it harder and harder to trust what their subordinates tell them. Though these types may have grown up with the knowledge and insights of the "operators," they increasingly have to abandon those insights and replace them with perceptions that in a tough competitive world, compromises have to be made, chances have to be taken, and financial criteria always has to be treated as paramount.

Schein concludes that organizations must reconcile the built-in conflict between and among these three cultures if they want to become a reliable learning system. Important questions to ask are: How do executives learn, given the realities of their roles, and how do we help them to become effective learners? How do engineers learn beyond the narrow confines of their technologies, and how do we help them learn? To achieve results, leaders must recognize that they are dealing with other cultures inside the organization and leaders naturally tend to impose their own culture biases on others. Schein believes there is a "humanistic bias" inherent in the field of organization studies that discounts the systemic and cultural influences on behavior. He says, "We spend our time advocating that 'they' should become more aware of the human factor, which is tantamount to saying give up your culture and become a member of ours" (p. 239).

CULTURE HALLMARKS

An organization's culture is also expressed through various culture hallmarks. These include symbols, core ideologies, rituals and ceremony, humor, and storytelling. Each of these culture hallmarks serves to strengthen and clarify what the organization is all about to both insiders and external audiences.

Symbols

An exciting first step in launching a company is deciding what symbol or logo best represents the organization. According to marketing research, some of the most recognizable corporate symbols include McDonalds' "golden arches", the red and white cursive logo and stripes of Coca-Cola, and Disney's Mickey Mouse ears. Harley-Davidson Motorcycles in-corporates an eagle and the American flag as symbols to express freedom and pride in an American-made product. When a company has really made it, they no longer need to put the company name next to the logo because the symbol is so widely recognized. Examples include, Nike, Target, and most recently with Starbucks' decision to remove the words Starbucks Coffee from its products and only use the mermaid symbol. Executives at Starbucks feel this move will help the company expand its brand beyond just coffee.

Core Ideology

Collins and Porras (1994) found that high-performing organizations have between three and six core values or "ideologies" (any more than six and it isn't "core"). They conclude that "the critical issue is not whether a company has the 'right' core ideology or a 'likeable' core ideology but rather whether it *has* a core ideology—likeable or not—that gives guidance and inspiration to people inside the company" (p.68). A few examples from the 18 companies included in their *Built to Last* study are:

3M

Innovation; "Thou shalt not kill a new product idea"
Absolute integrity
Respect for individual initiative and personal growth
Tolerance for honest mistakes
Product quality and reliability
"Our real business is solving problems"

IBM

Give full consideration to the individual employee
Spend a lot of time making customers happy
Go the last mile to do things right; seek superiority in all we undertake

Merck

"We are in the business of preserving and improving human life. All of our actions must be measured by our success in achieving this goal."
Honesty and integrity
Corporate social responsibility
Science-based innovation, not imitation
Unequivocal excellence in all aspects of the company
Profit, but profit from work that benefits humanity

Nordstrom

Service to the customer above all else
Hard work and productivity
Continuous improvement, never being satisfied
Excellence in reputation, being part of something special

Philip Morris

The right to personal freedom of choice (to smoke, to buy whatever one wants) is worth defending
Winning—being the best and beating others
Encouraging individual initiative
Opportunity to achieve based on merit, not gender, race, or class
Hard work and continuous self-improvement

Disney

No cynicism allowed
Fanatical attention to consistency and detail
Continuous progress via creativity, dreams, and imagination
Fanatical control and preservation of Disney's "magic" image
"To bring happiness to missions" and to celebrate, nurture, and promulgate "wholesome American values."

*Note from authors: These lists present the most historically consistent ideology for each of the visionary companies in our study. We did *not* merely paraphrase the company's most recent values, mission, vision, or purpose statement (if it had one) and we never relied on only one source; we looked for *historical consistency* through multiple generations of chief executives.

Using the examples above as a guide, think about your own organization. What are its core values? Would people inside the company agree on the core values? Are the core values unclear and in need of attention?

Rituals and Ceremony

Rituals are acts that are repeated regularly in an organization. Examples include Monday morning meetings and pre-store-opening huddles where managers discuss sales goals for the day and share words of encouragement. Ceremonies are "high ritual" or acts that occur less frequently but with greater emotion and spirit. Examples include, commencement exercises at the end of a school year, annual employee recognition ceremonies, or military change of command ceremonies. Often, rituals and ceremonies incorporate the use of cherished symbols from the organization that are passed out to individuals and groups. These events all have deep significance and mark an important milestone in individual or collective accomplishments. All organized religions understand the impact and importance of ritual and ceremony to create meaning in what could otherwise be seen as ordinary activity. It's been said that organizational life without ritual and ceremony is just an endless series of Wednesdays.

Humor

Humor is also an indicator of an organization's culture and the leadership style of those within the organization. When leading a contentious or controversial meeting, you will find that humor can relieve tension, break the ice, and get people talking to one another. Commenting on the role of humor in organizations, Trice and Beyer (1993) note, "Joking reduces conflict not only by releasing tensions and expressing hostilities in acceptable ways, but also because joking tends to set up and maintain social interactions. Joking by one party carries with it the expectation and license for the other to respond in kind" (p. 207). Similarly, Simon Ramo, co-founder of TRW, says, "Anyone in a leadership role will be handicapped in projecting influence if he or she is missing the humor gene" (Hiltzik, 2011, B7). Unfortunately, many leaders and managers don't understand how to use humor, or lack the good sense to know when they are about to tell the wrong joke to the wrong audience. As a general rule, self-deprecating humor is most effective while hostile or aggressive humor directed at others is never a good idea (and, by the way, not funny). Self-deprecating humor makes a leader more approachable and accessible. For example, as a business consultant, I can use jokes to poke fun at myself and the consulting profession in general (and then go on to offer invaluable advice!). Here are a couple good jokes about consultants:

A consultant is someone who borrows your watch to tell you what time it is . . . and then walks away with the watch.

✳✳✳

A consultant doesn't know any more than you do. She's just better organized and has slides.

✳✳✳

Peter Desberg (1996) has studied how leaders use humor in the workplace. He offers a number of helpful tips and examples on the effective use of humor:

1. *Avoid jokes that are discriminatory or dirty.*
2. *Learn jokes before telling them.*
3. *Make use of the Rule of Three.* Basic jokes are structured by the Rule of Three. In the first part you establish a pattern. In the second part you confirm the pattern. In the third part you violate that pattern with a surprise. Here is an example:

   > Three men were commuting into New York City, having a discussion about which man's wife loved him the most. The first man said, "My wife thinks I'm the most cultured man she has ever met."
   >
   > The second man said, "My wife thinks that I should have been an ambassador."
   >
   > The third man said, "Your wives certainly sound like they're impressed with you, but mine brags about me all the time. Every time I stay home from work and there's a knock at the door, my wife screams out . . . MY HUSBAND'S HOME!"

4. *Always end the joke with the climactic word.* If you tell the punch line and there are a few more words coming after it, you will "step on your own laughs."
5. *Don't laugh at your own jokes.* This is an obnoxious habit that seems to offend most audiences. Unless you are in character and have a particular reason for laughing at your joke, avoid doing it.
6. *Don't repeat the punch line for a joke that works.* Some people think that if a joke happened to get a laugh, they can repeat the punch line to get more laughs. They will not.
7. *Don't explain jokes that don't work.* If you want to get an audience to really dislike you, all you have to do is tell them a joke that is not

very funny. Then, when the audience does not laugh, assume that they did not get the joke, and explain it to them.

8. *Try to tell jokes or stories that can get laughs along the way.* Here is an example:

> An Englishman was visiting a New England fish cannery and the supervisor was giving him a tour. He decided to show the conservative Britisher that Americans had a clever sense of humor. He pointed to a shelf of cans and said, "We eat all we can, and all we can't we can."
>
> The Britisher just stared. Later that night he was having dinner with a friend and began chuckling. He said, "This American chap told me this frightfully amusing joke. We eat all we're able, and all we can't we tin."

Desberg (1996) provides the following examples of jokes you may be able to use (or simply find amusing).

> A new manager began by saying, "There are going to be a few changes in the system here. I'd like some input from you. Those who oppose these changes may signify by saying, "I QUIT!"
>
> ***
>
> The better the news, the higher ranking the official who announces it.
>
> ***
>
> Retreat into analogies and discuss them until everyone has forgotten the original problem.
>
> ***
>
> To spot the expert, pick the one who predicts the job will take the longest and cost the most.
>
> ***
>
> A leader shouldn't get too far in front of his troops . . . or he can get shot in the derriere.
>
> ***
>
> People would rather live with a problem they cannot solve, than a solution they don't understand.
>
> ***
>
> A true friend will not laugh at your joke until she retells it.
>
> ***
>
> There is no problem a good miracle can't solve.
>
> ***

Storytelling

In many ways, we are ancient beings in modern costumes; since the beginning of our species, people have always loved a good story. Drew Westen, professor of psychology at Emory University, notes that our species existed for more than 100,000 years before the earliest signs of literacy, and another 5,000 years would pass before the majority of humans would know how to read and write. Because of this, storytelling was the primary method of transmitting knowledge and values. Weston says, "The stories our leaders tell us matter, probably almost as much as the stories our parents tell us as children, because they orient us to what is, what could be, and what should be; to the worldviews they hold and to the values they hold sacred. Our brains evolved to 'expect' stories with a particular structure, with protagonists and villains, a hill to be climbed or a battle to be fought" (Weston, 2011, p. 1). For teachers, parents, and leaders, storytelling is also an effective technique to get others to remember an important point. For example, rather than wagging one's finger and lecturing others, an audience is much more likely to remember your message if you wrap it in a story. Even years later, people remember the stories they are told and consequently the lessons become much more powerful. It is likely that the mentors and leaders in your life that you look up to are also pretty good storytellers. Hence part of our leadership development involves always being on the lookout for a good story.

Storytelling also has an organizational impact. Steve Wynn, founder and CEO of Wynn Resorts, says "storytelling has changed my life and changed my business" (Esse, 2012, p. 30). Several hundred Wynn managers and leaders participate in intensive storytelling training aimed at understanding the power of stories to inspire meaning and significance among employees and communicate core values to customers. For example, at Wynn Las Vegas a guest was checking into the resort and realized that she'd left a vanity case at home containing some essential insulin to treat her husband's diabetes. The bellboy who'd taken her luggage talked the woman out of returning all the way home to retrieve the case, instead he called his brother who lived close to the guests' home. He arranged to have the medicine collected from the housekeeper, then left his shift and drove 150 miles through the night to collect the medicine and deliver it to the guests' room, so that it could be administered at exactly 7 am. Asked why he had taken it upon himself to do this, the bellboy said that both he and his line manager could see how his actions would contribute to the resort's "Story"—a simple and clear narrative co-created with the Executive team articulating the ambition of the business to provide the ultimate guest experience "so they never want to leave" (Esse, 2012, p. 30). Leaders at Wynn Resorts collect stories—from employees and managers at all levels of the company—that reinforce the core values of collaboration and involvement that are central to the company's culture. These stories are then publicized through a specially-branded social networking tool, StoryWeb, that keep the stories alive in the day-to-day operations of the company.

Here are a few stories—with the lesson each story is imparting—that you may find useful or amusing:

On admitting mistakes:

H.L. Mencken, the writer and atheist, was asked, "Mr. Mencken, now that you are getting on in years, have you thought about what you might say if on your passing, you should find yourself in heaven?" Mencken replied, "I should walk right up to St. Peter and say, 'My name is H.L. Mencken and I have made a terrible mistake!'"

On the wisdom of self-restraint:

Ronald Reagan, as governor of California, told a story about a speech he made in Mexico City. Reagan said, "As you know, I do not speak Spanish and so I made my speech in English and there was polite applause, but I thought pretty restrained enthusiasm. So when the next speaker began, to mask my failure to speak the language, I applauded at every opportunity and quite loudly. It was then that the American Ambassador to Mexico leaned over and said, 'I wouldn't do that if I were you Governor; he's translating your speech.'"

Truth in translation or trusting the messenger:

In 1994 Argentinean soccer coach, Jorge Solari, led Saudi Arabia to the World Cup for the first time. The Arabic translation of a comment by Solari said, "I have great pride in the courageous way our team played. I wish to dedicate this victory to the custodian of the two holy mosques, the King of Saudi Arabia and to all the Saudi Arabian people."

What he actually said in Spanish was, "I'm very happy with my boys, they played extremely well."

On the sometimes unknown influence of teachers:

Bolman and Deal (2008) share a story about a chancellor at Vanderbilt University who ended his speech to faculty at the beginning of the school year with this story. The chancellor said, "I'd like to tell you the story of a second-grade teacher in

Austin, Texas named Roberta Wright. Ms. Wright noticed that one of her second graders was stealing materials from the classroom at the end of each day—paper, markers, and other classroom items. Ms. Wright decided to call the young girl's mother to tell her that the daily thefts could not continue. The mother interrupted her and said, 'Oh, Ms. Wright you don't understand. She comes home every day and goes to her room and pretends she's still in school, she pretends she's you.'"

After telling the story the chancellor paused for a few moments, his eyes moving from person to person in the assembled crowd of university professors, and concluded by saying, "Ladies and gentlemen, that does not stop in the second grade."

As a college professor, I've attended countless events where a chancellor or college president has flatly proclaimed clichéd lines about the impact educators have on students. The results are usually less than memorable. However, when this idea is wrapped in a powerful story, like the one the chancellor at Vanderbilt told, teachers couldn't help but burst out of the auditorium and knock the doors down on the way to their classrooms. This is a great example of leadership and the power of storytelling.

? What Do You Think?

Apply the 5 Culture Hallmarks to your own organization. Write your ideas in the space below.

Culture Hallmark	Where is there a need for clarity or improvement in our organization? What can be done to strengthen the culture of our organization in each area?
Symbols	
Core Ideology, Values	
Rituals and Ceremony	
Humor	
Storytelling	

CULTURE PROFILES

Let's conclude this chapter with four culture profiles. As you read each description see which profile most closely aligns with your own organization. The profiles are especially helpful in describing norms, values, and assumptions, in addition to what it takes to survive and advance in each culture type. Organizational cultures can be characterized by how much risk is involved in the work and how quickly feedback is received on results. Most organizations don't fit precisely into one of the categories below, in fact, within any single organization, a mix of all four types of cultures will be found. Four culture profiles are:

Tough Guy/Girl, Macho

Types of jobs/industry: Law enforcement, military, construction, TV executives.
Risk level: High levels of risk, risk taking is expected and rewarded.
Feedback on results: Fast; Either you accomplished the mission or not, people loved the movie or it was rejected.
What it takes to survive and thrive: Tough attitude, "thick skin", competitive personality that doesn't shy away from confrontation, an appropriate saying for this culture is, "You're only as good as your last decision."

Work Hard, Play Hard

Types of jobs/industry: Sales, real estate, any commission based job.
Risk level: Moderate; You can always close another deal tomorrow.
Feedback on results: Fast; Either you made the sale or you didn't, you know quickly.
What it takes to survive and thrive: Heroes in this culture are the super salespeople who are charming, friendly, and outgoing. Success is measured by the team producing volume for the company rather than a distinct focus on individuals.

Bet Your Company

Types of jobs/industry: Aerospace, Investment banking.
Risk level: High; A long term investment that doesn't pay off can devastate the company.
Feedback on results: Slow; Have to wait a long time to see if things pay off.
What it takes to survive and thrive: These people are just as self-directed and tough as people in the macho culture, but they have the stamina to endure long-term ambiguity with little or no feedback. Decisions are

measured and deliberate but once a decision is made, people in this culture don't change their convictions easily. People respect authority and technical competence, and heroes provide psychological support during all of the rough times. Immaturity is not tolerated in this culture and evaluating the abilities of an employee could take decades. Top management makes statements like, "He's only been here five years, it's too early to tell." This is compared to the work/play culture where if someone has been with the company for a month and failed to get results, they are probably on their way out.

Process

Types of jobs/industry: Government agencies, schools.

Risk level: Low; Stability is valued, takes a long time to enact change.

Feedback on results: Slow; May take years for a student to realize, "That's what that class was all about!"

What it takes to survive and thrive: Protectiveness and caution are natural responses to the absence of feedback. People who are valued in this culture are those who are trying to protect the system's integrity more than their own. Survivors carry out the procedures as they are written down without asking whether they make sense in the real world. In fact, the real world ceases to exist, and most successful bureaucrats have trouble dealing with it when it infringes on their turf.

(Adapted from: Deal, T., & Kennedy, A. (1982). *Corporate cultures: The rites and rituals of corporate life.* Menlo Park: Addison-Wesley Publishing Company, pp. 107–123)

Questions for Review

1. What are the two definitions of organizational culture in this chapter? What key ideas do you think are most important in these definitions? How would you describe the culture of your organization?

2. What are the three cultures of management? Why do these three management cultures tend to clash in organizations?

3. How are symbols, core ideology, rituals and ceremony, humor, and storytelling related to culture? How are these culture hallmarks expressed in your own organization? Where is there room for improvement?

4. What are the four culture profiles? What characteristics determine each profile? How do these profiles relate to your own personality and organizational experiences?

CHAPTER 14:
Communication, Performance, and Culture Change

LEARNING OBJECTIVES

After studying this chapter, you should be able to:

1. Discuss examples of organizational communication.
2. Discuss the five roles of organizational members when communicating information.
3. Identify three elements of corporate culture that enhance long-term economic performance.
4. Discuss how culture type is related to organizational effectiveness.
5. Identify and discuss common practices in successful culture change initiatives.

ORGANIZATIONAL COMMUNICATION

We are witnessing a culture change in the way we communicate with one another. With the rise of electronic communication through email, texting, and social media sites, it is commonplace to send and receive messages without ever seeing the other person face-to-face. Often, when communication lacks nonverbal cues such as body language, intonation, and facial expressions, miscommunication ensues. Think about the role of vocal intonation when communicating the short message below. Say each sentence out loud and emphasize the bolded word in each sentence to see how the message changes dramatically.

I didn't hit him.
I **didn't** hit him.
I didn't **hit** him.
I didn't hit **him**.

With so many managers relying on email, instant messaging, and texts to communicate information, it's no wonder that so many messages are misinterpreted and require a lot of work on the back end to clarify what one really meant to say. One simple remedy to enhance effective communication is for managers to get off email, walk down the hall, and have a face-to-face conversation! Also, people tend to be more brazen or cruel when they are not looking the other person in the face. A recent study by the Pew Research Center found that 95% of all teens ages 12–17 are now online and 80% of those online teens use social media sites such as Facebook and Twitter. This study also found that 88% of social media-using teens have witnessed other people being mean or cruel on these sites. However, 78% report at least one positive outcome from their interactions on social media sites with 41% reporting at least one negative outcome (Pew Research Center's Internet & American Life Project, 2011).

Organizational leaders use a variety of methods to communicate with internal and external audiences. Keyton (2005) defines organizational communication as "a complex and continuous process through which organizational members create, maintain, and change the organization by communicating verbally, nonverbally, electronically, and in writing with individuals and groups of people engaged in roles as internal and external stakeholders" (p. 17). Keyton notes various examples of organizational communication such as:

- Communication among and between stakeholder groups including current and potential employees, current and potential clients and customers, current and potential suppliers, and regulators or those who may have a regulator role in the future.
- Communication aimed at socializing new members or negotiating one's position in the organization.
- Communication focused on structuring or controlling the organization.
- Communication devoted to negotiating and coordinating work activities.
- Communication devoted to positioning the organization within the marketplace and society.
- Communication associated with informal, day-to-day interactions and conversations. Which may include personal stories, gossip, rumors, and socializing that reveals important cultural information, especially when casual conversation begins or ends formal meetings.

Five Roles in Communication

Terrence Deal and Allan Kennedy's groundbreaking book, *Corporate Cultures*, continues to influence managers and researchers today. Deal and Kennedy (1982) offer five roles played by organizational members that serve to communicate messages and information. You will probably recognize individuals in your own organizational life that play many of these roles.

Storytellers. As previously noted, storytelling is a hallmark of organizational culture and an effective way to communicate important messages. For example, Thomas Watson Jr., son of IBM's founder, often told a story about a nature lover who liked to watch the wild ducks fly south in vast flocks each October. Out of charity, he took to putting feed for them in a nearby pond. After a while, some of the ducks no longer bothered to fly south; they wintered in the pond on what he fed them. In time, they flew less and less. After three to four years, they grew so fat and lazy that they found it difficult to fly at all. Watson always ended the story with the point that you can make wild ducks tame, but you can never make tame ducks wild again. He would say that at IBM, "we try not to tame them." Watson told this story again and again to impress upon people the value of deviance and tolerance for outlaw heroes in a company well known for conformity and standardization. To make the story even more powerful, one employee after hearing it, reminded Watson that "even wild ducks fly in formation" and that everyone in the company needed to be going the same direction. Many times there are retired leaders from the organization who have stories to tell but no one to listen. Always make an effort to listen to these stories because you might learn something.

Revered elders. These members tend to be older and more experienced members of the organization. There is a certain reverence and respect for these individuals. They can recite the history of the company and philosophical underpinnings to "why" the organization exists. Many of these people were around and worked with the founder or founders of the company. These people do not need to be senior managers; an administrative assistant who has been with the company longer than the CEO knows what it takes to survive.

Whisperers. These are the powers behind the throne. They are called whisperers because they have the ear of the CEO or senior managers and serve as trusted advisors. In George W. Bush's administration, Karl Rove is an excellent example of a whisperer. President Bush would take Rove's council so seriously that many dubbed him "Bush's brain." Many times when senior management changes, these people will be pushed out because they were too loyal to the previous administration.

Gossips. These individuals are not expected to be serious people and they are not always expected to get the news right. Even though gossips might not be accurate, many times their stories reflect the perception or "word on the street" as to how organizational members are reacting to a situation. These people tend to embellish stories, know how much money everyone makes, who is dating whom, and the real reason why the boss left the company (beyond the official memorandum that gets sent out!). Unlike whisperers they don't always have close proximity to power. Gossips can also be very destructive in the communication chain by distorting messages to their own advantage or by just stirring up trouble. However, skilled managers know that the gossips communicate information fast; therefore, managers can plant information with the gossips to get their own message out or combat an erroneous message that is circulating through the gossip chain.

Spies. These people are well-liked in the organization and have access to information across department boundaries. Spies are friendly to managers and can thus provide them with updates and information. There are obvious ethical concerns with using this communication channel. In 2007, Hewlett-Packard chairwoman Patricia Dunn acknowledged initiating an investigation to spy on other board members to determine the source of boardroom leaks to the news media. She subsequently resigned from the board and a private investigator was charged with conspiring to illegally obtain and transmit personal information on Hewlett-Packard directors, journalists, and employees. The news of the spying scandal rocked HP's well-known image as an ethical, transparent, employee centered company whose philosophy—known as the "HP way"—was legendary since its founding in 1938 by Bill Hewlett and Dave Packard.

(Adapted from: Deal, T., & Kennedy, A. (1982). *Corporate cultures: The rites and rituals of corporate life.* Menlo Park: Addison-Wesley Publishing Company, pp. 87–94)

ORGANIZATIONAL CULTURE AND PERFORMANCE

Is there a link between organizational culture and performance? Kotter and Heskett (1992) analyzed a variety of organizations and identified three elements of corporate cultures that enhance long-term economic performance:

> **Culture strength.** This is determined by goal alignment where employees focus efforts toward clearly established goals; strength is also

determined by shared values and behaviors which tend to boost intrinsic motivation; and culture strength impacts performance because organizational members don't rely on creative-killing bureaucracies to manage employees. Instead, cultural values guide employee behavior.

Strategic fit. Because a one-size-fits-all "winning" culture doesn't exist, organizations must find an appropriate match or "fit" between the values and behaviors that are needed to support the goals and needs of the organization. This fit is as important, if not more important, than the strength of the culture. The researchers put it this way:

> a culture characterized by rapid decision making and no bureaucratic behavior will enhance performance in the highly competitive deal-making environment of a mergers and acquisitions advisory firm but might hurt performance in a traditional life insurance company. Likewise, a culture in which managers place a very high value on excellent technology might help a computer manufacturer but would be inappropriate for a symphony orchestra . . . A culture in which people value stable and hierarchical structures might work well in a slow-moving environment but be totally inappropriate in a very fast-moving competitive industry (Kotter & Heskett, 1992, p. 29).

Adaptability to change. Organizations that achieve long-term results are able to anticipate and adapt to environmental change. Kotter and Heskett argue that three environmental factors managers must consider when leading change are: stockholders, customers, and employees. They found that "In the firms with more adaptive cultures, the cultural ideal is that managers throughout the hierarchy should provide leadership to initiate change in strategies and tactics whenever necessary to satisfy the legitimate interests of not just stockholders, or customers, or employees, but all three" (Kotter & Heskett, 1992, p. 50). This is because managers that care about stockholders will strive to get financial results over time, and to do this they must take care of their customers and this is only possible when they care for those who serve the customers—employees.

Cameron and Freeman (1991) found that culture "type" was related to organizational effectiveness. Their research reveals four types of cultures: clan, adhocracy, hierarchy, and market (see figure 14-1).

ORGANIC PROCESSES

TYPE: Clan
DOMINANT ATTRIBUTES: Cohesiveness,
   participation, teamwork, sense of family
LEADER STYLE: Mentor, facilitator,
   parent-figure
BONDING: Loyalty, tradition, interpersonal
   cohesion
STRATEGIC EMPHASES: Toward developing
   human resources, commitment, morale

TYPE: Adhocracy
DOMINANT ATTRIBUTES: Creativity
   entrepreneurship, adaptability, dynamism
LEADER STYLE: Entrepreneur, innovator,
   risk taker
BONDING: Entrepreneurship, flexibility,
   risk
STRATEGIC EMPHASES: Toward innovation,
   growth, new resources

INTERNAL MAINTENANCE ------------------------------------ EXTERNAL POSITIONING

TYPE: Hierarchy
DOMINANT ATTRIBUTES: Order, rules and
   regulations, uniformity, efficiency
LEADER STYLE: Coordinator, organizer,
   administrator
BONDING: Rules, policies and procedures,
   clear expectations
STRATEGIC EMPHASES: Toward stability,
   predictability, smooth operations

TYPE: Market
DOMINANT ATTRIBUTES: Competitiveness,
   goal achievement, environment exchange
LEADER STYLE: Decisive, production- and
   achievement-oriented
BONDING: Goal orientation, production,
   competition
STRATEGIC EMPHASES: Toward competitive
   advantage and market superiority

MECHANISTIC PROCESSES

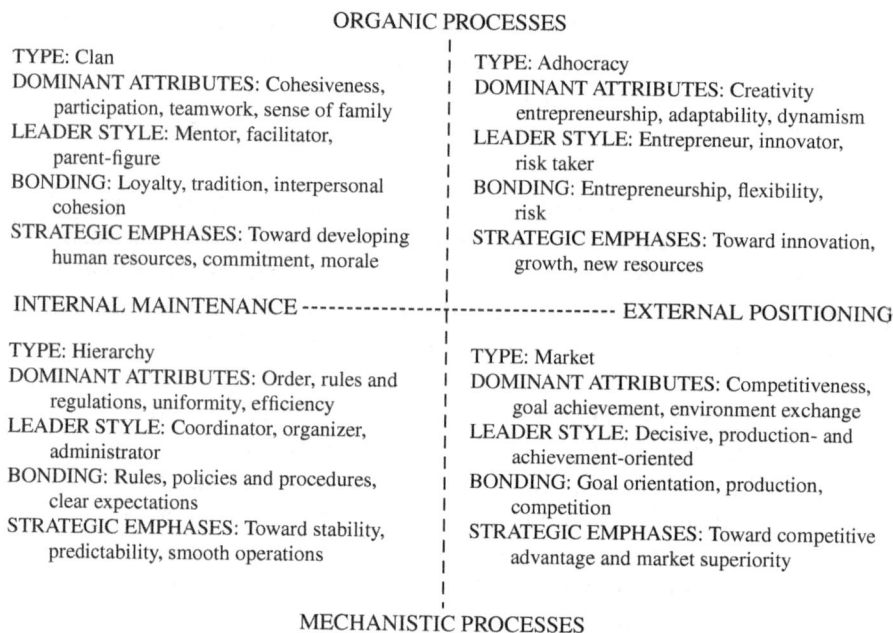

FIGURE 14-1 A Model of Cultural Congruence for Organizations

Reprinted from *Research in Organizational Change and Development* (1991), by permission of the authors.

It is important to note that *all* institutions possess attributes of several culture types; but organizations also can have a clearly dominant culture. The study just referenced was of educational institutions and the dominant characteristics of each culture predicted the organization's greatest level of effectiveness. For example, clan cultures were more effective than the others on dimensions related to morale and human resource concerns. Adhocracy cultures were more effective on dimensions related to the external environment and academic quality. Market cultures scored highest on the ability to acquire resources while hierarchy cultures did not score highest on any of the measured dimensions (this may be because the areas emphasized by these cultures were not part of the study's methodology). Cameron and Freeman suggest that their findings can be used by organizational leaders to assess and manage contradictory or paradoxical impulses from the presence of more than one culture type in an organization. Managers can also use the typology of clan, adhocracy, market, and hierarchical cultures, to successfully diagnose and facilitate change initiatives. For example, articulating a vision that contradicts the culture may lead to resistance and lack of direction that can derail change efforts. Finally, managers may want to capitalize on criteria of effectiveness that are consistent with their dominant cultures to build on organizational strengths.

Can Organizational Cultures be Changed to Enhance Economic Performance?

The answer to the question above is: Yes. Leaders can take specific actions to institutionalize a new vision and set of strategies in a culture (see Figure 14-2).

Kotter and Heskett (1992) studied ten successful cases of cultural change and identified common practices.

1. Hundreds of individuals initiated thousands of actions, all working within some general framework provided by more senior level leaders.

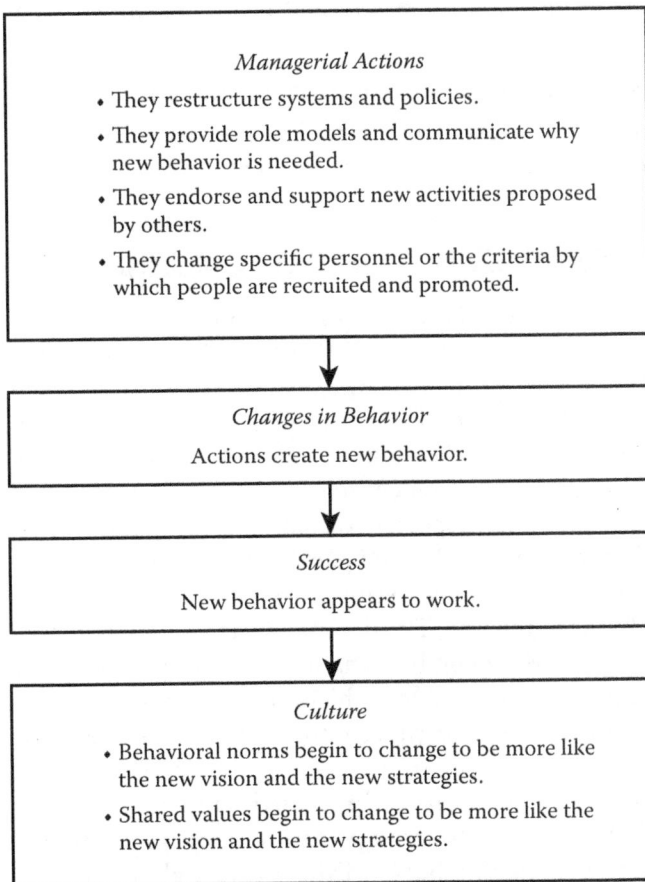

Managerial Actions

- They restructure systems and policies.
- They provide role models and communicate why new behavior is needed.
- They endorse and support new activities proposed by others.
- They change specific personnel or the criteria by which people are recruited and promoted.

↓

Changes in Behavior

Actions create new behavior.

↓

Success

New behavior appears to work.

↓

Culture

- Behavioral norms begin to change to be more like the new vision and the new strategies.
- Shared values begin to change to be more like the new vision and the new strategies.

FIGURE 14-2 Institutionalizing in a Culture a New Vision and a New Set of Business Strategies

Reprinted from *Corporate Culture and Performance* (1992), by permission of Simon & Schuster, Inc.

2. Specific emphasis was placed on changing people's behaviors.

3. People reorganized, often cutting levels and decentralizing responsibility, to put managers close to customers and to make employees more accountable for profits.

4. Managers were replaced by individuals whose values were more consistent with the culture they desired. Many of these managers were identified from business units that already had the healthiest and most adaptive cultures.

5. Leaders moved purposefully, without wasting time, and produced substantial positive results within the first two years. This was critical as early results created momentum to sustain the overall culture change.

6. Major cultural change took a while—more than two years.

7. Finally, and most fundamentally, the criteria used in selection and promotion decisions were changed to reflect the desired culture.

CULTURE CHANGE: THE CASE OF GM AND NUMMI

In the early 1980s, General Motors Company and Toyota Motor Corporation formed a partnership to operate GM's automobile manufacturing plant in Fremont, California. The partnership became known as New United Motor Manufacturing, Inc. or NUMMI. GM's Fremont plant was long considered the most dysfunctional plant within all of GM. It had a reputation for frequent strikes, routine absenteeism of over 20%, excessive grievances, and employees were even suspected of sabotaging quality. GM had three objectives in forming the NUMMI partnership. First, it didn't know how to make a small car profitably. Second, it wanted to put an idle plant and workforce back on the line. Third, it had heard about Toyota's production system, and NUMMI would be a chance to see it up close. For Toyota, they were facing pressure to produce vehicles in the United States, but Toyota's main goal was more about learning, rather than other more tangible business objectives.

John Shook, an industrial anthropologist and business consultant, was tasked with developing a training program to introduce the Toyota system to the American employees of NUMMI. Surprisingly, rather than the union and workers rejecting the Toyota way, they accepted and even *embraced* it with passion. Shook says, "The absenteeism that had regularly reached 20% or more? It immediately fell to a steady 2%. The quality that had been GM's worst? In just one year, it became GM's best. All with the exact same workers, including the old troublemakers. The only thing that had changed was the production and management system—and, somehow, the culture" (Shook, 2010, p. 64). So, how did this happen? Shook notes that traditional conceptualizations of culture change involve, first, changing how people think. He argues that this is the wrong approach. Instead, start by changing how people behave. "Those of us trying to change our organizations' culture need to define the things we want to do, the ways we want to behave and want each other to behave, to provide training and then to do what is necessary to reinforce those behaviors. The culture will change as a result" (Shook, 2010, p. 66). The figure below represents old and new versions of culture change.

The best example of changing behavior in order to change how people think is the introduction of the famous stop-the-line system (also known as *andon*) on the assembly line at NUMMI. This system allows an individual to stop the assembly line whenever they find a problem. First, all GM and NUMMI employees went through extensive training on the philosophy of the stop-the-line system (i.e., building quality into every process), precisely what is expected of each employee on the job, what to do when employees see a problem on the line, and exactly what will happen when an employee notifies the team leader of a problem. Shook notes that there was skepticism among some GM managers on implementing the *andon* process. Some questioned the wisdom by saying, "You intend to give these workers the right to stop the line?" Toyota managers responded: "No, we intend to give them the obligation to stop it—whenever they find a problem."

HOW CULTURE CHANGES – AND DOESN'T

The lessons from NUMMI are consistent with organizational development leader Edgar Schein's model of corporate culture. Schein proposed that the way to change culture is to change cultural artifacts—the observable data of an organization which include what people do and how they behave. *Anyone wanting to change a culture needs to define the actions and behaviors they desire, then design the work processes that are necessary to reinforce those behaviors.*

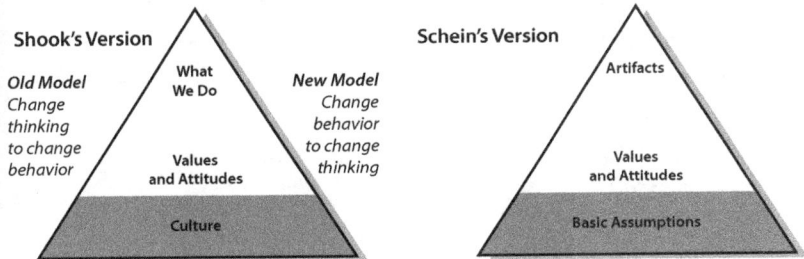

Shook's Version

Old Model Change thinking to change behavior

What We Do

Values and Attitudes

Culture

New Model Change behavior to change thinking

Schein's Version

Artifacts

Values and Attitudes

Basic Assumptions

Reprinted from "How to Change a Culture: Lessons from NUMMI," *MIT Sloan Management Review* 51, no. 2 (2010).

Shook summarizes how the Fremont plant changed by saying, "What changed the culture at NUMMI wasn't an abstract notion of 'employee involvement' or 'a learning organization' or even 'culture' at all. What changed the culture was giving employees the means by which they could

? What Do You Think?

Where might I/we improve in these areas? Think about: inspiration, culture hallmarks, use of symbols, ritual and ceremony, incorporating company history, heroes, clarifying core ideology, integration of values and mission into decision making, using self as symbol (modeling leadership), what sets us apart and makes us special compared to the competition?

_____

_____

_____

_____

_____

_____

_____

_____

_____

Are culture issues getting in the way of our performance? Think about: nonexistent or empty rituals and ceremonies, confusion regarding core values/mission, lack of meaning or significance beyond a paycheck, etc.

_____

_____

_____

_____

_____

_____

_____

_____

_____

successfully do their jobs. It was communicating clearly to employees what their jobs were and providing the training and tools to enable them to perform those jobs successfully" (Shook, 2010, p. 68). These changes allowed a powerful culture shift in how employees were viewed and treated by managers, and how the organization as a whole practiced continuous improvement by learning from mistakes on the job. Anyone in a supervisory position at NUMMI visited Toyota City in Japan for two or more weeks of training. At the end of each training tour, supervisors were asked what they would most want to take back with them to Fremont from all they had learned at Toyota. Shook notes that the answers were invariably the same: "The ability to focus on problem solving without pointing fingers and looking to place blame on someone. Here it's 'five whys' [which means simply asking "why?" until reaching the root cause of any problem]. Back home, we're used to the 'five whos'" (Shook, 2010, p. 68).

Questions for Review

1. What are some examples of organizational communication?
2. What five roles are played by organizational members in communicating messages and information? Provide examples for each role.
3. What three elements of corporate culture enhance long-term economic performance?
4. How is culture type related to organizational effectiveness? According to Cameron and Freeman (1991), what are the four types of cultures in organizations?
5. What common practices are present in successful culture change initiatives? What is the role of the leader?
6. Why was the culture change at NUMMI successful?

FOUR REQUIRED VIRTUES OF LEADERS

In addition to the skills, concepts, and practices discussed in this book, I'd like to conclude with a brief discussion of four virtues. When scholars profess that leaders must have character, an audience will invariably cheer and nod collectively with approval. But what exactly is character? Character is defined as a collection of virtues and the cardinal virtues—*prudence, justice, fortitude*, and *temperance*—have resonated for over two millennia. The cardinal virtues challenge human beings to attain the furthest potentialities of our nature. Pop psychology and cultural fads offer simplistic, transitory slogans on how to live one's life; however, this advice falls short because it lacks substance and permanence. The cardinal virtues have stood the test of time, appearing first in the writings of the ancient Greeks and Romans. They were then interpreted and applied within Judaism and Christianity. And they continue to be a source of inspiration, contemplation, and instruction in modern times. The word "cardinal" derives from the Latin word *cardo*, which means "a hinge." In this way, the cardinal virtues are the "hinge" upon which all of the other moral virtues depend.

Great leaders illuminate each of the cardinal virtues. This light influences the attitudes, thoughts, and actions of countless others now and into the future. This is a leader's greatest legacy. It is the pursuit of these virtues that matter because none of us can live up to them at all times. However, as a lighthouse guides a ship through stormy waters, the cardinal virtues call out and compel our attention and action. I am indebted to the work of Josef Pieper (1966) and his book *The Four Cardinal Virtues*. I have borrowed liberally from his ideas and used them as a springboard for my own interpretations.

CHAPTER 15:
The Cardinal Virtues: Prudence, Justice, Fortitude, and Temperance

LEARNING OBJECTIVES

After studying this chapter, you should be able to:

1. Identify and discuss the cardinal virtues.
2. Demonstrate how the cardinal virtues are related to leadership.

PRUDENCE

Prudence is known as the "charioteer of the virtues" because it guides the other virtues. "None but the prudent man can be just, brave, and temperate, and the good man is good in so far as he is prudent" (Pieper, 1966, p. 3). Prudence guides one's judgment and directs conduct in accordance with wisdom. Prudence is both the realization of the good and the courage to make right decisions. Prudent behavior probes for the truth in every situation—even if this truth is uncomfortable. The prudent leader makes a decision only after a period of discernment, evaluation, and the input of wise counsel. The prudent leader doesn't make decisions rashly or emotionally. As Pieper (1966) says:

> Prudence, then, is the mold and mother of all virtues, the circumspect and resolute shaping power of our minds which transforms knowledge of reality into realization of the good. It holds within itself the humility of silent, that is to say, of unbiased perception; the trueness-to-being of memory; the art of receiving counsel; alert, composed readiness for the unexpected. Prudence means the studied seriousness and, as it were, the filter of deliberation, and at the same time the brave boldness to make final decisions. It means purity, straightforwardness, candor, and simplicity of character; it means standing superior to the utilitarian complexities of mere "tactics" (p. 22).

Prudence is not shrewdness. It isn't focused on scheming or political calculations to determine the "right" answer. Instead, prudence requires moral action. Moral action is the fusion of cognition and will. It is not enough to simply want to do good works. Instead, prudent decisions require a true understanding and evaluation of the concrete reality in each given situation. Being cognizant of the situation and the right course of action then "clears the way for truth, so that truth can imprint upon will and action the seal of justness to the nature of things" (Pieper, 1966, p. 35). In other words, the good leader will create space for the truth of a given situation to emerge, and then armed with this newfound clarity, the leader will act. As I mentioned in the preface of this book, reflection without action is folly; action without reflection is dangerous.

JUSTICE

"Evil and suffering in our world have many names, but primarily that of 'injustice'" (Pieper, 1966, p. 43). Justice has more interpretations and definitions than any of the other cardinal virtues. Essentially, justice is the notion that each person is to be given what is his or her due. Therefore, injustice occurs when what rightfully belongs to a person is withheld or taken away. What is "due" another person can come from an agreement, treaty, promise, or legal decision. Also, just acts do not violate fundamental principles such as life and liberty. Justice demands that one person recognizes the other person as a separate human being who nevertheless is owed his or her due. In this way, justice is distinct from love because justice means giving to another person what is rightfully his even when love does not exist between the parties. Justice is an external act because the justice of an act can be judged by outsiders. "In the realm of justice good and evil are judged purely on the basis of the deed itself, regardless of the inner disposition of the doer; the point is not how the deed accords with the doer, but rather how it affects 'the other person'" (Pieper, 1966, p. 61). Along with external acts, the internal dimensions of a leader are also relevant. For example, one can imitate the actions of just people, but only the just person will derive pleasure from such actions.

Scholars have ranked the four cardinal virtues to answer the question: what makes a person fundamentally good and honorable? Justice ranks higher than fortitude and temperance because it reaches out beyond the individual and affects others. Quoting Aristotle's *Nicomachean Ethics*, Pieper demonstrates, "For as that man is utterly evil who allows his wickedness to hold sway not only over himself but over his friends as well; so is that man most utterly good who not only uses his goodness for himself but for others, too" (p. 65).

FORTITUDE

Reflecting on his life experiences, author Thomas McGuane says, "At our age you sort of accumulate a lot of scar tissue and the cold wind of the world just blows over your head" (McGrath, 2010, C1). Fortitude is expressed through acts of courage; however, fortitude emanates from goodness rather than brazen demonstrations of machismo—which is a caricature of courage. Fortitude must be guided by prudence which is the wisdom to know when and how to fight. Being fearless is not an expression of fortitude. "Fortitude presupposes in a certain sense that man is afraid of evil; its essence lies not in knowing no fear, but in not allowing oneself to be forced into evil by fear, or to be kept by fear from the realization of good" (Pieper, 1966, p. 126). Therefore, fighting to advance or preserve what is good by facing the threat of injury with grace and dignity marks the truly brave person.

As Josef Pieper frames the discussion, the practice of fortitude involves both *endurance* and *attack*. Because acts of courage require risk and the patience to endure a protracted struggle, in some situations endurance through suffering is the only possible form of resistance. Only in these times does the innermost and deepest strength of a person become revealed. The tremendous suffering endured by figures like Martin Luther King Jr. and Mahatma Gandhi are heroic demonstrations of fortitude that required endurance just as much as attack. Paraphrasing Thomas Aquinas, Pieper says, "Enduring comprises a strong activity of the soul, namely, a vigorous grasping of and clinging to the good; and only from this stout-hearted activity can the strength to support the physical and spiritual suffering of injury and death be nourished" (p. 128). During times of adversity and struggle, leaders must remain patient and remind their followers to do the same. Patience radiates hope, integrity, and the cheerful acceptance of all life's hardships. This is certainly a tall order to accept, let alone practice, but the cardinal virtues draw out the best in a person so the lesser impulses of our nature can be restrained.

However, fortitude also involves a willingness to fight. This means—with the guidance of prudence—one's passions (including anger) can be channeled to combat injustice through courage, self-confidence, and hope of success. Many times this requires a person to first attack those things within him or herself that need to be changed. Fortitude awakens within a person their strengths and weaknesses. The great leader enthusiastically embraces self-knowledge in an effort to leverage one's talents and honestly confront one's weaknesses. Self-awareness should disturb rather than give solace. Unfortunately, too often people will fill their days with activities in order to avoid deeper questions concerning who one is—or is becoming. But as Plato exhorts, "The first and best victory is to conquer self."

TEMPERANCE

Western movies warn that there are two types of people: the quick and the dead. However, in reality, sometimes those who hesitate are *saved*. The absence of restraint and self-control in many of today's leaders is often front page news. Anthony Weiner, Eliot Spitzer, Jeffrey Skilling, and Kenneth Lay were all talented leaders that failed the test of temperance. However, temperance goes beyond moderation or simply "temperateness in eating and drinking." The Greek origin of the word temperance means "directing reason" and the Latin *temperare* implies organizing various parts into one unified whole. In other words, temperance creates an inner order from which a person can experience serenity and harmony. Anything that complicates or disrupts this "inner order" in a person's life runs counter to temperance. In this sense, temperance does not deny pleasure; rather temperance is the fullest embodiment and expression of joy and peace.

What does temperance organize and direct? It channels our passions and desires. Passion and desire can serve to motivate and mobilize others to act. However, intemperate anger is contrary to the inner order just described as the cornerstone of temperance. Blind wrath, bitterness of spirit, and revengeful resentment oppose virtuous action. Instead, "temperate passion" is achieved through gentleness. This may seem paradoxical, but gentleness as a virtue doesn't weaken one's power. Instead, it signifies mastery of one's passions. Gentleness actually *strengthens* our ability to influence others. Witnessing temperance in others, or experiencing it in one's own self, engenders beauty and serves as a source of inspiration. In this sense, beauty is "the glow of the true and the good irradiating from every ordered state of being" (Pieper, 1966, p. 203). This gentleness of spirit fuses leader and follower together as a calming force for good.

Questions for Review

1. What are the cardinal virtues? Building on the ideas in this chapter, discuss each virtue in your own words.
2. How are the cardinal virtues related to leadership?

A PARTING STORY

There is an apocryphal story about a meeting between Henry David Thoreau and Ralph Waldo Emerson. In 1846, Thoreau was in jail for refusing to pay a poll tax. He felt justified in not paying the tax as a matter of principle because of the government's support of slavery and engagement in the Mexican War. When Emerson arrived at the jail, he asked, "What are you doing in here?" Thoreau replied, "What are you doing out there?"

The true measure of a leader is how one's actions impact the real world—"out there." In the spirit of Thoreau, what are *you* doing *out there*?

References

Adler, M. (1978). *Aristotle for everybody.* New York: Touchstone.

Ariely, D. (2012, May 26–27). Why we lie. *The Wall Street Journal,* p. C1.

Augustine, N. (2011, September 21). The education our economy needs. *The Wall Street Journal,* p. A17.

Avolio, B. (2005). *Leadership development in balance.* Mahwah, New Jersey: L. Erlbaum.

Badaracco, J. (1997). *Defining moments: When managers must choose between right and right.* Boston: Harvard Business School Press.

Bass, B. (1985). *Leadership and performance beyond expectation.* New York: The Free Press.

Bass, B. (1990). *Bass & Stogdill's handbook of leadership: Theory, research, and managerial applications.* New York: The Free Press.

Bass, B., & Avolio, B. (2000). *MLQ: Multifactor leadership questionnaire (2nd ed.).* Redwood City, CA: Mind Garden.

Bass, B., & Riggio, R. (2006). *Transformational leadership.* New Jersey: L. Erlbaum Associates.

Bennis, W. (2003). *On becoming a leader.* Cambridge, MA: Perseus Publishing.

Bennis, W., & Goldsmith, J. (2003). *Learning to lead.* New York: Basic Books.

Bennis, W., & Nanus, B. (2003). *Leaders: Strategies for taking charge.* New York: HarperCollins.

Bennis, W., Golemen, D., & Biederman, P. (2008). Creating a culture of candor. In W. Bennis, Goleman, & J. O'toole, *Transparency* (pp. 1–43). San Francisco: Jossey-Bass.

Bergmann, D. (1969). The original confidence man. *American Quarterly, 21*(3), 550–577.

Berns, L. (1987). In L. Strauss, & J. Cropsey, *History of political philosophy.* Chicago: The University of Chicago Press.

Birkinshaw, J., Bouquet, C., & Barsoux, J. (2011). The 5 myths of innovation. *MIT Sloan Management Review, 52*(2), 43–50.

Bloom, A. (1991). *The republic of plato.* New York: Basic Books.

Bolman, L., & Deal, T. (2008). *Reframing organizations.* San Francisco: Jossey-Bass.

Bridges, W. (2004). *Transitions: Making sense of life's changes.* Cambridge: Da Capo Press.

Brooks, D. (2010, May 25). Two theories of change. *New York Times,* p. A27.

Buckingham, M., & Clifton, D. (2001). *Now, discover your strengths.* New York: The Free Press.

Burns, J. (1978). *Leadership.* New York: Harper & Row.

Calmes, J. (2011, January 21). In Sperling, A political strategist known for getting it done. *New York Times,* p. B1.

Cameron, K., & Freeman, S. (1991). Cultural congruence, strength, and type: Relationships to effectiveness. *Research in Organizational Change and Development, 5,* 23–58.

Campbell, J. (1949). *The hero with a thousand faces.* Pantheon Publishers.

Carey, B. (2010, November 2). Cede political turf? never! well, maybe. *New York Times,* pp. Science, 1.

Carlyle, T. (1993). *On heroes, hero-worship & the heroic in history.* University of California Press.

Carr, N. (2010, June 5). Does the internet make you dumber? *The Wall Street Journal,* p. W1.

Carroll, J. (2006, October 9). *This I Believe.* Retrieved August 25, 2011, from National Public Radio: http://www.npr.org/templates/story/story.php?storyId=6196795

Cialdini, R., & Rhoads, K. (2001, Fall). Human behavior and the marketplace. *Marketing Research,* 9–13.

Cohen, N. (2011, August 29). In unsettled times, media can be a call to action, or a distraction. *New York Times,* p. B3.

Collins, J. (2005, July-August). Level 5 leadership: The triumph of humility and fierce resolve. *Harvard Business Review.*

Collins, J., & Porras, J. (1994). *Built to last: Successful habits of visionary companies.* New York: HarperCollins Publishers.

Coutu, D. (2009, May). Why teams don't work. *Harvard Business Review, 87*(5), 98–105.

Darley, J., & Batson, C. (1973). "From jerusalem to jericho": A study of situational and dispositional variables in helping behaviors. *Journal of Personality and Social Psychology, 27*(1), 100–108.

Dash, E. (2011, September 30). The lucrative fall from grace. *New York Times,* p. B1; B4.

Deal, T., & Kennedy, A. (1982). *Corporate cultures: The rites and rituals of corporate life.* Menlo Park: Addison-Wesley Publishing Company.

Desberg, P. (1996). *No more butterflies: Overcoming stagefright, shyness, interview anxiety, and fear of public speaking.* New Harbinger, Inc.

Dirks, K., & Ferrin, D. (2002). Trust in leadership: Meta-analytic findings and implications for research and practice. *Journal of Applied Psychology, 87*(4), 611–628.

Esse, A. (2012). Leading change through storytelling. *Strategic Communication Management,* 30–31.

Fackler, M. (2011, August 30). Japanese finance minister chosen by party as next premier. *New York Times,* p. A10.

Falbe, C., & Yukl, G. (1992). Consequences for managers of using single influence tactics and combinations of tactics. *Academy of Management Journal, 35*(3), 638–652.

Fiedler, F. (1967). *A theory of leadership effectiveness.* New York: McGraw Hill.

Fields, D. (2007). Determinants of follower perceptions of a leader's authenticity and integrity. *European Management Journal, 25*(3), 195–206.

French, J., & Raven, B. (1959). The bases of social power. In D. Cartwright, *Studies in social power* (pp. 150–167). Ann Arbor: The University of Michigan.

Gardner, J. (1990). *On leadership.* New York, NY: The Free Press.

Gardner, W., Avolio, B., Luthens, F., May, D., & Walumbwa, F. (2005). "Can you see the real me?" A self-based model of authentic leader and follower development. *The Leadership Quarterly, 16,* 343–372.

George, B. (2003). *Authentic leadership: Rediscovering the secrets to creating lasting value.* San Francisco, CA: Jossey-Bass.

George, B. (2004, Winter). The journey to authenticity. *Leader to Leader, 31,* 29–35.

Gergen, D. (2003). How presidents persuade. *Harvard Business Review, 81*(1), 20–21.

Gilbert, D. (2012, January-February). The science behind the smile. *Harvard Business Review,* 85–90.

Gino, F., & Pisano, G. (2011, April). Why leaders don't learn from success. *Harvard Business Review,* 69–74.

Goleman, D. (2000, March-April). Leadership that get's results. *Harvard Business Review,* 78–90.

Goleman, D., & Boyatzis, R. (2008, September). Social intelligence and the biology of leadership. *Harvard Business Review,* 74–81.

Golman, D., Boyatzis, R., & McKee, A. (2002). *Primal leadership: Realizing the power of emotional intelligence.* Boston, MA: Harvard Business School Press.

Greenhouse, S. (2011, September 5). Losing billions, postal service is near default. *New York Times,* p. A1.

Greenleaf, R. (1991). *The servant as leader.* IN: The Robert K. Greanleaf Center.

Greenleaf, R. (2002). *Servant leadership: A journey into the nature of legitimate power and greatness.* Mahwah, New Jersey: Paulist Press.

Harter, J., Schmidt, F., & Hayes, T. (2002). Business-unit-level relationship between employee satisfaction, employee engagement, and business outcomes: A meta-analysis. *Journal of Applied Psychology, 87*(2), 268–279.

Heifetz, R. (1994). *Leadership without easy answers.* Cambridge: The Belknap Press of Harvard University Press.

Heiligman, D. (2009, January 29). A marriage of science and religion. *Los Angeles Times,* p. A19.

Hernandez, S., & Hardesty, G. (2006, September 15). 'Freaking' inspires dance ban. *Orange County Register.*

Hersey, P., & Blanchard, K. (1993). *Management of organizational behavior.* Englewood Cliffs: Prentice Hall.

Herzberg, F. (1966). *Work and the nature of man.* New York: Thomas Y. Crowell.

Hiltzik, M. (2011, September 4). Lessons from a life as a manager. *Los Angeles Times,* p. B7.

Hobbes, T. (1962). *Leviathan.* New York: Collier Books.

Holmes, E., & Lublin, J. S. (2011, June 15). Penney picks boss from apple. *The Wall Street Journal,* pp. A1, A12.

Hsu, T. (2010, January 6). Satisfied at work? It's a rare benefit. *Los Angeles Times.*

Irvine, W. (2009). *A guide to the good life: The ancient art of stoic joy.* New York: Oxford University Press, Inc.

Isaacson, W. (2007). *Einstein: His life and universe.* New York: Simon & Schuster.

Jackson, J. (2006). *Organization development: The human and social dynamics of organizational change.* Lanham: University Press of America, Inc.

Jacobellis v. Ohio, 378 US 184 (The Supreme Court 1964).

Janis, I. (1971, November). Groupthink: The desperate drive for consensus at any cost that suppresses dissent among the mighty in the corridors of power. *Psychology Today,* 43–46, 74–76.

Janis, I., & Mann, L. (1977). *Decision Making: A psychological analysis of conflict, choice, and commitment.* New York: The Free Press.

Jordan, M. (2011, July 26). White-minority wealth gulf widens. *The Wall Street Journal,* p. A6.

Judge, T., Bono, J, Thoresen, C., & Patton, G. (2001). The job satisfaction-job performance relationship: A qualitative and quantitative review. *Psychological Bulletin, 127*(3), 376–407.

Katzenbach, J., & Smith, D. (2003). *The wisdom of teams: Creating the high-performance organization.* New York: HarperBusiness.

Kellerman, B. (2004). *Bad leadership.* Boston, MA: Harvard Business School Press.

Kellerman, B. (2008). *Followership.* Boston, MA: Harvard Business School Press.

Kelley, R. (2008). Rethinking followership. In R. Riggio, I. Chaleff, & J. Lipman-Blumen, *The art of followership: How great followers make great leaders and organizations* (pp. 5–15). San Francisco, CA: Jossey-Bass.

Keyton, J. (2005). *Communication & organizational culture.* Thousand Oaks: Sage Publications, Inc.

Kidder, R. (2009). *How good people make tough choices: Resolving the dilemmas of ethical living.* New York: HarperCollins.

Kilmann, R., & Thomas, K. (1977). Developing a forced-choice measure of conflict-handling behavior: The "mode" instrument. *Educational and Psychological Measurement, 37,* 309–325.

Kirkpatrick, S., & Locke, E. (1991). Leadership: Do traits matter? *Academy of Management, 5*(2), 48–60.

Kotter, J. (1990, May–June). What leaders really do. *Harvard Business Review, 68*(3), 103.

Kotter, J. (1997, January). Leading change: Why transformation efforts fail. *Harvard Business Review,* 96–103.

Kotter, J., & Heskett, J. (1992). *Corporate culture and performance.* New York: Free Press.

Kotter, J., & Schlesinger, L. (1979). Choosing strategies for change. *Harvard Business Review, 57*(2), 106–114.

Kouzes, J., & Posner, B. (2007). *The leadership challenge.* San Francisco, CA: Jossey-Bass.

Kramer, & R. (2009, June). Rethinking trust. *Harvard Business Review,* 69–77.

Lansing, A. (1999). *Endurance: Shackleton's Incredible Voyage.* Wheaton: Tyndale House Publishers.

Lazarus, D. (2008, December 17). Falling prices have appeal to those with stagnant pay. *Los Angeles Times.*

Lencioni, P. (2002). *The five dysfunctions of a team.* San Francisco: Jossey-Bass.

Lewicki, R., McAllister, D., & Bies, R. (1998). Trust and distrust: New relationships and realities. *Academy of Management Review, 23*(3), 438–458.

Lewis, M. (2000). Exploring paradox: Toward a more comprehensive guide. *Academy of Management Review, 25*(4), 760–776.

Lifsher, M. (2009, February 9). CalPERS to push reform, oversight. *Los Angeles Times*, p. C1.

Locke, J. (1988). *Two treatises of government.* Cambridge: Cambridge University Press.

Mansfield, H. (1985). *The prince.* Chicago: The University of Chicago Press.

Marciano, P. (2010). *Carrots and sticks don't work.* New York: McGraw Hill.

Maslow, A. (1954). *Motivation and personality.* New York: Harper & Brothers.

Maslow, A. (1970). *Motivation and personality* (2nd ed.). New York: Harper & Row.

McClelland, D., & Burnham, D. (2003, January). Power is the great motivator. *Harvard Business Review*, 117–126.

McGrath, C. (2010, October 21). An author still writing his way through big sky country. *New York Times*, p. C1.

McGregor, D. (1960). *The human side of enterprise.* New York: McGraw Hill.

Middleton, D. (2011, January 6). Schools give firms say amid though jobs market. *The Wall Street Journal*, p. B9.

Mintzberg, H. (1980). *The nature of managerial work.* Englewood Cliffs, New Jersey: Prentice-Hall, Inc.

Musa, M. (1995). *The portable dante.* New York: Penguin Group.

Naik, G. (2012, January 19). New insight into aging brains. *Wall Street Journal*, p. A3.

Nelson, B. (2002). Dump the cash, load on the praise. *Nelson Motivation, Inc.*

Pae, P. (2009, July 5). Quietly in command. *Los Angeles Times*, p. B1.

Pakaluk, M. (2005). *Aristotle's nicomachean ethics.* New York: Cambridge University Press.

Palanski, M., & Yammarino, F. (2007). Integrity and leadership: Clearing the conceptual confusion. *European Management Journal, 25*(3), 171–184.

Palanski, M., & Yammarino, F. (2009). Integrity and leadership: A multi-level conceptual framework. *The Leadership Quarterly, 20*, 405–420.

Palmer, P. (1998). *The courage to teach.* San Francisco: Jossey-Bass.

Peck, M. (1987). *The different drum.* New York: Simon and Schuster.

Perry, T. (2009, February 9). Out of the in-n-out loop. *Los Angeles Times,* p. B3.

Peterson, D. (2004). Perceived leader integrity and ethical intentions of subordinates. *The Leadership and Organization Journal, 25*(1), 7–23.

Pew Research Center's Internet & American Life Project. (2011). *Teens, kindness and cruelty on social network sites.* Washington, DC: Author.

Pfeffer, J. (2010, July-August). Power play. *Harvard Business Review,* 85–92.

Pieper, J. (1966). *The four cardinal virtues.* Notre Dame: University of Notre Dame Press.

Pink, D. (2006). *A whole new mind: Why right-brainers will rule the future.* New York: Riverhead Books.

Pink, D. (2009). *Drive: The surprising truth about what motivates us.* New York: Riverhead Books.

Porter, L. (1962). Job attitudes in management: Perceived deficiencies in need fulfillment as a function of job level. *Journal of Applied Psychology, 46*(6), 375–384.

Pullias, E., & Young, J. (1968). *A teacher is many things.* Bloomington, Indiana: Indiana University Press.

Richtel, M. (2010, November 21). Growing up digital, wired for distraction. *New York Times.*

Rivera, C. (2011, August 9). Cal state panel studies salary cap for campus presidents. *Los Angeles Times.*

Robertson, I., & Cooper, C. (2010). Full engagement: The integration of employee engagement and psychological well-being. *Leadership & Organization Development Journal, 31*(4), 324–336.

Roselli, M. (2004, September 30). *Kerry discusses $87 billion comment.* Retrieved September 4, 2011, from CNN.com: http://www.cnn.com/2004/ALLPOLITICS/09/30/kerry.comment/

Rost, J. (1991). *Leadership for the twenty-first century.* New York: Praeger Publishers.

Rothenberg, A. (1979). *The emerging goddess.* The University of Chicago Press.

Rousseau, D., Sitkin, S., Burt, R., & Camerer, C. (1998). Not so different after all: A cross-discipline view of trust. *Academy of Management Review, 23,* 393–404.

Schama, S. (1999). *Rembrandt's Eyes.* New York: Alfred A Knopf.

Schein, E. (1996, June). Culture: The missing concept in organization studies. *Administrative Science Quarterly, 41,* 229–240.

Schein, E. (2010). *Organizatinal culture and leadership.* San Francisco: Jossey-Bass.

Sendjaya, S., & Pekerti, A. (2010). Servant leadership as antecedent of trust in organizations. *Leadership & Organization Development Journal, 31*(7), 643–663.

Shook, J. (2010). How to change a culture: Lessons from NUMMI. *MIT Sloan Management Review, 51*(2), 63–68.

Silverman, R. (2012, February 14). Where's the boss? Trapped in a meeting. *The Wall Street Journal.*

Simons, T. (2002). Behavioral integrity: The perceived alignment between managers' words and deeds as a research focus. *Organization Science, 13*(1), 18–35.

Smith, A. (1976). *The wealth of nations.* Chicago: The University of Chicago Press.

Solomon, R., & Flores, F. (2001). *Building trust in business, politics, relationships, and life.* New York: Oxford University Press.

Spears, L. (1998). *The power of servant leadership.* CA: Berrett-Koehler.

Spreitzer, G., & Porath, C. (2012, January-February). Creating sustainable performance. *Harvard Business Review,* 93–99.

Stolberg, S. (2009, January 12). *Mistakes, I've made a few bush tells reporters.* Retrieved July 9, 2010, from New York Times: http://www.nytimes.com/2009/01/13/us/politics/13bush.html

Takamine, K. (2011). *The ethical conundrum.* Manuscript submitted for publication.

Tarcov, N., & Pangle, T. (1987). In L. Strauss, & J. Cropsey, *History of political philosophy.* Chicago: The University of Chicago Press.

The Neilson Company. (2011). *Blogpulse.* Retrieved June 11, 2011, from www.blogpulse.com

Thomas, K. (1977, July). Toward multi-dimensional values in teaching: The example of conflict behaviors. *Academy of Management Review,* 484–490.

Thomas, K. (1992). Conflict and negotiation process in organizations. In M. Dunnette, & L. Hough, *Handbook of Industrial & Organizational Psychology* (2nd ed., Vol. III, pp. 651–717). Palo Alto: Consulting Psychological Press, Inc.

Trice, H., & Beyer, J. (1993). *The cultures of work organizations.* Upper Saddle River: Prentice-Hall.

Verducci, T. (2011, May 30). Fred wilpon pays the price. *Sports Illustrated, 114*(22).

West, T. G., & West, G. S. (1984). *Four texts on socrates: Plato's euthyphro, apology, and crito and aristophanes' clouds.* Ithaca, New York: Cornell University Press.

Westenholz, A. (1993). Paradxical thinking and change in the frames of reference. *Organization Studies, 14*(1), 37–58.

Weston, D. (2011, August 7). What happened to Obama? *New York Times,* pp. 1, 6–7 Sunday Review.

White, T. (2008). *Discovering Philosophy 2nd edition.* Upper Saddle River, New Jersey: Pearson Education, Inc.

Wiley, C. (1997). What motivates employees according to over 40 years of motivation surveys. *International Journal of Manpower, 18*(3), 263–280.

Winerip, M. (2011, September 5). Power and obedience clash as catholic school teachers negotiate a contract. *New York Times,* p. A14.

Zaleznik, A. (1992, March-April). Managers and leaders: Are they different? *Harvard Business Review, 70*(2), 126.

Dr. Gregory D. Clark is professor of management and leadership studies at Orange Coast College. He also teaches graduate courses at the School of Business and Professional Studies, Brandman University. He received his BA in English and political science from the University of California, Davis, his MA from Chapman University in counseling and career development, and his doctorate in educational leadership and administration from the University of Southern California. Dr. Clark is a consultant to corporations, public agencies, universities, and schools. He lives in southern California with his wife, Kim, and sons, Anthony and Nathan.